I WAS A P.K....

Who Would Have Known

RITA RANGEL

WestBow®
PRESS
A DIVISION OF THOMAS NELSON
& ZONDERVAN

Scripture taken from the King James Version of the Bible.

Scripture taken from the Holy Bible, NEW INTERNATIONAL VERSION®. Copyright © 1973, 1978, 1984 by Biblica, Inc. All rights reserved worldwide. Used by permission. NEW INTERNATIONAL VERSION® and NIV® are registered trademarks of Biblica, Inc. Use of either trademark for the offering of goods or services requires the prior written consent of Biblica US, Inc.

WestBow Press books may be ordered through booksellers or by contacting:

WestBow Press
A Division of Thomas Nelson & Zondervan
1663 Liberty Drive
Bloomington, IN 47403
www.westbowpress.com
1 (866) 928-1240

Because of the dynamic nature of the Internet, any web addresses or links contained in this book may have changed since publication and may no longer be valid. The views expressed in this work are solely those of the author and do not necessarily reflect the views of the publisher, and the publisher hereby disclaims any responsibility for them.

Any people depicted in stock imagery provided by Thinkstock are models, and such images are being used for illustrative purposes only. Certain stock imagery © Thinkstock.

ISBN: 978-1-4908-5695-7 (sc)
ISBN: 978-1-4908-5696-4 (hc)
ISBN: 978-1-4908-5697-1 (e)

Library of Congress Control Number: 2015901180

Print information available on the last page.

WestBow Press rev. date: 2/27/2015

CONTENTS

INTRODUCTION

When someone thinks about a "PK" (*Pastors Kid*), there are many things that go through their mind because of the stigma attached to what a "PK" is or better said, what a PK should be — how they should behave, dress, speak or live. Most people assume we are nice, moral, caring, polite, loving, and decent people because our parents are pastors. Some might even think; *"Wow, I'd like a daughter-in-law or a son-in-law who was a PK"* because of the above assumptions. Well, we do have many of the above traits like any decent person, but not anything extra special just because we are pastor's kids. After all, we are just as human as anyone else. It's no wonder people are beside themselves when they hear of a crime committed by a PK. It's even worse if this person linked to the use of illicit drugs or alcohol. Why does it stand out more when they are connected to a church where their parents were pastors? What an embarrassment to us all. Why? I'm not really sure why. It's my opinion that standards are set higher for someone like a pastor or their kids. Everyone's reasons are different. What makes a PK different from the average person? It's my opinion that Christians and the general public are the ones that hold us to higher standards. We're supposed to know better! We're not expected to be engaged in criminal activities, promiscuous lifestyles, hanging out in clubs, dancing, drinking, using drugs or getting pregnant like everyone else in the community that is "normal"- whatever normal is. We are frowned upon when caught in activities that God forbid, were morally wrong because our parents are pastors. Unfortunately, this is the case in many of the minds of congregants for years! We PK's are normal too and desire a fare shake at life itself and need to be allowed mistakes as anyone else and not frowned upon because we are PK' s. I cannot speak for others including my siblings, nor do I want to say that all PK's experiences are like mine because we all have individual experiences that are different yet similar. There has been those who made it out and on their own successfully, happy and with no regrets or horrid stories about the ministry; but for the most part, most PK's don't have happy stories about ministry. I simply speak of my own experience and from meeting lots of fellow PKs through the many years I was out in my self-destructive journey.

Ever since I could remember, it was the same scenario with most of the Christian congregations my parents were associated with. Unfortunately, I see that this legalistic practice of criticism and condemnation still continues in some of the traditional churches today and it is so destructive. It turns people off and away from wanting to serve the Lord or come back to Christianity. The God I serve is a loving and forgiving God that knows our hearts, intentions and true motives. For me, it seemed like all the do's and don'ts were man-made and enforced because It wasn't the loving ways of the God that I serve today. It is my opinion that these legalistic practices keep thousands of PK's and backsliders away from a healthy relationship with our loving Lord Jesus Christ who is a forgiving, compassionate God who wants nothing more than to take us as we are full of mistakes and fumbles in life and make us his new creation and not live in condemnation all the time. There are thousands that remain lost, running from God and wanting nothing to do with *"religion" or "God"* today. Many of my parent's concerns were what the congregation would say or think. Everything seemed to be sin! There was so much emphasis on sin, condemnation and how we would go to hell if we went to the movies, a school dance, listened to secular music, wore make up, jewelry, dress suggestively, or God forbid we cut or dye our hair. There was no room for fun even if it was good, clean, harmless mischief fun. Being a teenager in a pastor's family setting was a drag and a painful ordeal. It was such a turn off to most of us growing up in church or ministry. Being a PK nearly destroyed my life and that of my siblings. It took many years to try and repair the damage or figure out how to exit the maze of legalism and condemnation.

Having pastors for parents was no picnic and always made me feel like I was on display wherever I went. Everyone in school knew I was the daughter of the "Rev". Sometimes I'd do something wrong and jokingly someone would say, *"Hey, you're not supposed to be doing that, what would your dad say"*? Oh how I hated that! Everyone seemed to be aware of what I was or was not suppose to be doing. I don't think my parents had any clue as to how pressuring this was at school for me; even my teachers all knew. Oh how I resented this. Cute guys at school knew my father was the *"Rev"* and it embarrassed me because I wanted more than anything to look cool and be normal like everyone else. I always felt different from others and under pressure to fit in. I desperately longed for *validation* and *acceptance* from everyone, especially my peers. My father was politically active in the community as well; so everyone knew him and could point out all the girls at the school that went to the *"Rev's"* church and there were many of us. We did things differently than other girls. We didn't shower in the gang showers like everyone else. We all showered at different periods of the day in the teachers' showers. We didn't have to wear shorts either. We wore culottes. These were the special accommodations that were made with the school district for all of the *"Rev's"* female students.

I have met countless PK's and backslidden pastors or leaders out in the streets, clubs and jails during my journey that shared a lot of my same personal experiences as a PK. It's funny how we all seemed to find ourselves, relate to each other and share a lot of the same stories about ministry. Every time I met another PK and shared my story, it grieved my heart that this stuff was still going on years later and they too were out lost like me when I knew we didn't have to be. We were basically good kids that went bad with a huge waste of a lot of talent. The vast majority of PKs I met were musically gifted either in singing and/or playing instruments with great potential for becoming phenomenal leaders but no one recognized it, tapped into us or nurtured any of the many gifts we possessed. Most people don't see the end results of damaged goods we later become. It's only the powerful touch of God Almighty that can repair and restore once again. It's a difficult, challenging and very demanding life in which we have no choice. For the most part, we are born into it. When our parents were called to ministry, so were we but people don't realize that! We are just as much of the ministry as anyone else. When we grow older, we should be able to make our own choices whether or not to stay connected to ministry and should not be frowned upon or gossiped about if we don't choose ministry. Some of my siblings didn't choose to participate in the ministry and that should have been okay too. Parents shouldn't discourage their children's choices if they want a career in something other than church or ministry. Pastors need to keep focused on their little flock at home first, then their congregation. As the Bible says in **I Timothy 3: 4-5**, *"If a man/woman is unable to rule his/her own home, then he/she isn't fit to care for his church either"*. A rebellious child such as I, was going through so many changes growing up; compounded by the fact that my parents were so busy with the ministry they loved so very much. Sadly, in the process they had no quality time for me or my siblings with school work, personal needs, wants, changes I was going through or problems. ***A man's children should be his most important responsibility.*** We PK's were often sacrificed for the church and I built up deep resentment because for the most part we ended up bearing the brunt of the weight and pressure associated with our parents in the ministry. It was bad enough that I was being scrutinized and under continuous surveillance. We too, needed to be continuously encouraged, loved, nurtured and appreciated. Our parents could have prompted us kids to strive for excellence in whatever activities we chose, not necessarily in the ministry. This should have been okay too. Not all of us are called to the ministry. I don't think we should feel obligated to work in ministry or be held to a certain standard just because our parents are pastors. The Holy Spirit will guide and give us the desires of our hearts which is far better than rebelling just because we felt the pressure. If the congregants are not pressured to be in ministry then PKs should also be given the same freedom to choose; that freedom should rightfully come from God. *For where the Spirit of the Lord is, there is liberty* (**2 Corinthians 3:17**).

There is much loss and waste with PKs because so many of us possess many talents, and strong leadership qualities. The Bible teaches that if we train up a child in the ways of the Lord, they will come back. Nothing or no one can pluck us out of the hand of the Almighty anyway. I could have so naturally been integrated into my parent's ministry and been used of God in my own unique way. It could have been instrumental in keeping me on the straight and narrow road too. I loved music and singing but I wasn't *"ministry material"* in the eyes of many, saved enough to play piano or get involved with the youth ministry. People had their eyes on my physical appearance and not on my heart's desire. This would have been a beginning for me because of how much I loved music and wanted to play the piano. So what if my music was different than the norm (*traditional*). It's just how I learned to play the piano (*by ear*) with an oldie twist but I wasn't given the chance! Unfortunately, I felt lost in the crowd never quite fitting in as part of my parent's ministry. Perhaps my parents didn't know how to integrate me into the ministry but it's a valuable lesson that should be learned from my experience.

It's my desire to share my experience from the point of view of a pastor's daughter. It is not my intent to bring attack upon my parents, other pastors, leaders in ministry or congregations; I only want to shed light upon my personal experience as I believe we can all learn from our past mistakes and there is always something to be redeemed and gained from any negative experiences. You may not be aware how your ministry will affect or may have already affected your children because as with my parents, they loved the Lord, they had a call on their lives and were deeply burdened to help the lost. I'm sure they never imagined it would bring pain to any us. I know now that they never meant for me to be affected negatively by their calling, but it happened. Still, God honored their calling and by the grace of God, eventually we were all restored. Thank the Lord for those whose children today chose to be a part of the ministry and are not affected negatively. Things are so much different today and most ministries today include pastor's kids which I think is great but hopefully, it is because they **want to** participate and not because they feel obligated to.

I would also like to shed just a little light on the issue of my over worked and unnecessarily criticized parents. There were many in the congregation who were ruthless and self-righteous in judging my parents on how they ran their ministry. I'm not sure why my father didn't' just kick these troublemakers out of his church; instead he stuck by them and loved the ministry all the more. I had always hoped there could have been more help and participation from the congregation. My poor overburdened mother; she ran herself ragged cooking, fund raising, cleaning the church and keeping our home up too until the time we all began to get older and we were put to help out. We were always the first to arrive at church and the last to leave. Most of the time; we went to church hungry. There was little help, compassion or consideration from the congregation to be mindful that we kids had school in the morning. God bless the few women who occasionally offered to help my mother on special occasions.

As the eldest daughter, I became my mother's main support system to help out at home with my siblings. I would like to encourage the church to offer whatever help you can to take the load off your pastors and their kids. I can see today that for the most part, a lot of churches do help the pastors and I'm thankful for that because it means less PKs that will have sad stories about the ministry taking a toll on their personal lives.

My parents didn't draw a salary, drive a nice car nor did we live in a nice (*not even decent*) home as most pastors do today. We lived in poverty and didn't know it. Dad drove a beat up station wagon, and we lived in a crowded two bedroom shack for all nine of us. We never received new school clothes at the beginning of the school year nor went anywhere with our parents on weekends for fun like a restaurant, a weekend together or any outing because that would be considered wasteful. This actually would have helped us to have some fun times away from the ministry and spend quality family time together. The only time we had together was *once a year* for a week in the mountains when we went camping.

Treat your pastors well. Remember we are a part of the ministry, part of the package, whether we or you like it or not. We have no choice! Pastors and their kids have bad days just like anyone else. Its' unfortunate the many backslidden pastors, PK's & people who were in ministry at one time are out there lost because of hurtful and unfortunate things that took place in their lives while in ministry. Many due to ministry burnout *(if there is such a thing)*, hurtful things like ruthless criticisms by the very same people they served or not enough help. Yes, some pastors backslide, yes they fall in sin but how many of the "*regulars*" have slipped and no one knows because they never got caught or aren't in the front lines where people can see them. Don't judge your pastors just because you sin differently.

I never met one fallen minister or PK that was happier and better off backslidden. All were miserable, bitter, tired and lonely for their fellowship with God again but found it hard to get back up. I've met too many spiritually wounded, powerful fallen anointed soldiers out there needing our prayers. I should know, I was one of them and it was one of the most difficult challenges of my life to get back up and stay up. I believe the enemy wants us wounded and broken. I believe he wants Christians this way so that he can gloat over our desolation and thereby discourage others as well. It's not easy for fallen backsliders to get back up. It was my biggest stronghold and my restoration took years to work through. I'm so thankful to my

Lord Jesus Christ for my inner healing, revelation, forgiveness and finally the restoration he has given me over my past. He has made me a better woman and not a bitter one. It was for this reason that I was compelled to finish this book of my experience in hopes of sharing my story with people, especially pastors, church leaders, congregates and PKs to shed some awareness to all in and out of ministry. I am reminded of the Word of God that says *"My people perish for the lack of knowledge"* (Hosea 4:6, NIV). If you don't know the subtleties and strategies of the enemy, you can never overcome him. God reminds us to *"Be not overcome of evil, but overcome evil with good.(*(Romans 12:21, KJV). Thank God that what was meant for evil, discouragement, and destruction, God through His sovereign love and mercy, turned it all around for good. His ultimate grace and power restored, renewed and redeemed my life. For that I now give him all the honor and glory that He allowed me to be a PK. It is with sincerity and good motives that I have allowed my life to be an open book with transparency and narration of my experiences as a PK with you.

DEDICATION

I dedicate this book to my parents who completely and wholeheartedly devoted their lives to the ministry as young as they were. They sacrificed everything to win the lost at any cost and bring hope to the hopeless. I sincerely applaud them for doing what they did and accepting their assignment to "serve" without complaining. It was a difficult, challenging and strenuous task to do with seven children. I didn't always understand or agree with them but they persevered even though. In spite of all the hardships, I owe so much to my beautiful mother, who taught me about modesty, forgiveness and understanding. She lived a life of compassion to those that were in need and to those through the years who had gravely offended her. She gave me the priceless tools I would later benefit from because of her "consejos" (*Spanish for wise counsels*) and the forgiving example she lived. I now honor her by living her legacy.

To all my siblings, who endured and sacrificed so much through the many years of ministry because we had pastors for parents. We were a total of seven, three boys and four girls. I was the eldest of the girls. We all went through so much together and were affected in one way or another. Some chose to serve the Lord, others scattered different ways because of our past PK experiences. We all eventually (*years later*) found our way back to the Lord and serve Him the best we know how today.

I want to include all ***other PKs*** who share some of my experiences and are out lost or wounded from past ministry experiences or who no longer want anything to do with Christianity. My heartfelt desire is to find you, share my experience and serve as an example and encouragement. We share camaraderie as PK's because of the many similar experiences never talked about or understood by church congregations.

And to my cousin *David* who died without the opportunity to read this book about so much of what we talked about. He went to his grave grossly wounded from his experiences as a PK and chose not to share his experience with anyone other than when we would sit and talk. No one could imagine the devastating pain he carried from his past, not even his own family that he hid it from. One would not know it because he appeared normal on the outside but was severely wounded and was a silent walking time bomb on the inside. He struggled to trust people in his life because of ministry. He hated the fact that he was violated by someone in his dad's church that got away with it. He could have been rescued and mightily used of God with his awesome musical talents like so many other PKs. He chose not to try and repair any of it when he could have. He encouraged me to finish this book even when we both were out lost in our crazy worlds and destructive journeys.

Finally, special thanks to my friend *Julie Amaya* who was my ghost writer for this book. She took time from her busy schedule at work, home life and personal ministry to take on this assignment as a labor of love. The goal was always excellence to the best of our combined abilities. She has always been there with me through the good times and the most critical times of my life. She never judged me but rather loved unconditionally. When we first met we became fast friends and I was able to lead her to the Lord when she was in her lowest valley and at the point of taking her own life. Ironically, years later, our roles were reversed and she became my encourager when I was in my valley. The grand finale of our life-long friendship has been working together to complete this book. Thank you, Julie.

DISCLAIMER

Be advised that although this book is my autobiography based on my personal memoirs, many of the names, dates and stories of which I speak about have been changed to protect the innocent and to minimize any negative implications this might have on anyone.

Simple Beginnings

As was common practice back in the day, my parents were married extremely young. Dad was only 15 and mom was 14 years old. They were a typical poverty young couple living in a ranch in 1956. My older brother was seven, I was six and my baby sister was four at the time. There were few families living on this ranch. Our families regularly got together for weekend parties with lots of drinking, music and dancing that usually lasted through the weekend. When it got late at night, my brother, sister and I would stay in the bedroom watching television or play with our toys. My mom would constantly check in on us and bring us snacks. My brother and I would take turns looking through the peep hole in the door to watch our uncles, aunts and friends party all night until we fell asleep. This went on for several years. My parents were bikers and rode old Harley Davidson motorcycles (choppers).

On Sundays we would routinely go high up into the hills. My dad, along with others, would drive his Harley up into the hills to see who could reach the top of the mountain. It was so steep that sometimes the bikes would slowly come tumbling down backwards. For us, it was entertaining, exciting and a lot of fun. The drinking and partying went on all day. Mom would bring homemade burritos and drinks for us kids because we'd be there all day long. It was *"family time."*

Many family and friends would show up either on their Harley's or in cars with their kids too.

One very early Sunday morning at the ranch, my father was highly intoxicated and playing his guitar with other family members. To my mother's surprise, he asked her to pull out her mothers the old church hymnal and they began singing hymns. Unbeknownst to my dad, the Spirit of God began to move within him. He was about to experience his divinely ordained appointment that day. At one point, he found it difficult to continue singing and got all choked up and emotional. He didn't understand what was going on or why he was feeling like this. Out of the clear blue sky he decided to go visit an uncle who was an ordained minister. He hadn't seen this uncle for many years. When he arrived at his uncle's house, he told him that he had heard he was ill and wanted to see him before it was too late. Of course, this was only a story my dad told him as an excuse for his sudden visit. To my father's surprise, his uncle (*being lead of the spirit*) replied, *"That's not true. You are here because you are under conviction and the Spirit of the Lord brought you here"*. My father fell to his knees weeping. His uncle began praying for him and thanked the Lord for what was taking place in my dad's life that morning. After a long while, he stopped crying and his uncle invited him to go with him that same morning to Sunday service at a local church. My dad, who was still hung over, agreed to meet him at the church in a while. He returned to the ranch and told everyone to get up and get ready because they were **ALL** going to church that morning! Everyone laughed; but got ready anyway. They all went to church on their Harleys and in some cars with the kids. They were all either still intoxicated or hung over. Some went inside and others waited outside on their bikes. There was a loud speaker outside so everything in church could be heard. Church went on and the Pastor spoke, he asked my dad if he was willing to testify on the microphone of how the Lord had touched him that morning and declare his salvation publically. The Pastor knew all the bikers were outside listening. Dad was also aware that he would be heard and might possibly be mocked later but he went up anyway and began to testify how the Lord had touched him and changed his life that morning. He shared how God had touched him in a powerful way he had never known before and spoke of his life changing experience that very morning. He said he wasn't sure how but he knew that he was not the same man anymore. Dad was very emotional during the whole experience as he poured out his heart in front of the entire church and all those who were outside listening. He knew he might be made fun of later but he didn't care because he knew something amazing had happened to him.

Dad began taking us all to this small church for every service he could. This humble little church was not far from the area where they used to ride their bikes. He began to feel his call to ministry right away and a burden to preach God's word to save souls. Funny thing was that my mother did not understand exactly what he was doing as she wasn't converted yet. My dad continued to trust God for her salvation. One day when mom was pregnant with one of my sisters, we were at a special revival service and the power of God began to deal in her life. She fought the tears as she resisted the power of God that was dealing with her. However, before the night was over, she had yielded to the beautiful presence of God that touched her in a way she had never known before. That night she gave her life to the Lord even though she had told my father she wanted nothing to do with Christianity. She tells of how the power of God overcame of her and how she wept and wept feeling the sweet Spirit of God go right through her. Her entire being was instantly cleansed and renewed that night. Shortly after, she too began to share how she was never the same from that night on. The Lord had answered my father's prayers and gave her the same desire to serve God. They began serving the Lord together and soon they felt the call into the ministry at the young age of 25.

A few more years passed and two more siblings were born. My father had a real passion to start his own church. They began holding services in our small house. Our dining and living rooms together made for the church area where services were held. So many people were getting saved and delivered that it wasn't too long after that they outgrew our little house-church and so we went to another house to hold services. The new location was a house that was only a frame being constructed around the corner in the neighborhood. This framed house just sat with the construction on hold because the owners had run out of money. They offered my parents the place to start holding services. I suppose this was the beginning of what would be our PK memories. The enemy wasted no time in his attempts to discourage my parents as young pastors.

There was a time that we lived in a little small house across the street from the place we used for church. One day we went somewhere and when we returned home, all of our personal belongings were out on the curb of the street. We had been evicted from our home. As kids we didn't quite understand everything but we knew it meant we wouldn't live there anymore and we had to find another place to live. It didn't seem to discourage my parents much because they both continued to press even harder and stayed faithful and strong to their calling. My mother was completely supportive of dad and the calling. As far as us kids were concerned, it was all fun and entertaining because we were always busy doing something and each day brought new experiences and challenges. It was all so new and we were all so very innocent.

We spent a lot of time together as a family. No more parties or drinking that went on for days. Church services went on for hours but it seemed to pass quickly. People didn't seem to be concerned about time and schedules during these years. People only came to praise the Lord and be in the house of God. We witnessed so many miracles. People were delivered from the craziest things in their lives. It was the early 1960s and God was doing a fresh new thing in the church. At the house church, we kids all slept on top of or under the benches when we were tired. We struggled financially because my parents began to live completely by faith. Dad gave up his daily job to go full time into the ministry as there was so much to do. Through the years, the congregation quickly grew but so many times people failed to pay their tithes which were supposed to help keep the ministry going. It put a severe strain on my parents because by now there were seven of us to feed and care for.

We continued to move a lot. There were times we did not have groceries. My parents would get us all together and bring our need for groceries in prayer. We all just believed that the Lord would provide and incredibly, absolutely incredibly, God always did!! This was always such an amazing sight to see and experience firsthand at such an early age. We witnessed (*sometimes in a matter of hours*) how suddenly from out of nowhere, there would be a knock at the door. When dad would answer, it was someone being obedient to the Lord's prompting to deliver bags of groceries to our doorstep. Wow, what an awesome sight. We all knew not to touch anything until we all gathered together to thank the Lord for meeting our need. We continued to witness the miraculous power of God in action in many ways. To this day, we still remember these experiences. Every time we prayed, we would all pray believing in our hearts because we just knew (*at an early age*) that God was faithful! Without fail he would move on our behalf. The same prayers went on whenever one of us was ill. We didn't have medical insurance and by this time we were a family of nine. When one of us got sick, it was like a domino effect. I can't tell you how many times we would witness God's miraculous healing power HE touched us and made us whole. I guess you could say it was a way of life for us to totally trust God because we were taught by example that God would always come through. My parents trusted God for everything and refused to consider "*no*" or "*maybe*" as an option. They prayed, believing wholeheartedly for everything in the ministry.

One of our lifetime family memories was that every year my dad would take us all for a week-long camping trip. It's amazing to me now when I look back and remember the junkie car we had, the many pints of oil it would take to drive up there and the constant pulling over to the side of the road to let the engine cool off. We didn't care. We just wanted to get there. We were all crowded in this car going up there and back. Thank God this was before the seat belt law because all nine of us were stuffed in that car on top of each other. There wouldn't have been enough seat belts anyway. We didn't mind because we were going camping!

Mom would make fresh tortillas every morning using her famous metal pipe and dad was very camp savvy. He knew all the ins and outs of camping. Our one week would pass so quickly. We didn't want to come back. It was our one and only greatest treat every year. It's funny that as poor as we were, we didn't know it. Mom cooked very healthy, tasty food in the mountains like beans, rice, tortillas and meat cut up with potatoes because it stretched our food to make more! Looking back now, my parents were in love with Jesus and each other. They were totally sold out for Him.

It was the-mid sixties and God was miraculously moving in our neighborhood delivering drug addicts, alcoholics, and restoring many broken families. As the years quickly passed, my parents were continually dependent on the mighty hand of God to meet all our needs. It's awesome to look back at such powerful faith in a young couple doing their best to serve the Lord with all their children. My dad enrolled in Bible school. He loved his books and learning. When he was studying, we were not allowed to bother him and we had to keep the noise level down. This was hard because we were seven children who were usually running around playing most of the time as children do.

By this time I was a preteen growing up quickly. It was my job to help my mom with the kids, cooking and cleaning house. It was my older brother (*oldest by one year*). The other five were all younger and required constant supervision so I helped mom with whatever I could do which included lots of laundry. The ministry began to put a strain on the household and mom needed more and more help. There were the church meetings, fund raisers, prayer meetings, on and on. Mom pretty much led the women in all church activities, meetings and preparing food to sell after services during special events to raise money for the ministry. During the week, she was also busy making tamales to sell on weekends to help church finances. Saturday was the day we all went door-to-door selling tamales. My sister under me (Klu) would sell the most and when some of us didn't go, she always did. Most of the customers already knew my sister by her first name since it is a unique name. They would ask for her by name, "Klu-klu". We had our regular clientele each week that waited for our tasty tamales. The majority of finances came from the sale of these tamales. It was a lot of work and the ladies would have what looked like an assembly line going on in the church kitchen. Mom had a few faithful sisters that would help her. My siblings would play outside during this time. Most of the time I was doing household chores to help mom. Since I was the oldest of the girls, it was what I was expected to do while mom was busy with the tamales. It's just the way it was.

I Thought Our Life Was Normal

Growing up in the ministry for several years now it seems to be the norm because it was all we knew. Church seemed to be fun. People were always around, my parents had their busy schedules and we all continued the routine of always doing church things. We usually ate oatmeal for breakfast. It was the cheapest way to feed a lot of us and the way mom made it was really good with cinnamon toast. There were times we didn't have any breakfasts at all because we either didn't have any and or we were running late for school. There was no such thing of *free breakfast* nutrition programs at school for us like they have now. We were seven children and it was hard for my parents to provide for us at times. I remember a school program being a big part of providing clothes and shoes for us. We thought it was the greatest surprise when they would bring us some groceries. My dad was also very good at cutting out cardboard to put inside our shoes as patches when they had holes. We thought it was so cool. At times the school saw fit to purchase us shoes off and on throughout the year. I suppose they knew we had needs but it never dawned on any of us where the shoes or food came from because we just thanked the Lord for sending us the blessings and providing for our needs. Unfortunately, I don't have very many memories of either parents sitting down and helping us with homework, projects, sports or music activities because of the ministry and/or limited funds. School events were a luxury. My father was still in his four year Bible College as well. He had his own homework due at school and he was always busy preparing sermons to preach at church too.

Whenever pastors or evangelists came in from out of town, we automatically knew we would be giving up our room or beds so the guests could have a place to stay. I'm not sure if it was cool for my parents to bring these evangelists in to stay with us but it's what people did back then. We didn't really mind. We were used to having guests or visitors. We knew it was temporary. Mom would cook to feed them and us. We always had fresh homemade tortillas; she made them so fast and stacked them high. By the end of all meals, they were all gone. She used a metal roller to make them, nothing fancy but man, those tortillas were great! Mom really knew how to use that metal roller. I helped her set up and clean after all meals because my siblings were much younger. She cooked, served food to guests, entertained and also fed us too. We all then got ready for church. Little by little, it became harder to complete homework because we would get home, do our chores, eat and then get ready for church services or a church-related activity. We never had any real quality time to sit and complete school work comfortably. We did our homework the best we could whenever we could. Our parents were just so busy all the time with the ministry. They loved the Lord, winning souls and were totally sold out for God. They did whatever it took to keep the ministry going. I think being young and sold out for God as they were was great except for the fact that our home life took major blows for lack of quality time with us, the lack of finances, and nurturing. We all had different needs which seemed to go unnoticed. How I wanted a *"dad"* and not a *pastor* for a parent like my friends. I wanted a normal dad that could be playful and joke around; someone who would take us on outings on weekends like other families I saw. Although their hearts were in the right place, we were sort of left out. Sharing my parents with everyone, anytime, anyplace and at any given time of the night was such a drag. Today someone has to make an appointment to see their pastor. Our parents were out serving the congregation and the community needs all week long at all hours of the day or night. People would call on them for prayer and hospital visits. Shortly after, they would go leaving my older brother and me to watch the kids. I don't think anyone ever had any clue what a sacrifice it was for us to share my parents. It caused me to begin feeling resentful that anyone could call on them at any time and expect them to be at their beck and call because, after all, they were pastors. As I got older, I became frustrated with it all and wanted so badly to be a normal family without all this outside ministerial pressure. My parents were called to ministry and unfortunately, we were too. We had no choice in the matter. My dad worked hard to balance his schooling, pastoral responsibilities and a family at home. The congregation never knew how we felt. I began feeling cheated that my parents went out praying for others, counseling people, dealing with deaths and funerals etc. in the neighborhood. It was our family time that was being sacrificed. I think my dad somehow saw us as part of his congregation. Dad dictated what was right and wrong, sin or not sin! I was so tired of what the Bible had to say and all the do's and don'ts. There was always so much chastising that came with anything we wanted to do like listen to rock and roll music, our hair and clothing styles or any other fun things we wanted to do. I began feeling resentful of being talked at instead of talked to for fear of what I might make my parents look like to the congregation. It was all tolerable when I was younger but things radically changed as I got older and I began to think for myself. No one but no one ever asked me how I felt about my future, personal life desires, or my likes or dislikes. It was as though, I didn't exist. There came a time I felt like I was always competing for my parent's time. School (college) or careers were never discussed as an option either.

Evening services usually ended at 10 or 11pm. People back then didn't care how long services went. Again, we were always the first to arrive and the last to leave, after locking the doors, picking up trash, putting things away or taking people home after church

11

services. For the most part, we went to sleep late. Mom washed our clothes with an old-fashioned ringer washing machine. She would feed the clothes through the ringer to squeeze out the excess water off before hanging them out on the clothes line which was also time-consuming. No such thing as automatic clothes dryer. Everything was hung out by hand out in the back yard on a rope with lots of wooden clothespins. Looking back, it was a lot of work for mom with seven children, a husband, a church and full time ministry. My father still didn't have a regular day job because they were both in full time ministry and he was still in Bible school. As a matter of fact, we all were! Yes even us kids. We didn't have a choice. We lived by faith which meant we were dependent on any tithes that came in because it took care of all church expenses, our rent, groceries, household utilities and all necessities like laundry soap, toiletries and gas for the car to pick up people and take them home because my parents were also the church taxi drivers. They used to pick up anyone who didn't have a ride to church services. It was just what that they did. Once church was over, we were usually the last ones leaving and my parents also drove everyone back home in our station wagon which took so much wear and tear. They would pick up people from everywhere in several other distant communities. Sometimes some of us would go with my dad after church which was kind of fun because we got to go for long rides. He would first drop off all the locals and then come back for the second batch of people who lived farther away. By the time we got home, it would be very late and we had school next morning. We probably should have been in bed. We didn't mind at the time because it was normal for us. This was what we did after church services.

I will never forget one night after church. I went with my dad to take people home and as usual, the station wagon was fully loaded. I was about 10 years old. Some of us had to sit on people's lap until one by one people would get off and there would be more room. We were driving along and one of my father's church elders (*an elderly man*) sat behind my father and I had to sit on his lap. He was a dynamic preacher and an awesome guitar player. He molested me! I didn't understand what was happening or what it meant because we were taught to trust and respect our elders. I was so scared. I didn't know how to react and I remember asking myself why he was doing this? What it meant and what should I do? He kept putting his hand under my dress and touching me inappropriately. He continued talking to my dad as though everything was perfectly normal. I was confused and scared frozen all at the same time. I wanted to cry and scream and get away. I even tried to move away but he kept pulling on me and held me there tight on his lap. I didn't say anything because I thought I would get in trouble. Somehow I thought it was my fault! I looked around at all the other people in the car and no one had a clue what was going on. It was dark, crowded and busy. What was really puzzling is how he just continued conversing with my dad and everyone else as though everything was fine and kept touching me. They were talking about the service and how the power of God really moved. It just blew my mind and freaked me out at the same time. I kept looking around to get someone's attention and trying to move. It didn't help. He kept a firm grip on me to stay on his lap. By the time we stopped to let him off (*which felt like hours*), he exited the car and amazingly continued talking to my father. He casually just looked over to me with absolutely no expression. I was still afraid and now sick to my stomach. I kept staring at him as he continued talking to my father. I wondered if this was okay or if this was supposed to be something that normally happened in life since there was no expression from him or anyone else in the car. I remember giving him a dirty look as he waved goodbye. I was confused, scared and dumbfounded at what had just taken place. All the way home I was quiet in the car. I wanted to tell my dad about this brother and what he did to me but somehow, I couldn't muster enough words to tell dad what had just happened. I began to feel choked up and emotional. I wondered what he would say or if he would even believe me because after all, this was a "*man of God*," and one of his elders. My dad just drove along as he always did singing and making small talk. He never detected anything was wrong. Everything in me wanted to tell him. I felt like crying and yelling but nothing came out. I think I was in shock and just held it in. I figured I'd tell my mom when we got home. I could hardly wait to get home. Our trip that night seemed extra long.

We finally reached home but when we did, mom was already lying down. She was so tired. She had not been feeling good that night as she often struggled with female physical complications. I wasn't sure if she was sleeping so I stood at the door and just looked in. As I was contemplating telling her, I became emotional and wanted to cry. I'm not sure why but part of me thought somehow I would get in trouble or she wouldn't believe me. I just didn't know how to start the conversation. I slowly walked in staring at her as she lay there in her bed. She saw me standing there and just looked at me. I didn't say anything for few seconds. She asked me if I needed something. I panicked and said no. She prompted me then to get ready for bed. I kissed her goodnight turned around and went to the room instead. I got ready for bed very slowly, pondering over and over if I should just run back in and tell or just wait till morning. I even thought about telling my brother whom I was so close to but the moment didn't quite lend itself and I didn't know how to tell him or what he would say. I went to bed feeling dirty and nasty about what had just taken place and I couldn't get the nerve to tell someone, anyone! I thought about my ordeal all night long. I told myself I would tell mom in the morning. I silently cried for a long, long time until I fell asleep.

Next morning as we were all getting ready for school, I kept waiting for the perfect time to tell my mom but somehow in the rush of things, I couldn't find the right time to sit her down and explain what had happened to me the night before and besides, I still felt very emotional. She was so busy with all the many mouths to be fed. It was always a noisy rush getting us all out on time. I just went along to school as normal. Unfortunately, there was nothing normal about my entire day at school. I kept thinking about my ordeal all day long at school and I remember feeling sadness. I wanted to go hide somewhere. At all my recess, I sat alone and thought about it some more. I looked out at all the girls playing and wondered how many other girls had shared my experience and if this was normal. I was pretending I was talking to my mother and telling her about this pig that touched me. Well, that day led to another day and another and another. I never mustered enough courage to tell my parents, my brother or anyone else. It was my secret for a very long time. I saw this man again and again in church services and I kept staring at him from behind. Every time I saw him in church playing his guitar and *"praising the Lord,"* I felt sad and empty inside. I wondered how he could just play his guitar, preach and praise the Lord as though nothing was wrong. He had traumatized me and it left me feeling shameful around him and others. I hated that he was a so-called hermano, (*Christian man*), yet so evil. My life changed from that day on and my ordeal would remain my secret for many years to come. I sometimes fantasized about standing up in church one day and telling everyone what a nasty pig he was and what he had done to me. It made me wonder how many other girls he had done this to. I even thought it might have been because I was the pastor's daughter or because I was a bad person? It occurred to me that maybe he had done this to my sisters or some of the other youth. I couldn't risk asking them in case he hadn't so I never said a word. He disgusted me. I simply avoided going around him and or going with my dad anymore when he was taking this brother home. I didn't want my sisters going with my dad anymore either just in case he'd want to touch them too. I don't know why, I just couldn't get the words out or why I thought I would get in trouble. I hadn't done anything wrong; at least I didn't think so. I had a feeling that someone would think I was lying about this spiritual leader. After all, this was my dad's church elder, a powerful preacher and well respected man. I wondered how he could do what he did and simply go on in church as though nothing had ever happened. I questioned why God didn't just strike him dead right where he stood. I always watched out for my sisters around him after my ordeal. When we would pass each other in church, I would glare at him. His wife and daughter also went to our church. They were very nice people. It made me wonder if he ever touched his daughter like that at home. I use to feel sorry for them because they didn't know what a pig he was. There were a couple of times after this incident that my dad took me to drive congregation people home again. I only went with my dad when this man wasn't with us and I never sat on any man's lap again. Oh how I hated to see him in church and I wondered how he could play the role of such a highly spiritual person when all along, he was nothing but a dirty pervert. My world of innocence was shattered from that night on. I learned not to trust people and I began to wonder about other people in the church, especially the men. I wondered if they also did inappropriate things like this that no one knew about.

There was another time when I went with my dad to take people home. There was this older Indian woman who didn't live so far but far enough that she couldn't walk to church. She was one of the persons my dad had in the full station wagon. I was forced to sit on this lady's lap. Again, there was no room but I figured it was safe because she was a women and mother like my mom. I knew that soon I would have a seat of my own. Kids always sat on the lap of an adult. We made several stops dropping people off. I dozed off because I was so tired but I awoke to this lady removing my turquoise bracelet and ring set that my parents had recently bought and given me. I thought I was dreaming. My parents could hardly ever afford to buy us nice things so this was really special. She had already removed my bracelet as I was waking up and had successfully slipped off my ring as I fought with her to keep it. I looked at her as we were pulling into her driveway and yelled out *"Hey, what are you doing, give me back my bracelet and ring"*. She acted as though she didn't hear me. She got off the car and thanked my dad for the ride. I stuck my head out the window and told her to give me back my bracelet and ring. Again, she acted like she didn't hear me or know what I was talking about. She thanked my dad for the ride and said the usual, *"God Bless You Pastor."* I was so angry and as we were about to drive off, I yelled out again, *"Hey! I want my bracelet and ring back!*" My dad asked me to sit down and asked what I was talking about. She just waved good bye. I was infuriated with her.

This time I did tell my dad what she did. He told me perhaps I had just dropped it somewhere. I told him *"No dad! I felt when she was taking both the ring and bracelet off".* He said I would probably end up finding it somewhere in the car later as though he didn't believe me and it crushed me inside. Needless to say, I never found it. Of course, it was because she took it off me. I couldn't prove it to anyone but to this day, I have a vivid memory of this traumatizing incident of her hands on my wrists and finger removing my jewelry. After this day, I didn't want to go with my dad after church anymore - period! I began to build such resentment towards these hypocrites in my parents' church that called them Christians. One was a pervert and the other a thief. One was a man and the other a woman. I couldn't trust anybody! I would go to church and begin to see people and wonder what secrets they all had and what kind of people they really were away from church. I suppose this was the beginning of my resentments towards people of the church that called themselves Christians and were actively involved in ministry. I didn't like some of them and I began to build up grudges and negative attitudes towards them all. Suddenly, things around me that pertained to church began to take on a different meaning.

When I hit the age of 15, I wanted my own room. Our little two bedroom house was already small for all nine of us, my parents and 7 other siblings. I began to demand my own privacy. My dad miraculously thought of cutting the big room where we all slept, in two. It would be a small area enough to fit a twin size bed and a drawer but I didn't care, I could finally have my own room, put up my own things and dress in private. I thought it was the greatest thing! I had stuffed animals on my little bed fixed up to be what I felt was me. It wasn't much to the average person but for me, it meant a lot.

3

I'm Not Liking This Anymore

It's hard to imagine that we kids actually used to enjoy all the action that went along with ministry for all the wrong reasons. There were all those special events, out-of-town revivals, and all the visiting churches that came to attend dad's church. My parents had one of the biggest cutting-edge Spanish Pentecostal churches in the 1960s in our area. People were witnessing many modern day miracles and deliverances with drug addicts, gang members, alcoholics and people getting delivered from demonic spirits. It was scary and very real. I was now older. As I was growing up I began changing and wanted to be involved in the usual teen-aged activities with my friends in junior high school. I wanted to do things like going to the movies and school dances and sometimes hang out with friends at the mall. It was always such a conflict to go have fun doing what I thought were normal things with my school friends. Everything conflicted with our religious values and we were not allowed to participate. We rarely even went to the beach either and when we did, we had to go in a dress or skirt because we weren't allowed to wear pants, shorts or God forbid, a swim suit to get into the water. The times we did go, no one, but NO ONE there wore a dress or pants to swim. Looking back now, we were living a life of extreme legalistic religious rules and not anything sincere of Godly values.

By this I mean we were bound by man-made religious legalistic rules which meant women didn't wear pants, make-up or jewelry and no listening to secular music like rock and roll or oldies. We very rarely watched television. We were forbidden to wear any up-to-date hair styles like the dancing curls or beehives that were the style at the time. Those hair styles were considered carnal or worldly. Supposedly, it was because it brought attention to us. I remember thinking, *"I'm not liking this anymore."* We were encouraged to wear simple hair-dos which didn't include dying our hair or anything that attracted unnecessary attention to ourselves. It was okay while I was younger and didn't know any better but I was now a teenager. My mother always spoke about modesty. I wanted to try some of these new hairdos and clothing styles but everything I liked, seem to be a sin and contrary to Christian standards. My motives were pure because I didn't know any better but it didn't matter, according to the church, it was sin. My poor mother, as overburdened as she was always balancing her ministry duties and home life. In time, I could see how she was beginning to look worn down and tired. On top of all this, she struggled with physical female complications which seemed all the time. I never quite understood what her condition was but I knew she was often in pain throughout the years. Sadly enough, I don't ever remember her going to see doctors. She didn't wear anything stylish because she was the pastor's wife and had to lead by example (*whatever that was*). I can remember her always talking to the young women about doing things with modesty. Ninety percent of the congregation practiced what they thought was *"holiness"*. It was all just too strict and too much! It caused a lot of us to go underground with makeup, pants, music and what would have been considered a non-Christian lifestyle.

My parents continued thriving in the ministry. Services were always full especially on Monday nights followed by special fellowship afterwards. People looked forward to attending these services and didn't' seem to mind that they lasted an average of three to four hours long, sometimes longer. It's sad that today, people want to be out in and out no more than two hours.

The church had doubled in size and was still growing. I helped at home a lot more since I was the eldest of the girls. We were put to work with cleaning or picking up at church and at home. School became even more difficult because we got home from church too late and tired. We would have to get up early for school the next morning. The only times we had to ourselves were when there were no church services. As the years continued to pass, money was even more limited because my parents still continued to live by faith in the ministry and all seven of us were growing with bigger needs. By now dad was in his fourth year in bible school. He still didn't draw a salary as most pastors do today. I remember a few times when we would go behind the markets to the trash bins and get potatoes, carrots and other vegetables that had been discarded. Mom cleaned it all, and made very good soup! The income from the church tithes was supposed to take care of everything but unfortunately, it didn't. Many car repairs also had to be made because of all the wear and tear on our station wagon which my dad was always working on. My parents had a lot of favor with other people in the community and other churches. Dad was a radical for God, way ahead of his time. It was the 1960s and he was doing things differently from the norm in the Spanish Pentecostal churches at that time. He had a lot of fresh ideas and wasn't afraid to implement them. He began fundraising to build one of the largest churches in our city. It was still very rural at that time. We lived next door to a large dairy that was just a few yards away from our home.

Everyone knew about "The Rev". He was young and on fire for God. After much fundraising, which mainly came from selling tamales and pledge efforts, he began to build on a property they had purchased. Everyone was excited about the big new church being built. The construction work was headed up by a brother in our church who was a contractor. Some of the other men from our church periodically came to help. My mother got the ladies to prepare food and drinks to feed the laborers. There was so much excitement within the whole community. Sometimes people driving by would pull over just to watch what was going on.

People came from everywhere for the grand opening. My parents were thrilled about this thriving little church that grew explosively. I was happy for them too. By this time I never wanted to see tamales again for the rest of my life! I know my sister, Klu, felt the same too because she sold the most. It was a huge labor of love making all those tamales month after month. Thank God, my parents had so many kids because we sold them on the streets and in businesses. We took orders, delivered them and sold them out of our car too. Wow! I will never forget the tamale season of our lives.

Many more people began to come and not long after, dad was running the largest church in our city. With a large church; there also came more challenges, obstacles and sacrifices. There were special three-day revivals with guest speakers which still required us kids to give up our rooms and beds for those speakers that came in from out-of-town. There wasn't any money to house them in hotels and they certainly didn't eat at coffee shops or restaurants like they do today. Almost always they stayed at our house. They rested and ate all their meals with us. Mom was cooking more and trying to balance home life with ministry which was pretty hectic at times. Sometimes I would see my mom looking so run down. I felt so helpless to do something nice for her. Anything! Since I was the eldest of the girls, I was expected to help with the laundry, housework and cooking. I remember wanting to try some of the popular clothing styles of the 1960s which included brightly colored floral patterns, miniskirts and the dancing curl hairdos. I would practice hairdos on my sister Klu. My mom would try hard to get me some cute material patterns so I could make my clothes. Everything was made by hand, no sewing machines. That would be a luxury. We couldn't afford to go shopping at the mall for ready-made, store-bought clothes.

Meanwhile, the church continued growing by leaps and bounds every month. It was the fabulous Sixties. The mini-skirts styles were in style but that was absolutely non-negotiable with my dad. I was *NOT* going to be allowed to wear any short skirts. I practiced wearing makeup too. My mom would simply remind me to keep it modest. She recognized I was growing up and tried to incorporate what was going on in the world and letting me grow up too. She was as nurturing as she could be under the circumstances. She didn't wear makeup or nice clothes because the women in that time mostly wore black skirts and white blouses with a red flower on the blouse. God forbid she would wear anything fashionable! She had to look holy and spiritual which actually made her look older. She dressed very modestly and because she was already a lovely lady, she still looked very nice. She never wore any upbeat hairdos, hair tints, make-up or (*God forbid!*) jewelry. My mom was always on the front lines with my dad. I truly don't think she was aware of how run down and matronly she was starting to appear. In those days, any female that went up to the pulpit had to wear nylon hosiery. There never was any extra money to buy nylons and so, in the name of "**holiness**" she often wore hosiery with runners. If she didn't wear hosiery, the ladies would notice. I used to watch the ladies look her over from the top of her head to the heels of her feet. The congregation was highly critical of my parents' walk with the Lord. It was as though they were on a pedestal for everyone to either approve or disapprove of. It seemed as though the more plain, simple and bland looking you were, the more spiritual and holy you were thought to be. If a woman was made up, she was considered carnal or trying to attract attention to herself. There was one sister that always had my mother's best interest at heart. She would bring my mom goodies like chocolate, nylons, hair spray, pins for her long hair, or a few dollars for whatever personal mom might have. She would say, "*This is for you Sister Chia (my mother's nick name) not the church.*" It's like she knew of my mother's personal unspoken struggles. We all knew she cared for mom in a special way. She was very strict with her own children but she definitely looked out for our mom. She must have discerned what my mother went through. She was a quiet but very observant woman, sitting back and just watching people. When she spoke, everyone listened because she was bold and aggressive. She wasn't shy with words and she definitely spoke her mind. She knew my mom was young and inexperienced. I was so grateful for her and her husband in my parent's life. They would later become two of my parent's church elders as well. This was Sister Emma and her husband Rudy Chavez. He was also one of dad's comrades that he often hung out with. Brother Rudy became my dad's right hand helper and an awesome guitar player. Rudy was dad's personal friend. They spent a lot of time together. He would help dad *(and sometimes a couple other brothers)* with any plans or ideas dad wanted to implement. Unfortunately, all these brethren are now deceased. My parents didn't have many personal friends or people they could call on but I do remember this couple (Rudy and Emma Chavez) in the front lines serving in any capacity needed. I can count maybe five couples and a few single ladies that stood faithfully by my parents through time. It wasn't much and certainly not enough because the church was so big and the needs were many. There was also Tony and Lena Pompa *(now deceased)* and their many children. They had their share of problems with their older sons but they were supportive of my parents and the ministry. They lived 45 minutes away from the church but despite the distance, they were faithful. There was also Sisters Cuca Rodriguez and Grace Fuentes *(deceased)*. They had their share of problems with their unsaved spouses and children too but they were strong ministry helpers. Funny how certain things stick in our memory like the few faithful people and the acts of love and loyalty they demonstrated to my parents. All seven of us kids have loving memories of these few people who stood by our parents during our childhood. And even though they were few, they were loyal. We all knew they were there to help. All these people have now gone on to their eternal rewards with the Lord. God bless them for their life of loving and serving my parents.

As time went on, I got better at styling the dancing curls and doing makeup. I began to notice the frowns of disapproval from the women in the congregation. It seemed like things began to take a turn for the worse. I was finding my identity and I wanted to fit in at school too but there was one big problem. Everyone at school and in the community knew who I was. I was the daughter of *"The Rev."* Everyone knew everyone especially in our *(barrio)* community either by association or because they were related. By now I was about 16 years old. I began talking to mom about my likes and dislikes. My dad had no idea of what I was going through. He was busy with the ministry. I don't think he even realized we were all growing up right under his nose because he didn't see us or deal with us on a day-to-day basis like Mom did. I guess like any other parents, they just see us as children. Before you know it, we were all grown up and they never realized when it happened. Dad had very strict dress codes for us, including the all the other girls in church. Even in junior high school we didn't take showers with the rest of the girls. We had to use the teachers' showers. The teachers didn't like it either but my dad went to the school district and fought for this issue until they agreed to accommodate all the Rev's students.

One outstanding memory I have is that our parents never argued. If they had any disagreements, we didn't know because they honestly NEVER fought or argued around us. We all spent a lot of time together too. Our family lived in poverty but for the most part, we were content and happy. Our parents never discussed church issues around us either. Back then children were raised to be seen and not heard. We were never allowed to participate in grown-up conversations. It's just the way it was.

My parents had a wonderful love life. They were openly demonstrative about how much they loved each other and we all knew when it was their quiet, private time to be alone in their room. Mom would feed us, make sure our chores were done and allow us to watch television or the younger kids could play so my parents could retire to their bedroom for private time. It was a given. We all knew it was their love time. I suppose we had no idea what that really meant accept that it was their private time to be alone and it was what grownups did. We thought it was normal. That's the way they taught us. There were those rare days when there weren't church activities and we did other things with our free time. I remember spending this time to get my clothes together for school the next day, doing some sketching which I liked to do, or sewing clothes by hand. We all had plenty to do whenever we had free time which wasn't often enough. As usual, I practiced hairdos on my sister Klu. My poor sister hated it but I bribed her with favors I would do for her at school, let her hang out with us older girls or give her a ride (*cruise*) around after school. The four of us girls all slept in the same bed up until the time my dad divided one of the bedrooms in half and made me my own bedroom. My brothers all slept in another bed. We were good at making the best of whatever we had. We really didn't know any different either.

The women of the church didn't take on a whole lot of responsibilities to help our mom as the women in churches do today. Mom pretty much spearheaded everything and had to ask the ladies for help. She had a few good women that helped her in the kitchen whenever she did ask. Don't wait for your pastor or his wife to ask for help. Offer your help, or get the women together and take the load off her back. It's unfortunate that many pastors (*like my parents*) are out trying to reach the lost and needy, yet have to sacrifice their own families at home. We children are people with lives, desires and feelings too. We needed nurturing but somehow we ended up with our parents left-over's at the end of the day. I wanted so many times to speak my mind but we were raised to keep quiet and respect our elders.

Does Anyone Really Care?

During the fabulous Sixties we had the Beatles. Wood Stock was about to take place. Of course, as a pastor's daughter I NEVER expected that I'd be able to attend anything like that. I was also very young. Everyone at school was talking about it like it would be the greatest thing in the world to go. The mini-skirts, the bangs with our long hair were the fashion. It was the era of the flower children and free love. The Women's Equality Rights movement was just kicking into high gear. The world was rapidly changing and we couldn't avoid it because it was all we talked about at school. The Beatles had taken the world by storm. I liked listening to the Beatles. I thought they were so cool. Sex was what everyone was doing more freely and abstinence was slowly becoming an outdated thing of the past.

My parents were fully consumed with ministry and completely devoted to their calling. I was in high school still wanting to try some of the popular clothing and hair styles. We never owned a sewing machine either so I sewed everything by hand. My parents had a problem (*especially my dad*) with the mini-skirts. I longed for more independence and like any healthy teen aged girl, I was boy crazy! My parents were stressing over people in the congregation noticing the changes I was going through. Church colors were always dark and bland, nothing fancy or loud. I loved everything loud, bright with radical patterns like paisley. The church women begin criticizing my choices of dress, hair, makeup and mannerisms. It wasn't just me they were talking about but the youth in general along with my poor-hard working mother. The ladies were constantly gossiping about her and the fact that she didn't always wear nylon hosiery when she went up on the pulpit to lead praise and worship. Yeah, can you believe it? Hosiery! What is sad about all this is that these same sisters in the Lord had no idea that there just wasn't enough money for things like nylons. It was a toss-up between feeding us, nylons or buying gas for our station wagon to pick up people for church. Making sure my mom had nylon stockings was not a priority except in the critical minds of the legalistic, sanctimonious, spiritual ones. I still struggled with my grades in school because I could never spend enough time completing my homework like I should have or didn't understand the work. There was always too much to do and continued to go to bed late and tired.

I began to notice how much nicer my friends dressed. I saw that they lived in nicer homes with nicer furnishings and their parents drove nicer cars. Most of my girlfriends I visited all had their own big bedrooms while I had a little small little cubby section of a room for which I was so grateful. Their lives were so different from mine. I began to feel so "ghetto" and ashamed of my lifestyle. Everyone seemed to have more fun, freedom and lived nicer. At least it seemed so in my mind. They went to the movies and other activities that I wasn't allowed to participate in because of my family's religious legalistic views and convictions. My living situation as a pastor's daughter felt more like a drag. The answer to most anything I ever wanted to do was always "*NO*!" I was criticized over how short my skirts were and how much make-up I wore. For me, being a Christian was such a drag! Everything I wanted to do was a sin, a big sin! I wasn't allowed to do anything or go anywhere like school activities because we were Christians and weren't supposed to go to movies, school dances, or listen to worldly music. I began to think more and more about when I could leave the house never look back or have to deal with church restrictions again.

When my brother or I listened to secular music, it was away from my parents. We used to sneak around to listen to rock and roll. We would listen to music at school and later in his car when he was old enough to get one. I always tried to fit in with my girlfriends at school and would go along with whatever they wanted to do. Sometimes we would ditch school to go meet boys or go to parks where they would blast the music and we would dance. At times it included drinking and smoking pot. I could remember thinking that God was going to strike me dead. I could picture God as a big strong, strict, angry powerful person that would punish me for committing such ungodly things and for not following biblical teachings. Well it didn't take me long to figure out I wasn't going to die if I drank beer, smoked pot and danced -- at least not anytime soon. At first I felt so guilty like such a dirty, sinful person for betraying God and my parents. My mom always knew our schedules and knew what time we got out of school and what time we should be home. I hung around with several crazy girls from the neighborhood. It was such a drag at the end of the day to go home after cutting school all day and pretend I had a normal school day. I had to put on a straight face with my alcohol breath for which I chewed gum to kill the odor until I could brush my teeth. I'd get right to my chores and keep myself busy to avoid my parents. At school I participated in activities that everyone knew would not be cool with my parents. Most of the girls and the guys I hung around with were friends since elementary school so everyone knew each others families. They knew that my church didn't allow me do a lot of stuff. I suppose I felt like I needed to prove to them that I could hang with them and I was just as normal as anyone else. I could be just as hip and cool as they were. I wanted to fit in with everyone no matter what the cost. I was basically a good girl in that I wasn't sleeping around with the guys like some of my girlfriends. God forbid! I knew God would strike me dead for sure if I did! At any rate, I had good values instilled in me through the years in church and I knew what my boundaries were.

My father was a civic activist in the community. He was involved in community activities that required attending many City Hall meetings. He was involved with *"Urban Renewal"* where they wanted to knock down old community houses and rebuild a new community. Dad was often quoted in the daily newspapers, giving public statements for the rights of the poor. Everyone knew who *"The Rev"* was. I can remember (twice) that a guy I was interested in at school asked me, *"Hey, aren't you the Rev's. daughter?"* I just wanted to die of embarrassment! For me, it was embarrassing to have pastors for parents. In another sense, I suppose it was a good thing because they all respected me and would apologize whenever they used foul language. I didn't like this label and felt embarrassed over my parents' position in the community. I know I should have been proud but I wasn't. I wondered to myself, *"Why can't we just be a normal family, why can't my parents just be regular non-religious people like other parents?"* This limited me in everything I wanted to do. It was like ninety percent of whatever I wanted to do was a sin or worldly. It was a constant bummer. I really didn't understand or agree with it all but I believe that my heart was pure none the less. I was pure and innocent and all I ever wanted was to fit in have a little fun instead of church, church and more church! Deep inside it really did bother me about what I would make my parents look like to my friends or at the church but I rebelled anyway.

My mother was the one that kept things in perspective. She was more sensitive to my needs and wants. I know my dad didn't know half of what was going on with us. She never wanted to bother him with family problems so he could be clear-minded to study because he was finishing up in Bible school. As I grew older, I increasingly rebelled against it all; the church, the people, the rules and the pressures because I felt like I was always under a microscope and under close scrutiny from my parents and the congregation. They all seemed to be so concerned with what I was doing, wearing, how

I was acting, combed my hair, the amount of makeup I wore and what guys I talked to! I didn't consider myself a part of ministry. I was only the pastor's daughter. It was too hard to be part of ministry even though I wanted to play the piano and be a part of the youth but there were those in the church that felt that I should not be dressing like I did or wearing any make-up. My mother was always working behind the scenes making things happen like the women's activities, meetings, cooking food, etc. She continued to press in for the ministry and for us. She and my father continued to have a strong marriage relationship which kept them close together. It's a wonder they even had time for themselves. It was probably their solid love life and communication which kept them united. I never wanted to walk in my mother shoes. I knew that the Christian lifestyle was *NOT* something I ever wanted to follow after. Many times I sat in the pews and listened to my dad preach his heart out. Everything was in Spanish and seemed to be on how we should live our lives and what would happen if we didn't follow what the Bible said. Oh how I wanted a dad and NOT a pastor. I think pastors should talk *"to"* their kids and not *"at"* them as though they were the congregation. There was no room for discussion. It was how the Bible said things were and that was it! We never discussed the Bible at home amongst ourselves or how it could be applied to our lives in moderation. It was as though we kids were just part of the congregation. We should have been separated from being the pastor's children at home. It would have been healthier to speak more about moderation rather than black and white sin. As a pastor's daughter, I couldn't care less about a special speaker who wrote a book about things in the Bible. I wanted a normal mom, dad and family without all the rhetoric about what was right or wrong and what people thought. As a teen, I just wanted to be home and listen to cool music and do the normal things other kids did with regular parents. I wanted them to participate in my hobbies and all the things at school that mattered to me. I wanted to feel free to explore things in life without feeling condemned like hair and makeup but I knew it was against church teachings and there

31

probably wouldn't be any money for those kinds of things. I had no idea until later I could have qualified for a grant or a student loan to go to college. Going to college wasn't an option for any of us. No one ever spoke or encouraged me about my future or attending college.

So many times I just rolled my eyes as my father preached about love, grace and Christian living. I felt like my parents were more concerned about having their kids under control and looking like good kids to the public. Hogwash! We were normal kids and normal human beings that made mistakes along the way like any other kids. I didn't like the feeling of competing for my parents' attention. It was unfortunate how often I entertained the thought of someday leaving home, going on my own, sinning all I wanted because I felt like it and breaking all Biblical rules just because I could!.

Sadly (*looking back now*) my mother was so overworked. She was expected to carry out most church operations while my dad was either busy with Bible school, studying to preach at church services or speak at other churches. When he wasn't preaching, he was out on hospital visits praying for the sick, out in the community or out picking up people for church. Mom cooked at home for after church fellowships because by now, we lived next door to the church. By this time I absolutely knew without a doubt this was not a life I ever wanted to do or participate in when I got old enough to leave. Everyone took it for granted that we lived next door because every time they needed something, they'd come knocking or walking in. Well so much for our privacy.

We seven were so many yet we were all very close. Unfortunately, as we got older, we always seemed to be in the way. Sometimes mom would give us a pep talk when we went without dinner (*which was often*). We were told that we had to wait until church was over before we could eat. Ironically, my father would be served big plates of food because he was "*the pastor*". Mother never sat and ate with him. She would be busy serving and cleaning up later. I observed and thought to myself, "wow"! There were times we were pushed away (*scolded*) from the fellowship table by our grandmother. It didn't take me long to resent this and I never did it again regardless of how hungry I felt. No one had a clue we were often hungry and hadn't eaten. It was harder for the little ones because no matter how many times my older brother and I told them to stay away from the table; they would still tell mom they were hungry.

As the years continued to pass, I built up such resentment towards everyone and all the rules we were expected to follow. It all sickened me to the point where I plotted how I would leave first chance I got. No one seemed to have an idea about our family needs, our financial status, or how emotionally hard the ministry was on all us kids. I often wondered, *"**Does anyone really care**"?*

I wondered about what I was going to do when I left high school. I had very good artistic abilities and had even won a couple of first place awards for my work in high school. This would have been a good time to tap into my talent and consider attending art school. I had natural musical abilities inclined but that's as far as it went. I designed and created really nice clothes that sometimes included beads, sea shells and other wearable art sewed into the clothes which many found very attractive and unique. I could have capitalized on this because I was always complemented by my art teachers who found it amazing that I had created the things I did. It would have prepared me for something more substantial in my future.

My older brother was in gymnastics in high school and he was very, very good. It was most unfortunate that my parents not once were able to attend any of his practices much less any of his performances due to their busy ministry schedules. It wasn't a priority for them at the time. My brother and I would talk about it and I could see it in his face that it bothered him. He and I often talked about how we felt about church and God. Both my brother and I agreed that as soon as we were of age, we would bail out and never look back. Our only concern would be our siblings we'd leave behind. It was always about struggling to make ends meet which was a bummer. We were teens now and we were understanding things more, especially the financial struggle. It was a given that pastors were poor and always struggling financially. It was as though the poorer you looked the more humble and spiritual you were. How unfortunate that we just got used to going without the basic necessities because there was never any money!

My parents were in full time ministry in every sense of the word for years. There were a couple incidents that will always stay with me as a sad memory. When the finances were really bad, my dad took on a part time job at a local gas station to make ends meet at home. Unfortunately, when the congregation found out, they began to criticize and accuse him of wanting to make money. Well, hello? What do you think? We were so desperately poor and without the basic needs; dad had to do something! No one but NO ONE came to my parent's defense except for the Chavez family. No one knew when our utilities were turned off, which was often. It seemed every month one of the utilities turned off. I know my parents were grieved over it. I don't know exactly how it was resolved I only know my dad was ruthlessly pressured until he was forced to quit the job. I never understood why my parents never told these small-minded trouble-makers to back off or leave the church; maybe my parents were just too naïve, humble or prideful to tell anyone about our needs at home. One thing I do know, there was no mercy spared by anyone in the church to try and understand what was really going on. Another time dad invested in a small *"used"* typewriter that he needed for Bible school and church sermons. He was accused of spending church monies on himself without permission. I remember overhearing him tell my mother that he didn't think he needed to call a board meeting to make such a small necessary purchase. I never knew how that all panned out either but I know the typewriter stayed.

By now, I was a teenager and more often I remember overhearing talk about these things and it made me so angry within. I wanted so much to express my feelings to the congregation. One day I was sitting in the pew fantasizing how I would just walk up to the pulpit and say what was on my mind for my parents and put everyone on notice about all the hardships our family was forced to survive. I wanted to tell everyone to just give us a break and shut their gossiping mouths. It was only out of pure respect for my parents that I didn't go through with it. I didn't want to humiliate them or get in trouble; even though at that point, I didn't really care about much anyway. My father eventually completed Bible school, thank God!

As a teenager, I began to voice my concerns and complaints to my mother who took the brunt of it all so as not to stress my dad out. I don't think she ever told him anything that would go on at home. I saw everyone as critics and hypocrites because of the way they acted. There were only a small handful of people that genuinely supported my parents. I was becoming more rebellious; or maybe I was just fed up with it all. No one ever tried to reach out to me or understand me as a youth. I can't speak for my other siblings except that they too, began to see things going on and it wasn't pleasant. There was no communication between the pastor's kids and the congregation. How sad that the memory of this solitary, Sister Emma Chavez watching out for mom, sticks out so strongly in our memories to this day. She impacted all our lives by her small, loving, seemingly insignificant thing like making sure mom had nylons because it was such a big deal at that time. Even after all these years, we still talk about her.

As far back as I can remember mom never went shopping for herself. She went to thrift stores to make affordable purchases like a blouse or skirt to wear. She was very thrifty but then again, because there was no money, she had to be! God forbid she would spend any money on personal things for herself! This pastor's wife was young and pretty but looked homely because of the bland style of dressing and combing of her long, beautiful hair. This wasn't sending me any good messages about Christianity. She loved the Lord and I could see her genuine focus on ministry. She never fussed to dad about wanting or needing personal things. She just made the best with what she had. Sister Emma was the only woman who took the time to visit mom when she did and bring her little surprises. The funny thing was that so many congregation members were afraid of this very bold and outspoken woman. She was somewhat dominant, very outspoken and extremely strict with her five children in. I liked the fact that she had the gumption to speak out for my mother and us. She wasn't afraid of anyone. Even I was afraid to speak out of line around her. I respected her and knew she had our best interests at heart. No one took the time to ask my parents what they needed or to reach out to us children. Later I often wondered if other pastors had special people in their lives like these two. It was as though we lived on separate planets. I didn't want to be around church people. There didn't seem to be anything kind or changed about them. I remember looking around during church services and brainstorming. Many thoughts went through my head about all these people in my Dad's church and wondered if all other churches and pastors kids would go through the same things we did. There wasn't any warmth or connection with any of the congregation towards me or any of my siblings. I can remember a few times that we had revivals and special guest speakers that preached powerful moving messages. One time, it moved me to the point where I actually responded to the altar call. I cried out to God in those times and wanted to convert my life to him but didn't really know how to or what to say. I suppose I was definitely touched by God because I was broken and cried out to him. A part of me wanted Jesus in my life but it was always a spiritual tug of war and the enemy would remind me of the horrible church people who wouldn't believe me or would criticize me if I tried to do anything in the church. Unfortunately, it was on one of those nights that I truly had an encounter with God and spent a long time at the altar praying. I remember that no one prayed for me and maybe it was for the best because it would have thrown me off. After this service, I later learned that the ladies had been making comments about my hair and the fact that I was wearing makeup, most of which I had cried off anyway. The sad part of this altar call experience was that I had cried to God to help me be a better person, to change me to be different from the others who attended my dad's church. I asked God not to let me be bothered with these people and perhaps use me someday, somehow to work for Him with the youth with fresh ideas. I wanted to do things differently. I asked God to help me play the piano and sing someday. I can't say for sure that I was actually saved or that I had a genuine born again experience then, because I didn't confess to anyone that I had invited Jesus into my life just in case I couldn't live the proper Christian life. Funny how **NO ONE** in our church did any follow up with me about my walk with God. No one checked to see if I needed anything or to pray with me for direction in my life. Maybe everyone thought since I was the pastor's daughter, I would just know when I was saved. I really had no idea. I know that on this one night I felt a tugging in my heart that was different than anything I had ever felt before. My parents were always busy with the ministry and never sat with me *(or any of us)* about where we were with Jesus or where we could be used in ministry. They were sincerely excited about the many miracles and deliverances taking place. They were radically on fire for God and at the peak of their ministry. With the exception of the ministry, our life was actually pretty simple. I know we were all very close despite abusive ministry experiences beyond our control. I still never told my parents about the elder who had molested me in my dad's car.

Now it was 1967. Through the power of God more miracles were taking place. People were miraculously delivered from cancer, deafness, blindness and many other physical ailments. My older brother and I continued our talks about leaving home when we became of age. We would vent to each other about everything. He finally got a car and my parents began to trust us both to go out but we had to go together. Our curfew was ten o'clock. We would leave together to go cruise up and down a popular cruising strip where young people hung out. I would find my friends and leave with them. Man! What a treat it was to get out and do this. We would make sure to get all our chores done and do everything our parents asked of us during the week so we could go out on the weekends. My parents didn't know that although we left together, we would split up with our own friends and go our separate ways. Later we would meet again and come home together like a good brother and sister as if we had been together the whole night. This went on for a long time. There was nothing spiritual or PK about us when we went out because we would blast our rock and roll music and hang out with friends that had absolutely nothing to do with church and we loved it! It was a terrific feeling of freedom to go out and have what we thought was fun, fun, fun! We really thought we were getting away with so much but it was all done in innocence because we really were good kids. God forbid, the congregation found out that we were cruising on the strip! We never told our parents. We would lie about where we went and come home when we were supposed to. At first we were allowed to stay out till 10 pm. Later we were trusted to be back by midnight. We had so much fun. \We would laugh and talk about it all the way home. What an awesome lifetime memory.

My poor brother continued in gymnastics in school. He was very good at it too. My sister and I would stick around to watch him after school sometimes. Unfortunately, this would be a lifetime wound for him because he won a few times and neither one of my parents were ever able to be there to support him at any workouts or matches where he actually won. I don't think it was because they didn't care but because they were busy with the ministry and home life. It was important for my brother's self-esteem and confidence that my parents attend but unfortunately, it never happened. It's sad to say that the ministry robbed us all because it took priority over anything we had going on at school. Pastors and those in ministry need to make their family a top priority to prevent ill feelings from developing as they did in my life. I always felt like no one ever really genuinely cared about me. I don't think people appreciated the fact that we sacrificed our parents and shared them all the time; day or night. Seven children was an excess of little lives to sacrifice. We were all different and unique with different needs that went unnoticed.

Congregations need to be sensitive to pastor's kids because we too sacrifice our parents for you. It's a package deal! I'm not sure congregations get this. One would think it is a warm life-changing experience with wonderful memories of being surrounded by people who love the Lord and not a life of such emotional pain, struggle, resentment and hardship. It was my experience watching my parents in ministry that pastors can be overloaded from having a ministry and a church that can cause them to feel overwhelmed, discouraged and eventually experience ministry burnout. It's a wonder my mother didn't get completely discouraged. I'm convinced today that my parents genuinely loved the Lord and never dreamed ministry would affect us in a negative way. We learn from experience that you only get one chance at raising your own children and once they're grown, it's next to impossible to undo the damage. There are no *"do-overs."* As PK's our memories shouldn't have all been of horrible struggles, poverty, and endless nights in church with not enough time for what was important to us.

One of the most detrimental turn offs as a PK, was all the legalistic rhetoric from the congregation. There were those who interpreted the Bible in such a way that they came up with all these rules of do's and don'ts **they** felt was indisputable law to be followed in order to be in God's will or be considered holy, sanctified and be accepted as a good, God-fearing Christian. All along, there was actually nothing damning (*in my opinion*) with going to see good clean movie at the theater. Instead we were taught to believe it wasn't Godly to go to movies or hang out with unsaved people. To a certain point yes, I could see the truth in that but as a young person, I should have been trusted to make a sound value judgment so that I didn't have to be sneaking around as I did for years.

Today I would encourage you to take an extra step to engage in dialogue to get to know your pastors' children. Try doing simple little random acts of kindness as a token of appreciation; things like remembering their birthdays or giving simple little *"just because"* gifts. How sad that I don't have any memories (at all) of any birthday parties for me or any of my siblings. Mom would bake a cake; but that was it! There was never any money for things like that. Embrace you pastors' children. This is especially true when they are teens because we go through the normal teen-age changes other kids do. Make them feel wanted; loved and needed. I remember feeling like a complete "*misfit*" to the church; always left out and felt like I was only in the way. How sad that I wasn't ever able to find my place in my own father's church because of ignorant people who didn't possess the true love and understanding of the God they served. They just didn't get it! PKs shouldn't want to run the other way as soon as they become of age! We want/need to know that you genuinely care about our lives too. Parents can only do so much. The church today needs to display a more nurturing and unconditionally loving attitude towards PKs. I challenge you to ask yourself where you are with your pastors and their children.

A Marriage Made In Heaven

(Or was it?)

My parents often hosted special fellowship services that occurred every Monday night. It was called "La Confraternidad" (*Spanish for,* **The Fellowship**). It consisted of several Pentecostal Spanish churches that came from several cities to congregate and praise the Lord together with different preachers and special songs. It was held at different locations every week. I liked it because lots of people came. We teen girls looked forward to it because lots of cute guys would come. Everyone knew my dad's church had the highest number of youth and girls. It was fun to look forward to having all these cute guys come to talk either before or after services. It was the normal teenage hormones going crazy. It was a lot of fun because it was an exciting break from my father's regular congregation. These fellowship services were a lot of extra work for my mother because she would prepare the food for after service fellowship and then stay to clean up later. In those days, no one went out for fellowship after church to local restaurants or coffee shops as they do today. All the after service fellowship took place in the back kitchen or patio areas of the churches.

There was an elderly lady pastor and her daughter who were regulars at these special fellowship services. They didn't include the youth from their church as their congregation was predominately elderly. However, they did have a 20 year old grandson who transported them to and from these services. He would bring them, drop them off and leave. He would return on time to pick them up at the end of service.

When services began, everyone had to be inside church (*especially the youth*), with no one outside! Church rules were very strict and no one questioned authority. We knew we had to be inside the church or be reprimanded later. My Aunt Rosie used to police the grounds. She made sure everyone was indoors and not out clowning around. We all feared getting caught by her. When we walked out to use the restroom, you better believe she was looking for us if we weren't back in a reasonable amount of time. If someone got caught outdoors breaking the rules or just hanging out, she would reprimand them, tell my dad and their parents' later.

One day before I actually became aware of it, this certain grandson started coming right back when services began. He would go to the window and look in. He would just stand there at the window during services looking in. He had been watching me for quite some time but never went inside for services. When church was over, he would go back to his car watch us and wait for his mother and grandmother who were visiting pastors. This went on for quite a while. One day when services were over, he walked over to where we were all hanging out and began to mingle with us. Several weeks went by and he began to actually attend the services because I noticed him sitting in the back. He began waiting around to talk to me after church. His name was Carlos. They called him "JR". Not long after, I learned who his mother and grandmother were. He and I began talking and getting to know each other better. It was amazing how much we had in common. He told me how his grandma and mother were pastors of a church too in another county. One day he commented how his grandma and mother noticed him talking to me and they thought it was nice but reminded him that I was "*la hija del pastor*" (*Spanish for the pastor's daughter*) so he better be on his best behavior and respectful. He told them he was thinking about asking me out on a date. They immediately discouraged him against it and told him to just get that idea out of his head. They didn't want bad vibes or any trouble from the pastor (*my dad*) if he learned their grandson was interested in his daughter. We continued talking and always looked forward to these Monday night services and could hardly wait for church to be over so we could talk. Not only was this guy fun but he was also very funny. He continued coming to church and hanging out with me. After a while, his grandmother and mother started waiting for him while he was talking to me and didn't want to leave right away. Of course, by now, my parents and the congregation had noticed us talking. It was the church gossip.

After several months, Carlos finally got up enough nerve to ask me out. My biggest fear was telling my parents. I was sure they would say "*NO*" so I simply told him I needed more time. He told me what his family said about us dating. By this time he and his family had been talking about us and the dating thing. He said they offered to speak to my parents on his behalf because it was the right thing to do but he wouldn't have it and insisted they stay out of it and let him talk to my parents. A few weeks later he asked me out again. I had practiced what I was going to tell him when the time came. He insisted we go out on a date and was willing to ask my parents. I froze and like a dummy, I forgot to say what I had practiced. I just told him I didn't think it was a good idea because my parents were very strict. Dating was a sensitive subject with my parents because of what had happened on my last date a year ago that went terribly wrong. I told him how it had left me completely devastated. I had never mentioned anything about this to Carlos because I was so embarrassed. I simply told him I didn't think it was a good idea but he insisted on asking my parents himself and gave me the date he was going to ask which was to be in two weeks after the Monday night service. He talked about what we would do on our date. But I once again reminded him how strict my parents were and if they let me go at all, I would have a curfew. He didn't care and said it was fine.

He just wanted to spend time with me and get to know me without a bunch of people around. Well, I got enough nerve to agree and told him that we would probably need to have a date plan because my father was sure to ask where he planned to take me. Well, he suggested something simple like dinner and the movies. I quickly told him I wasn't allowed to go to the movies and asked him *NOT* to say movies. He asked what was wrong with movies. I explained how my parents didn't allow us to go to the theater because of our religious convictions. I suggested something like dinner and maybe go for a drive. I thought about how cool it would be to go on a date with another PK who could totally relate to me because we came from the same background. I thought, "*Wow! My parents will like this guy because he was funny too!*" I think they already liked him. By now I was 17 years old and quickly approaching my 18th birthday; he was 20. I had been on two other dates before him so this one would be my third official date. The two prior dates had been with someone that either came to my parent's church or were connected somehow to church family. Carlos wanted to know what actually happened on my last date and why it was a disaster. I told him I really didn't want to talk about it. This only made him that much more curious and politely insisted I tell him. Reluctantly, I explained how this guy and all his family attended my father's church. My date had asked my dad if we could go out and to my amazement, he let me go. However, when we were on our date, we had spent some time kissing (*necking*) - nothing vulgar but I had never made out with anyone like I did with him. No sex involved, of course. We had to check in with my parents who would be in the back of the church kitchen making tamales with other ladies from the fellowship. We were 15 minutes late and quickly exited the car to check in. As we were walking to the church kitchen, he commented to me; "*Hey, watch your neck.*" I didn't know what he meant and I just laughingly said it back to him, "*Watch your neck silly*" When we walked in, I saw all the "hermanas" (*sisters*) and greeted them all. I commented to my parents that we were back. Everyone just looked at us. I was used to the congregation always staring at me anyway so I didn't think anything of it. I was a little anxious because we were a late and my dad was very strict. Both my parents had an angry look on their face. I just knew I was in trouble. I honestly didn't have any idea what my parents long faces were all about. My dad told us both to wait outside and they'd be out to talk to us soon. We walked out and were wondering what they were going to tell us. Shortly after, both my parents walked out, closed the kitchen door behind them and walked towards us. I was so nervous and scared. My date quickly began to apologize for bringing me home a bit late. My dad asked him to be quiet. I tried to explain how time just slipped by. I had a slight smile to my face out of pure nervousness and embarrassment. My mother assumed I was laughing at her. She asked me *"Do you really think this is funny?"* But before I could answer or ask her what was wrong, she slapped me across the face! She thought I was smirking at her but I was just nervous and embarrassed in front of my date. I had so many thoughts crossing my mind and just couldn't believe what had just happened. I continued to try and talk to my mother again (*still nervous*) but I guess my nervous smile angered her more. I attempted to talk to my date and before I could continue, she asked me once again if I really thought all this was funny and slapped me again on the other side of my face! I looked at him and could tell he was mortified as he stood there stunned and speechless. He stumbled to find words to apologize to my dad for being a late. My father ordered me in the house immediately and told my date to never come around me again. My date still kept trying to apologize but it just fell on deaf ears because my parents were both infuriated and didn't want to hear it. They both walked back into the kitchen where they were making their tamales. We started walking back to the house (*next door*). He kept saying he was so sorry and would call me during the week or catch up with me at school and left. I was still in shock as to what had just happened not to mention the heat to my cheeks from the slaps to my face. I began crying from humiliation and hurt with my parents for embarrassing me this way. I was devastated because I really had feelings for this guy. I proceeded straight to my room and cried. A few minutes later, I walked over to the bathroom to wash my face because I knew my makeup was a mess and probably all smeared. Nothing could prepare me for what I saw next. I looked in the mirror and was shocked by what I saw. My neck was full of hickeys from one end of my neck to the other! I suddenly realized why he had said, "*Watch your neck*". I ran to my room, turned on the light and looked in my mirror up close. As naive as I was, I wondered if I'd get pregnant too. It all came together and now I knew what my parents were so upset about and all this time I was thinking it was because we were late. My parents stood in the kitchen finishing up their tamales. It must have just killed my parents to stay calm until they were finished. A couple of hours later, they returned to the house. I suppose they were feeling humiliated in front of all the brethren and having to act normal until they were all done. It was honestly my first experience having hickeys and I really didn't know they were on my neck. I was mortified and ashamed by what I saw. It scared me too!

As I continued telling Carlos the rest of my embarrassing story, he looked dumbfounded. All he could say was, "*Are you kidding?*" as though he couldn't believe what he had just heard. I explained to him that my parents were very, very strict and didn't mess around. I told him that I knew I really hadn't done anything wrong and was still pure. I told him I hadn't had sex with this guy; it was only necking and I felt awful about it because it was nothing like my parents thought. I explained how my father later came to my room to scold me again for humiliating them in front of church members. His concerns were that the church members that had seen me. I was angry that he didn't believe me. We argued for a while until I lost it and told my dad "*I really didn't give a darn what church people said*". He assumed we had sex. I reached a breaking point where I broke down crying from hurt and yelled out that my date and I did in fact have sex, I loved it and I'd do it again and again! It was then that my father slapped me across the face and somehow I lost my balance and fell to the floor as he was reminding me how people were going to talk about this night to everyone; and then walked out. I remembered feeling so hurt with dad because it was the first time had he ever hit me. I told Carlos how I cried more about the hurt I felt with my parents because I hadn't done anything wrong, hadn't had sex or anything as they thought I did because of those hickeys. I knew I was innocent. I didn't know about sex yet. I told Carlos that's why it was going to be really tough for my parents to agree to let me go on a date again.

Carlos promised this would never ever happen with us and he would assure my parents they had nothing to worry about. I told him I didn't think it was a good idea right away and asked him to give it few more weeks or even months. I explained how I had been grounded for months after that disaster. My parents and I never talked about the incident again. This boyfriend didn't come to my dad's church anymore. His sisters and parents still attended my parent's church and told me that their brother told them what had happened that night. I was so embarrassed for a long, long time. Weeks after this incident, all those people that were in the kitchen that night continued to look at me but said nothing. I could see "*those looks*" on their faces each time they saw me and it made me feel embarrassed and like a real loser. I explained to Carlos that "*if*" my parents let me go, this would be my first date since that incident. The designated Monday was quickly approaching. I did everything I could to earn my "*brownie points*" at home to impress my parents so they would say yes when Carlos asked to take me out.

The day that we had been waiting for finally arrived. I had huge butterflies in my stomach during service that night. He was waiting until after church to ask them. The whole service seemed to take extra long and I couldn't stop thinking about what my parents would say and hoping they wouldn't embarrass me again and say something cruel. Naturally I was hopeful they'd have mercy and just give me a chance and let me go. The moment finally came when church was over and casually; Carlos approached my parents. My mom stood beside dad. There were a lot of people there that night. I couldn't bear to watch and pretended to be preoccupied while he was talking

47

to them. Every now and then I would look over towards them. My dad was looking very serious as my mother just looked on. Oh how I wanted the ground to open up and swallow me. I just walked around trying to keep busy. By the time they had finished talking, I was serving drinks to his mother and grandmother in the fellowship hall. My parents and Carlos later walked into the fellowship hall and acted normal. Carlos motioned me to meet him outside. We met and sat to talk. He had a serious look on his face as he said I was right about my father being very strict. My father told him he was hesitant about letting me go and had a feeling this was going to happen but because of his (*Carlos*) parents, he was going to make an exception and let me go. By now he is smiling and my heart sank with surprise that my dad agreed to let me go. Of course they spelled out all the rules (*just as I told him they would*) which we had to follow or I'd never be allowed to go out again. I didn't care, I knew it helped that Carlos mother and grandmother were ministers too and Carlos was also a PK.

It is now 1967. On the evening of our date, he came to pick me up in his new big beautiful deep forest green Cadillac, El Dorado of the year. It blew my mind how big and beautiful this car was. I learned a lot about him during our date. He was active in motorcycle movies with his motorcycle which was a 1954 Harley Davison with suicide gears. It was all news to me that he was an actor too. In fact, he had just bought this car in cash, with the monies he made from one of the latest movies he was in. He had been in a couple of other movies before this one. Motorcycle movies were hot during the sixties. He explained how the movie director let him wear his special helmet which was a German chrome helmet with a spear coming out of the top. I thought it was cool. It all seemed so exciting. But I also learned that his family was strict with him and imposed rules on him as well. It felt so good to relate perfectly to someone else in my similar shoes.

We dated for months before my parents finally allowed me to begin coming home by midnight instead of 10 pm as before. We had dated about a year, always following all the rules set up by my parents before he popped the question about marriage. He talked about how perfect our lives would be because of our common Godly upbringing and that it would be a marriage made in heaven. I thought it was too soon and told him I would think about it. I couldn't imagine what my parents would say except that we were too young. Actually, I was 18 by now and he was 21. The more I thought about it, I believed like this would be my big opportunity to make my exit from our house and get to finally leave home with all the church rules, regulations, legalistic nonsense and religious practices. I wanted to be on my own and be free to go to movies and have fun like everyone else.

Ten months after he had first mentioned marriage, I dropped the bomb on my parents about Carlos wanting to marry me. They were both shocked. They thought we were too young and neither of us was ready for marriage. They begged me to reconsider and think it over because it wasn't going to be as easy as we thought. Well, their advice fell upon deaf ears because I just wanted *OUT*! I felt certain that I loved him as much as he loved me and we could make it work. After all, we were both PK's. I wanted to prove everyone wrong and show them all that marriage for us could work! To my surprise, his parents also thought we were too young but they didn't want us to do anything dumb like elope. They all knew we were dead set on getting married. Not long after, his parents came to my parents to hold a meeting and officially asked for my hand in marriage which was the proper thing to do at that time. His family was pleased that their son was marrying a good girl. He told me how his family was so pleased that he was marrying another PK that came from a good family. They liked me for him and were in agreement to pay for most of the wedding. Neither Carlos nor I attended this meeting. We would have to wait till later to find out what was discussed, arranged and agreed upon.

The wedding was set for September 28, 1968. My father would perform the ceremony at his church. The wedding planning began. We strategically set the date for nine months later so people wouldn't think we were getting married because "*I had to*". In those days one assumed if you got married quickly, it was because you were (**P.G.**) pregnant! At any rate, I was scared but happy about making wedding plans especially since I was still a virgin. I was sure this would be a wedding made in heaven because of our sincerity to do things right and everyone would know the pastor's daughter was getting married the right way and not because I was pregnant. I wanted my parents to feel proud of this wedding even though I knew they weren't exactly thrilled about me getting married so soon after graduation from high school. I remember feeling so sure that God would be pleased with us and that we would have a wonderful life because we were doing things the right way. We knew when we began a family, our children would attend Sunday school like we did and go to church as well. We weren't going to have religious arguments about religion or where our kids would attend church. Neither Carlos nor I had a real relationship with God. Neither one of us confessed to having Jesus Christ in our lives. We continued dating and I made a sacred vow to myself, God, my parents and my husband-to-be; that I would save myself until marriage and give my parents at least this one honor. I wanted to be remembered that this pastor's daughter was married proper and pure. Virginity was an important thing back then. I didn't want to walk down the aisle in shame and pregnant on my wedding day like many weddings I had witnessed. It was my way of leaving my home and family with honor and making parents proud of me. For sure, it was one thing I wasn't going to ruin. It was exciting shopping for a dress. We found a big white dress and an extremely long, long veil. I felt so pretty and right. After months and months of planning, the wedding day finally arrived. I had butterflies in my stomach and I was happy, scared and excited all at the same time. As my uncle (*my dad's younger brother*) walked me down the aisle, my father stood at the front watching me. He was a bit emotional and tearful the whole time but he managed to get through the ceremony. It was truly "**a marriage made in heaven**". Everything was perfect and wonderful including the reception.

Our married life was great for the first year. After that we began having problems. I found out that he had begun smoking marijuana and continued in his acting career as well. He was hardly ever home. He also began to sing with a band in the neighborhood. They called themselves; **"Lil Jr. & Odyssey."** He was the featured lead vocalist. His acting career took off and he spent a lot of time in acting classes too. This went on for quite some time. He was always either at band practice or at his acting (*Improve*) classes. He began playing gigs with the band everywhere and they quickly became very popular. He loved it and bragged about how everyone liked them. He was actually a very good singer but began having serious mood swings that were completely foreign to me. By our second year of our marriage I realized that I had made a huge mistake. Yes he was a PK like me but he was nowhere near ready to make a commitment to the Lord and in fact, was high on marijuana most of the time. I begin to miss my family and sadly remembered my parents telling me that "*he wasn't ready for marriage, it's too soon*". I spent most of my time alone at home like a good wife. I did a lot of crying and wishing I had listened to my parents. I figured this would be my punishment from God for my disobedience and not listening. In our second year I became pregnant with our first son. Everyone (*including Carlos*) was very happy about a baby coming. He promised to change and spend more time at home. He said things would get better. It worked for a while but it didn't take long before he returned to his old self again; leaving me alone, getting high with his friends and coming home in the wee hours of the morning. I was no longer making dinners for him because I never knew if or when he would be home. So many nights I cried myself to sleep.

My pregnancy was a sad and lonely one because of his partying lifestyle. I spent most of the time alone, crying, feeling lonely and regretting that I had ever married this guy. One day during the fifth month of my pregnancy, I asked him to take me to visit my parents for a while. He didn't want to. This went on for weeks and months during my pregnancy. One day I asked him again to please take me to see my family. I actually knew that on that day, they were all going to be at their morning prayer. We went to the house first but they weren't there. I went to the church next door and found quite a few people there praying. I asked him to leave me there for a while to visit. He gladly left me and drove off. He was in a bad mood. As I sat on the bench in the back of my dad's church listening to everyone praying, I began to get a weird feeling as I had felt before when the power of God got a hold of me. As everyone was praying, I began sort of trembling within and I thought I should pray about my problems so I made my way down the aisle to the front of the church. I somehow knew as I was walking, that something (*life changing*) was about to take place in my life. I just felt it coming as I knelt at the altar. I surrendered my life to God that day and asked him to come into my life, change me, forgive me and use my life for His honor and glory. I was at that alter for hours and by the time I got up; God had spoken to me about sing for him, playing my piano and work with the youth. I had never felt this before but on this day, I knew I wanted to do something for God. Unbeknownst to me, Carlos had come back for me while I was at the altar praying. He sat and waited but became angry because I was taking too long. My father told him he would give me a ride home later if he didn't mind. Later, I remember thinking I didn't care. I felt so good, lighter, happy and different. I remember feeling for the first time that I had definitely made a decision to receive Jesus Christ into my life as my personal savior that day. I had a genuine encounter with God and felt totally transformed like NEVER before. I couldn't stop crying tears of joy and thanked God for coming into my life. I was genuinely transformed that day and I promised to serve Him the rest of my days. It was an awesome feeling. I knew I was changed inside! My parents and others that were there that day were so happy for me. My parents took me home later that afternoon and counseled me about how I would be tried and tested in my new walk and decision to serve the Lord. They told me that even though Carlos knew of God, he wasn't ready for a commitment; I needed to continue praying for him and let the Lord deal with him. They reminded me of the power of prayer and how I simply needed to put my marriage in God's hands. I began to attend church as often as I could. It wasn't long after, I gave birth to out first son. I was also baptized in water. My dad baptized me in water. That experience was even more amazing. I knew that I wanted to be totally radical for God and I was called for a special purpose in my life. I just felt it in my spirit. I wasn't sure exactly what it was I wanted to do, but I would wait on God. All my hurt and feelings towards all those ladies in my parents church who had talked, offended and hurt me, no longer meant anything to me. I didn't care what people thought of me anymore either because God had taken away all that pain. I knew I wanted my walk with the Lord to be different and just wanted to keep it real! I felt God's calling on my life to minister in song and maybe someday preach.

As time went on, I would try and get to church early and stay afterwards just to practice on the piano at dad's church every time I got the chance. It was hard because we only had one car. My husband would give me a ride to church and my parents would give me a ride home. He liked this because he didn't have to worry about coming home early. He was free to go out to do his thing knowing his good little wife was in church. I didn't care because I couldn't seem to get enough of God in my life. My husband began rebelling against my decision to serve God and my desire to be in church. Most of the time he was out having band practice or on the road holding concerts on weekends so I was able to go to church pretty much all I wanted. I loved going to church, singing and praising the Lord. It was like I was on my own spiritual honeymoon. This worked out great for him and his agenda which included drugs, weekend travel and by now, other women.

His parents continuously apologized to me for their son's behavior. They had no idea what their son was truly involved in and I didn't want to volunteer the information. They continued attending services at dad's church on Monday nights as well. I always asked for prayer for my husband. I would try and talk to Carlos about the

Lord and how much we needed to attend church together. He always told me he didn't want anything to do with God at this time and he wasn't ready to make a commitment. He said it was fine for me but not to expect him to do the same until he was ready. He didn't want me to talk about God because he already knew all about God. He said that when he was ready, he would make his own decision; he just didn't want to hear it for now. I sometimes talked to him about living for God and giving his singing talents to the Lord. It was often hard NOT to talk about God, especially when there was a great service where the power of God had moved touched and changed people's lives. I always had a burning desire to share with him especially since I knew he knew about God. After all, I was on fire for God. I took risks sharing with him knowing he didn't want to hear it. I would remind him that his singing talent was from the Lord and he could be used mightily to win souls! He still, didn't want to hear it and would ask me to be quiet.

When our first son was born, Carlos was so very happy and again promised to make changes for our sake and spend more time with us. I suppose a part of him meant it but he was so caught up in his other crazy life that he could only keep his promise for a short time. He lasted only a little while before I began to see those familiar behaviors in him again. I learned later that he was beginning to experiment with harder drugs like PCP and super cools. He'd come home in the early hours of the morning if at all. It was sad and lonely because I had no one to share my joy with except my baby.

His group, *"Lil Jr. & Odyssey"* sang Oldies but Goodies. They were very popular at the time and for many years to come. His head and heart were filled with so much pride. He didn't think he needed God or me. Many years went by and he wouldn't change. I grew tired of living alone and finally left him indefinitely for the first time on the fifth year of our marriage. He couldn't believe that I had actually left. He begged me to come back home promising that he would make changes for good. He asked for forgiveness and promised me the world. He said he really needed his family in his life. Naturally, I wanted to believe him and in time, reluctantly, I returned home. It was only a matter of time before once again; I began to see all the old familiar signs. I knew it wouldn't be too long before his addiction would take over getting the best of him and he would completely return to his old ways. That's exactly what happened. He began to stay out for days at a time now. There were many times when I worried because I hadn't heard from him and I would think maybe something was terribly wrong. He did this over and over until it became the norm that he didn't always come home. I continued to pray and trust God for his deliverance from drugs. Unfortunately, he grew worse with physical assaults on me and began violent behaviors at home that caused me to be afraid of him. I didn't know he was anymore as he had changed significantly. I felt shame that the marriage wasn't working. I hid a lot of what was going on from his parents. They began to realize that he wasn't coming home for days because his car wasn't there. We lived in the back house behind his family's home. His grandmother would take him aside and remind him that he had a good woman and asked him if this was what he wanted a good wife for? She'd told him how he was an embarrassment to both families and warned him that if he didn't change his ways, he would end up losing us. He listened respectfully but later came home and accused me of talking to his parents about all our personal business; which I hadn't.

Business was booming big time for his band. He let his acting career go and began traveling with the band full time up and down the state. They began performing with well known oldie artist. He felt so confident that he was headed for the big time. He would tell me he didn't care or have time for small things like home life and family. He ran around with other women all the time. He continued using hard drugs and lashing out at me physically and emotionally. Our marriage by now was constantly violent. I never knew what mood he would be in when he did come home. I often had bruises that I hid from my parents, my friends at church and his family. I often remembered my parents telling me this would happen. Oh how I regretted getting married. One of my main reasons was to just get the out of the house (*respectfully*) and just be on my own. It was too late because not only did I have our two year old son but now I was pregnant from our second son and four years later, our daughter was born. The children were the love of my life. I loved being a mommy. They too, were brought up in the ministry. Although I knew I had grounds for divorce because of his promiscuity, I chose to believe for his change through prayer. I believed God could and would change him.

After 15 years of an abusive marriage, 3 children, several separations including a move to the State of Florida, his countless adulterous affairs, drugs, arrests and numerous acts of violence towards me and the kids, I decided to file for a divorce. It took so much from me to do this as I had prayed and fasted for years (*off and on*) that he would repent from his ways and change. The kids were older now and their living environment was definitely not healthy. Even so, I became an expert at hiding all my pain, tears, and bruises from the world around me. I was so tired of all the fighting at home whenever I would see or talk to him due to his addiction. It was becoming harder and harder to explain things to the kids. By now they were asking more questions like why I was crying. My oldest son one day asked why I was always sad when daddy was around and why I was crying. I told him, it was because I was praying. *He responded "I know you're not praying because it only happens when he comes to the house and makes you sad"*. Carlos was totally unwilling to make the necessary changes for our marriage to work. For years I wondered how our lives could have turned out this way. I was so deeply wounded that our marriage hadn't work out. I never wanted divorce in my life but I was the one making all the sacrifices, including the kids. I was brought up believing divorce was not an option! Not only did he not have any time for family in his life, but he made it clear he wanted no part of God either. What a devastating reality and disappointment for me/us. I truly believed in my heart we would have a great marriage and yet, it went quite the opposite

Church Doors Close
New Door Opens

Several years went by and urban renewal came in through our city. My parents were forced to sell the church property they had worked so hard to build and eventually purchased another church in another city not far away. They were there for a few short years. Nothing could have ever prepared any of us for what would come to pass shortly after. My father went through a period of discouragement and fell from grace. He left the ministry altogether. It was one of the most heartbreaking, difficult and saddest time for our entire family and congregation. It was also one of the most challenging times for my faith. My parents had always been my pillars of strength and role models. They were held in the highest regard by the congregation and the community as well. But in spite of it all, they ultimately separated. Their separation brought about a church split and it sent their flock scattering to different churches. His fall was so crushing to us all and it would affect all our lives in an inconceivable way for a pastor's family, especially my siblings. Who would have ever thought this could and would hit our parent's? After all, they had a thriving church, well-respected and esteemed by many. Truthfully, there was a time that even I began to question the reality of what kind of a chance I stood of making my marriage work too (*we hadn't divorced yet*). I thought to myself, if this could happen to my parents who were strong Christians, in ministry and married for 25 years, what guarantee did I have of making my marriage work? I asked God "Why?" This wasn't supposed to happen. My wounded spirit searched for answers which I didn't have and didn't know where to begin. I knew it was going to be a big scandal when people found out, especially those that were the most self-righteous and critical of my parent's ministry anyway.

It was embarrassing to say the least and the gossip spread like wildfire. It was a horrible time for our family. We were all at a loss for words. My dad eventually left the home. We could not imagine what was next! My mother stayed back making the best of what was left of our family but she stopped going to church too. She made the mistake of isolating herself in her room. In time, she grew cold. She was grief-stricken and inconsolable. What was remarkable was how no one ever came to visit, encourage or offer to pray for the family. Maybe people just didn't know what to say; so they simply stayed away. How I wished anyone would have come over to talk with her. It was as though she had a plague and had disappeared from the face of the earth. I guess it was way too scandalous for anyone to deal with; so they stayed away.

I continued strong in my faith serving the Lord full force and spiritually supporting my mother and my siblings as much as I could through this unspeakably difficult time. I was married and had my own cross to bear at home. I didn't want Carlos to know about my parents. My younger brothers began to act up in school. They too were miserably unhappy after the separation. Nothing would ever be normal to them again. They were understandably angry but didn't know how to channel their anger and grief. They began to hang out with "*undesirables*" from the neighborhood. I thought our home couldn't possibly get any worse but guess what? It did, in a big way. My brothers began cutting school and acting up towards their teachers. My younger sisters tried to compensate for the boys the best they could at home. My brothers friends began coming over and hanging out at the house blasting music and drinking. In time, I noticed by brothers began getting tattooed which was a no-no in our home. It didn't take the local Sheriffs too long to red flag our once respectable *"pastors"* home as a troubled, chaotic local hang out where gang members came to party. By now, they knew my brothers by their new street nick names because they had been called out to our home on numerous occasions. My poor mother took the brunt of it all still trying to balance the home, the kids, and the lack of money with our utilities constantly getting turned off or on the verge of getting turned off over and over again. My sisters began changing the way they talked and even dressed. For me, this was worse than a horror movie. Everything my parents preached against was now the day-to-day norm in our home.

Whenever we ran into people in public, their concern was more about *"What happened, we heard or was such and such true?"* instead of lifting my parents in prayer. It seemed all they wanted was to get the straight scoop of what was going on. Apprehensively I would just tell them all to pray for our family. My mother continued to withdraw from everyone. She hardly came out anymore and eventually she began drinking in her room to numb her pain. I kept praying and took time to fast over my family's situation and asking God for guidance, strength and encouragement. There were times when my emotions got in the way and I felt like I would cave in but I knew things would only get worse if there was no supportive balance. Everything went from bad to worst. My younger brothers refused to listen to anyone anymore. They were angry and rebellious.

My father announced he was going to close the doors of the church. I was involved in drug prevention outreach in the local community where my dad's church was. One day two of my associates and I met to discuss and strategize our program in the community. After the meeting, one of the brothers I worked with asked me how I was doing because he had noticed that I was somewhat withdrawn that day and unusually quiet during the meeting. I told him how my dad, as the pastor of our church, was considering closing the doors to his church and how he had fallen from grace. I shared how badly I felt about all this and asked they keep us in prayer because I truly believed that we needed to keep the church open in our community. We all prayed together that day believing God for guidance and direction in keeping the church doors open. One of the men I worked with was named Sal who was a converted, ex-drug addict. Sal strongly agreed that a church was needed in this barrio (*Spanish for neighborhood*). We talked about the possibility of getting some of the people from his church to come and hold services at dad's church. Later I spoke to my dad about this and asked if he could hold off on closing the doors so we could get someone in to hold services. He said that wasn't what he wanted to do. He just wanted it closed. I asked if he would just think about it. He reluctantly agreed to give it some thought.

A couple of these men were Christian brothers who a local church not far away. The pastors were Sonny and Julie. These pastors had a heart for the same kind of community we were working with, the drug addicts, prostitutes, gang members, alcoholics, and the low lives. They shared how God was miraculously moving in their church with this community. I told my friends that I had asked my dad about letting us use the church for services and he would think about it. It started with just an idea. The brothers thought it was a great idea. One day the three of us walked over to the church on the corner and stretched out our hands towards the chapel. We prayed that if it was God's will, then so be it. They too, were excited and said they would talk to their pastor as well.

My dad insisted to close the doors. There have been stories that said my dad was desperately looking for someone to take the church off his hands. That's not true. He only wanted to quietly close the church doors and take some time off so as to get his life in order. After a few weeks, my dad agreed to speak to Pastor Sonny. What a small world! It turned out that my dad had gone to Bible school with both Sonny, Julie and in fact, Julie's family commonly attended my father's Spanish church. Not long after this meeting with Pastor

Sonny, an agreement was worked out for the use of the church. We began holding services. Unbeknownst to us, Pastor Sonny had already been praying about branching out more Victory Temples but the finances were limited. Most of Sonny's congregation was ex-drug addicts, alcoholics; people with high risk lives. There wasn't a whole lot of money available to expand the ministry. Its funny how out of the tragedy of my father's fall and his plans to close his church, a new little church was about to be birthed.

Our first leader who served as our Pastor was Gilbert, along with his wife and three small children. In time we thought we should give the church an official name. The church wasn't as big as Victory Temple. It was more like a little chapel so we named it *The Chapel*". It would be the first of many other Chapels born out of this Outreach Ministry in the mid-seventies. It was a bittersweet deal in that it was my father's church but now would be occupied by other people unfamiliar to me. Pastor Sonny's vision to expand would become reality out of this little church in a big way. Unfortunately, my father's flock scattered. Some members stayed and began to attend The Chapel while others went to other ministries and some just stopped going to church altogether after the closing of his church. My sister, Klu, and I continued attending the Chapel services. I played the piano and led the worship services. I can remember feeling so awkward seeing someone else preaching up there on the pulpit instead of my dad. It was the same piano, offering baskets, kitchen, and fellowship hall but different people. As bittersweet as it was, we hung in there and adjusted. The people were different and dressed differently from what we were used to. The women wore pants to church which was a no-no in my dad's church. There were street people who came in just "*as is*". I observed and took it all in. It took some getting used to and a whole lot of adjusting. Although it was different, it sustained me through my grief and struggle with what was going on in our home with my parents and my marriage. The people didn't seem to care about all the specifics of how we got this building. They just enjoyed going to the services. The power of God was moving in a huge way in this little Chapel in the heart of a very hardcore neighborhood.

Unfortunately, not long after the start of great things happening in the chapel, our dear Pastor Gilbert became ill and died. Once again we were all devastated. As a new congregation, we were challenged with yet another major change. Pastor Sonny sent us temporary help like (Bro Phillip) until he could send someone permanently. This was an on fire preacher in the making. He was young and radical for God who had come out of the men's recovery home. At that time he was single and dating his girlfriend. Not too long after coming to Victory Chapel, my sister, a few others and I orchestrated a wedding shower for Phillip and his bride to be there at the Chapel because they announced they were getting married. It was fun and exciting growing together in this ministry because it was so very new. Oh, sure, we made our share of mistakes but we grew through it all. We were all learning together. My sister and I were making new friends and working this challenging ministry through its unique beginnings. As time went on, Pastor Sonny sent a couple more helpers until the time came when he sent us our final pastors Bobby and Dolores who would stay for the next twelve years.

During those years we had many visitors from the mother church, Victory Temple, and from the various men's rehabilitation homes. Our services were always exciting. The men's homes launched many mighty men of God who were powerful preachers and evangelist like brother's Rudy, Cal, Ray, Calki, and several other powerful men who had graduated from the men's homes. We always had a packed house. I continued playing the piano and assisting each pastor that came along with the worship ministry.

Each pastor had his own unique way of doing things. Following them came natural to me because of my earlier experience at my parent's church. I was used to logging in offerings, tithes, cleaning of the sanctuary and everything else that goes on in the ministry. The time came when other ministries would be birthed. These little Chapels were the beginning of numerous Chapels launched out in the 80's.

Through the years my sister, brother-n-law and I started a gospel group called *"The Chapel Singers"*, some called it *"Judy and the Chapel Singers"*. Everyone knew me as *"Sister Judy"* and that's the name people got to know me by. We would minister in many churches and not long after, we also began going into the prisons with different ministries. At church, I directed the Chapel choir which would go back and forth singing at other churches. I was encouraged by what I saw and heard at our little Chapel and my faith continued growing stronger to believe for my heart-broken mother and lost ex-pastor father. I prayed that they would be restored to their faith someday. I kept sharing with my mother what was going on at the Chapel but she didn't want to hear about church. It was too hurtful as she had once pastored this church with my dad and she couldn't find the strength to return as a visitor. I imagine this must have been very awkward for her. Even so, I continued to tell mom all about what God was doing at the church. I felt this ministry could help to restore her to wholeness. I began to invite her to hear and see the awesome things the Lord was doing at the Chapel for herself. I asked her to just come check it out. I could feel how difficult this was for her but I never stopped talking about Victory Chapel and the miracles and deliverances going on there. I was building my faith as well. We were holding street rallies and all sorts of activities in the community. By now the entire community knew about this Chapel. We continued singing with the choir and at one point; we even went out and purchased matching outfits for us all to wear. Keeping busy with this ministry helped my restoration too. By this time I was living near the church just up the street and it was convenient to walk to and from church. My three children were all little. I continued to pray and fast that the Lord would break the strongholds of drugs from my husband. He continued out of control.

The unpredictable, tumultuous drama continued to escalate even more with my family and the kids. My mother was like a pressure cooker under pressure all the time and one day she blew! She suffered a stroke which left her face and hands twisted. The worse it got, the more I fasted and prayed. It was so painful to see this once strong and powerful pastor's wife alone without any support from anyone. I was always feeling my faith tested. I also had my own drama at home with my unsaved, rebellious husband. I continued working in the ministry keeping busy and trusting God for a breakthrough in our family and in my marriage. I don't think our dad had any idea of the catastrophic chaos and devastation the home was left in but I never stopped praying that God's power would prevail and He would restore our family to wholeness once again.

One day I was sitting outside alone, praying and crying. I was pondering to myself how helpful it would have been for my parents to have had a support system they could have gone to for help or restoration. I wondered what other pastors do for help when something like this happens? Where do they go when they're in trouble, having marital problems, midlife crisis of any sort, a partner has an extra-marital affair, they experience ministry burnout or financial devastation, just to mention a few? What about the pastors' kids? What were we supposed do or where could we have gone? Regardless of all our various ages, we all carried so much unnecessary emotional baggage, shame, and disconnection from what use to be normal. We had more questions than answers. There was no comfort or support from anywhere. I thought about how these problems didn't make my pastor parent's bad people. After all, they were in the middle of personal crisis. What is the difference when anyone, anywhere has had an affair or marital problems? Why is it worse because they are pastors? I suppose because pastors and their kids (*again*) are held to higher standards. God forbid any one on them should fall from grace! I don't think it should have been the end of the world for either of my parents. They/we needed restoration not criticism. We need to have more compassion and understanding supported with prayer. It was trauma for us all! We were left to figure it out by ourselves and it felt like the end of the world for us to be shunned by the congregation and others we thought were caring, loving Christians. It was hurtful and devastating to our belief in God.

Even though we had no part in what had happened, our lives were tremendously affected. It cut deep to the core and permanently altered all our lives. I can remember one day sitting on the porch crying out to God to give me understanding and direction for my family. Although I believed God could work it all out, I still had a lot of unanswered questions and it tore me up inside. It's like no one was saying anything. I never gave up on God coming through for us all.

A real breaking point came when my younger 21-year old brother, Jonathan, was found dead of a heroin overdose. He had never been a drug user. He had just given up on life little by little and would always say how much he hated his life and everything around him. He always questioned why he was even born? Every time he drank, got high or frustrated, he questioned why he was born? He began experimenting with heroin after our parent's separation. Prior to this we *NEVER* had drugs around the house. The day my brother died a piece of my mother died as well. She mourned very hard as did our whole family. The enemy doesn't play around and he doesn't play fair! Bitterness had set in and everyone was already running on high emotions of our broken family and the shock that my little brother was suddenly dead. Our family was so broken and the wreckage was beyond human repair. It could only be salvaged by God Almighty. It was hard getting through all the funeral arrangements and later, the public display of our now shattered, dysfunctional family. It's a miracle that we even got through it at all. At the services it felt more like people were spectators of what was going on with our family. Many people were affected by my parent's marriage and church break up. I found it remarkable that in spite of it all, my mother still felt bad for the flock having to make the decision to find another church. She truly had a pastor's heart to feel what members were probably feeling. I continued to pray with mom and believe for her restoration. She was angry, hurt, humiliated and confused about what to do. There was such a sense of hopelessness. She would say she really didn't want to backslide and go to the world because she only knew the Christian way of life with my dad. My two younger sisters stood by her at home when I couldn't because I had my own family to care for and couldn't always be there. My younger siblings were all still at home and left to sink or swim on their own the best they could. In time it all affected all the bills, utilities and mortgage because it all came to a head. There was nothing normal left anymore. It felt like a bad dream unfolding before our eyes in slow motion. Many times there was no food and no extra money for things like laundry soap or gas for the car. I prayed hard for a God to intervene.

The Pico Rivera church finally got going in a powerful way. The Lord continued moving in the miraculous. The lost were being touched and delivered from drugs, gangs, alcohol and more. Despite the wreckage in my family, God was still on the throne performing modern day miracles which kept me greatly encouraged. We had people come out to the Chapel and help us with evangelistic work in the neighborhood. There were also a couple of the Men's homes who would also come and help us out with street rallies. Seems every other weekend we were having street rallies there on the corner in front of the church. God was giving us favor with the community and the vato locos, (*Spanish for the homeboys*) in the neighborhood. The ministry was new. We all used whatever talents we had to make things happen. Everyone seemed to be on the same page of soul winning at any cost. One afternoon we were setting up for a street rally when a Christian brother we called Cal asked me if I could play an accordion because we needed some music and didn't have a portable piano. I told him that I had never played one and didn't know how. Minutes later, he walked up to me and put an accordion in my arms and said, *"We'll Sister, here, you have thirty minutes to learn before we get started"*. As he walked away I tried to explain how I had never played one before and wasn't sure how. He kept walking and said; *"We'll you now have twenty-nine minutes, do your best"*. It blew my mind but I went into the church, prayed and started slowly pushing buttons to figure out how it worked and make music come out. In those days we used whatever we had to get the job done and didn't think about what we didn't have. We just used what was at hand coupled with FAITH. I continued to push the buttons, pulling and pressing to figure out how the music came out. I had no knowledge whatsoever how to play it but somehow, it slowly began to come together. By the time they were ready to start, Brother Cal asked me, *"Well, are you ready"?* And off we went. He put a microphone on the accordion and to my amazement, it sounded like music and I started off with *"I'm so glad Jesus set me free"* with no problems. I myself was amazed because I had never, ever played an accordion before. Many people from the streets gave their lives to God that day. Many were touched and changed from that simple street outreach and many more that came after. It was a joy to have had a part in it. Needless to say, I learned to play the accordion that day. We talked about these rallies for years. There was the music, the testimonies and preaching's, what a combination. Brother Cal and so many people were so on fire for God. One day after one of these street rallies as we were tearing down all the equipment, Brother Cal walked over to me and gave me a word he said was from the Lord. He was so right on! He also said he needed to pray strength into my life because I would be going through major testing. Little did he know what had transpired with my father's fall, the church split, our family falling apart, our parents' divorce and my mother experiencing mental breakdowns at home? The Lord used me to hold things together and help my mom get restored. Bro Cal said the Lord had told him to pray an anointing over me so that the power of God would come upon my life like never before. He asked me to raise my hands. I asked, *"right now, here on the street corner"?* He said *"Yes, here on the corner, right here and right now, lift up your hands; the anointing is here in a powerful way and is about to touch you"* I closed my eyes and as soon as he started to pray I felt the power of God go completely through me like a surge of electricity from the top of my head to the souls of my feet. I cried and was so broken before the presence of God. I spent a couple of hours broken before the presence of God. My life would never be the same after that.

From that day on, I began to feel such a sense of holy boldness in serving God and began deep praying and fasting for my mother and restoration for my entire family situation. I never stopped inviting my mom to church services as I felt so burdened for her. I continued to share with her how God was moving at the church and all the miracles that were taking place. She wouldn't say much, only that she wasn't ready. I faithfully continue to lead worship services on the piano and work with the church choir. This was done completely by Holy Spirit on-the-job training because I had never taken any piano lessons and yet God's anointing was obviously on my hands and voice. By this time, mom was drinking and getting high at home. I could see how difficult this was for her and discerned how her heart had hardened too. She had shut down from within from a world of ministry she had once loved and cared for people. She found a new life in her room that was totally cut off from people in her own self-imposed exile. It was as though the four walls of her room were her lonely prison cell. So much occurred through the years at the house ranging from violence, overdoses, fights where police were called, ambulances coming to the house because my mother was having a strokes, mental breakdowns and suicide attempts. When I thought it couldn't get any worse, again it did! I kept sharing with my mom what the Lord was doing at the Chapel and kept telling her that no one would recognize her at the Chapel because these were all a new crowd and the ministry itself was different; not like the traditional Spanish style of church we were used to. She said she would think about it. I was excited and thanked the Lord for this small hope.

Meanwhile, my older brother had been wounded in Viet Nam pretty badly and had been in the hospital. Mom was petrified with fear at the thought that she could lose her son. Worse than that, was the thought of telling my brother about our broken home. After several months, my brother was healthy enough to be flown back to the United States. We were all excited yet dreaded how he would react to the news of our now broken family. When he was told, he had a stoic look on his face. He was quiet, in disbelief and showed little emotion. He acted cool with no comments. I will never forget the talk we had later when he shared with me in private. He said, "*You know sis, after all the years we spent in church, this wasn't supposed to happen and if this happened to our parents and they were pastors, what kind a chance do any of us have with our marriages?*" I had little words of comfort to share with him except to fight back the tears. All I could say was that with the help of the Lord somehow things would work out. He quickly commented how he didn't want to hear anything about "*the Lord*". I could feel his hurt and anger. He kept talking about how strict dad was with us all and couldn't understand how something like this could happen to a family as strong as we were or at least he thought we were. He sarcastically commented how we, being the oldest, were put through so much of church restrictions of dos and don'ts and now none of it mattered. He said he wasn't sure what was worse for him, getting shot or getting the news that your family was no longer intact and your parents were divorcing. I could feel his anger manifesting in a subtle way. I felt bad for the whole idea of Christianity that day. He commented how if this was Christianity, he would never become a Christian.

One day to my surprise, my mom agreed to go to church with me. My heart bubbled with joy. I tried so hard to keep calm and told her I would pick her up. As she was getting off the car, she commented how she felt butterflies in her stomach going back in her church. I totally understood and applauded her bravery. I got her a seat near me and went to sit at the piano to do worship. I prayed in spirit that the Lord would touch her that day. The service was completely different from what she was used to. I kept looking at her during the service and kept interceding for her. People who didn't know her just welcomed her. She too noted that people were wearing pants to church which was different. No one seemed to be concerned with people's attire. They were just glad to see you there and welcomed each other. I know my mom was touched because it wasn't the usual Pentecostal community she was used to. It was a church full of ex-vatos locos (*homies*) and what looked like common street people coming to church, happy and praising God. This was refreshing to see how happy everyone looked. I think this blew her mind. As I had predicted, she didn't know anyone there. She went up for prayer, cried and cried at the altar. I was overjoyed and broke down in tears myself. The Lord had answered my prayer to allow mama to come to church. God began to restore her back from that day forward. It wasn't long after this, that she began going to church on her own and liking the services. God was moving in her life and restoring her. She began bringing my siblings too. I could see she was trying and the spirit of God quickened me several months later, to put her in the choir so that she would be even more encouraged. At our old church, they would never have allowed this because she was a baby in Christ by only a few months. It was the craziest thing because here she was an ex-pastor getting restored. Nevertheless, I followed the urging of the Holy Spirit. I kept encouraging her to join the choir so she could get stronger and walk the straight and narrow path. She thought this was a crazy idea. I knew she was struggling with self-condemnation. I just keep serving in my church and being faithful. One amazing day she came to me and said she wanted to go ahead and join the choir after all. After several more months in the choir, I asked her to learn that old song "*The Broken Vessel*" which I thought she could relate to. This song would be her signature song for years to come. She sang it with such a powerful anointing. With time and prayer, she gained new Christian friends, began to trust again, laugh and do new things in her life like have fellowship which was new to her. God began to use her in singing and I began to see the transformation and healing taking place right before my eyes. It was an answer to my prayers to see her talking to people, smiling and laughing again. Home life was still a wreck but she began trusting God for a new home transformation. Soon she began to take the bull by its horn and make changes in the house too.

One day a brother friend of mine, who was in the Men's Home had come with the others to visit our services at the Chapel. We would always chat a while after church during coffee and fellowship.

God had changed his life in a tremendous way. He had come from the apostolic faith. Ironically, he was the son of a pastor whose father had also fallen from grace. His name was Pete Gomez. He would always share about what God was doing in his life. After greeting him as usual, he inquired about my pretty friend, referring to my mother. I told him to be cool and she wasn't just my friend. He assumed she was my sister. I told him she wasn't my sister either, she was my mother. He was taken aback and said he didn't believe it. I nicely told him she was a backslider getting restored right now and wasn't interested in meeting any men. I suggested he continue to pray to God about someone else for his life. Needless to say more time went by and many more services. I eventually introduced Pete to my mom. They became friends and to all our surprise, several months later, they began to date. My mother once saw him at the altar crying out to God (*in Spanish*) and she commented how it blessed her heart to see an ex-drug addict man crying out to God in this sincere fashion. She hadn't seen that before. Another year went by and they were married. Months later, Pastor Sonny baptized Pete in water. Both Pete, mom and my little sister moved away to another state far away where they were fully restored and began their own (original) "*Set Free Prison Ministry*" that would last over 25 years. The Lord opened many doors for them and used their lives in a tremendous way. What an awesome sight to see. I would have never believed that things would turn out the way they did for my mom. Only God could have restored and fixed someone so hopeless and broken. Once again, God made a way out of no way. I was on a spiritual high.

I continued serving the Lord and still believing for my husband's conversion. He continued in his "*oldies*" music concerts with his secular band. I believed for his change and that he would use his talent for the Lord someday. I honestly believed I would see him serving the Lord with his talents. I simply believed in my heart that the great God I served was greater than any problem. I had also prayed that when and if it was his time, the Lord would remove him out of my heart as painlessly as possible. I continued serving God and He was faithful to continue doing new things in my life that I never experienced in my Christian walk. I was also in contact with my dad and would encourage him to find his way back to the cross. He did a lot of crying during our visits. I prayed with him each time I saw him. It was difficult to be in between both my parents because I loved them both.

Several years later, my dad also found his way back to the Lord in a Spanish church and remarried. He started a new family. He had returned to church and begun his restoration. The Lord began to open many, many doors everywhere to the prison ministry. By now we had combined both ministries. We would do the singing and my step dad preached. There were not a whole lot of prison ministries in the 70s and 80's as unique as ours representing the family and the restoration that could take place. It was comprised of my step-dad and my mom, us 3 sisters singing and my brother-in-law. The Lord really used us all in a tremendous way. He put a unique anointing on all our voices. More than anything, it was awesome to see what the Lord had done in our immediate family with restoration, needed healing in us all that nearly wipe out our entire family both physically, mentally and spiritually. This included the tragic death of our little brother Jonathan. It's hard to imagine all this could happen to a pastor's family. Seems like this sort of stuff should not have to happen when people are serving God, but it does and it did to us all in a big way. However in the end, what was meant for evil, harm and destruction, God turned it around for good. That's the kind of God we serve that when a door is closed to us, He is already preparing us to walk through a new one.

"Wear & Tear"

Judy & the Chapel Singers continued ministering in churches, street rallies and prisons for over twenty two years. We ministered for years at many prisons and States from one year to the next. We spent our holidays in the prisons so we would celebrate with our own families either the day before or the day after. We were fully committed! It was easier traveling because we were all family and we shared in all the expenses, rooms and food. We brought hope to inmates that God could salvage any situation including broken families like ours.

Through the years, I felt myself begin to wear down in ministry. I had also by now divorced Carlos after 16 years of an abusive marriage. It broke my heart that my husband chose not to change his ways and continue in his addiction with loose women and bizarre behaviors. He still refused a relationship with God. He always said he just wasn't' ready to sober up and felt like his world (*singing career*) was at its peak. What should have been a great, healthy and a good life for our little family, by now had turned disastrous. It was a huge letdown for me and in time, it took a real toll on me. Not only had our "**marriage made in heaven**" failed, but he never chose to serve the Lord with us either.

The children were growing up and began needing more attention with their own needs. It all was such a strain on me. I guess you could say I began to let my guard down because I lost my joy and my first love. I remember telling my family who was doing great in prison ministry that I wanted to take an indefinite leave of absence (*sabbatical*) from the ministry. They didn't feel this was a good idea and cautioned me about the possibilities of growing spiritually cold and discouraged. They reminded me that it was the ministry that had actually helped me through my circumstances. At this point, I didn't care. I just wanted out! My cold heart just wasn't in ministry as before. My family felt let down and disenchanted. They continued to tell me that I was making a big mistake and now they would have no music either in the prisons. I was the music arranger for the group too so now that would be gone!

I took the leave of absence anyway and went my own way. I kept working and coming home to my children. I concentrated on my family life. As disappointed as my family was, they went on ministering in the prisons without me. Everywhere they went people would ask for me. I'm sure it was a strain on my family to explain I would be gone for a while. No one played our songs for the group anymore. They were on their own. This was absolutely the biggest spiritual mistake I could have ever made. Just as they warned me, I slowly began to grow cold. I still went to church and occasionally helped out but I began to lose interest. In a way I was glad to stop the traveling because my heart wasn't in it anymore. On top of all this, I was gainfully employed full time and traveled substantially for the job. It took a lot of my time from everything and family life at home. God knows I didn't want to repeat my childhood ministry experiences with my children too. But it was exactly what was happening. I was so busy with ministry and my job that I had no quality time at home for my growing children. By this time I had moved away from my family and was pretty much on my own. Little by little, I didn't go to church as often anymore. I was visiting a couple churches in my area with some friends of mine but not like I should have been or was called to be. God just seemed so far away.

One day while coming home from work, I noticed two men who looked like undercover police parked near my parking space where I lived. Something about the car they were in was alarming to me. I exited my car and walked into my house. A good thirty minutes later, I heard a knock on the door. Looking through the peephole, I saw it was the men whom I had noticed earlier. I opened the door and they identified themselves as law enforcement. They were detectives who asked to come inside and speak to me. As I let them in my heart sank to the floor. Nothing could have prepared me for what they would tell me. They explained how something very serious had recently happened locally where someone had lost their life. One of my sons had been identified as a friend of a detainee they had. I was speechless. My sons were in their room where I had instructed them to stay unless I called them. The detective explained how these individuals were all in their twenties and my son was the youngest of them all. He was only 16 years old at the time. They wanted to talk to my son and question him about what he knew. I called my oldest son to the living room where they sat and they asked him a few questions. He told them he didn't know anything and the detectives stated they didn't believe him and were going to take him in for further questioning. Being as he was a minor, they asked me to come along. I made arrangements with the neighbor to take care of the other two until I got back.

We all left. I followed them in my car. All the way to the station I kept telling my son he needed to tell the truth about what he knew and it would go much better than if he tried lying or covering up for someone. He was quiet the whole time and gave me those famous three words teens often respond with, "I know, mom." I prayed as I drove and held his hand at the same time. I told him we would trust the Lord to help us know what to do. It was an ordeal walking into the interviewing room. It was intimidating and scary to say the least. My son was afraid and didn't want to give up any names of guys in his area, who he knew or who he hung out with. I didn't know any of them either because he wasn't allowed to bring any friends over as he had a little sister at h home and boys (friends) weren't allowed at the house. How I'd wished I knew some of his friends so that I could have approached them myself.

We couldn't afford an attorney. My son looked like he was not feeling well. When I asked him what was wrong, he stated he felt sick to his stomach and felt faint. I stopped the questioning and asked if I could pray with my son. They allowed me to pray for him. I felt awkward because I wasn't in ministry or going to church anymore and yet I was going to pray. I didn't care and proceeded to pray the best I could. I prayed that he would simply tell the truth, do the right thing and that everything would turn out in his favor, in Jesus name. They questioned him for a very long time and I continued to silently pray. Later, they decided they were going to hold him. I was asked to leave and told I could return the next day. Now it was my turn to feel sick to my stomach. It was one of the hardest things I ever had to do. They walked me out to the front office and I had to leave him there. At this very moment, I thought about his dad. He was still not saved and only God knew where he was running around. I sat in my car feeling so alone and deserted. I sobbed and sobbed as I wondered and worried what would happen to my son. I wondered where his father was; not that he had ever been around for his children anyway but for that moment, I was so broken and confused about what to do. Inside, I knew I would have to face this ordeal alone. Oh how I needed his help, his advice and an attorney. I thought about what I was going to do if they decided to charge him with this crime. I was so scared and felt myself emotionally collapsing. I could only imagine what my son was feeling too. He had never been away from home. I remembered I had left the kids with the neighbor and had to get back to get them but couldn't control myself. I was crying, shaking, scared, angry and terrified as to what I should do next. I finally started my car and began to drive. I didn't go home for quite a while. I don't remember where I parked I only know I did. I just sat there and sobbed because I didn't want the kids to see me this way but had to tell them he wasn't coming home. I cried out to God and pleaded with Him to intervene on our behalf. I thought about my family and what they would say when they found out.

Everything I had prayed for that afternoon and night didn't seem to matter because nothing had happened in our favor. In fact, it was quite the opposite. I came home without him with a sense that my son's life was over. I wanted to call someone, anyone and ask for prayer but being as I wasn't in fellowship anymore, I felt like I had NOTHING, *(not even a prayer)* coming to me and it dawned on me that perhaps, this was my punishment from God for quitting on ministry and walking away from my calling. I was sure God was punishing me. After beating myself up for a while, it dawned on me I still had to tell my kids that their brother wasn't coming home for a long time.

Still sitting there with my mind going a hundred miles an hour, I reminded myself that I had to be strong for the kids and take it one day at a time. I had no other choice. I needed to go get the kids who looked very worried and scared when I them left hours ago. I decided I would put myself on "*survival mode*". When I finally got them home we sat down at the kitchen table and I explained what had happened. Since I was taking the day off from work the next day, I told them they could stay home from school with me. My daughter, who was only nine years old, suggested that we should pray and God would help him and us. It struck a raw nerve with me. I began to cry and told her I had already been praying since we first left and now we just had to wait and see what would happen. I didn't want to discourage them.

That night, I talked to God and asked for His help. Early in the morning I called in sick to my job. The next day, I was even worst so I called my doctor to ask him to take me off work for a couple of weeks and prescribe something to help me sleep. He saw that I was an emotional wreck and recommended I take at least thirty days off work and so he gave me a thirty-day leave of absence. He gave me a prescription for a sleep aid and something to calm my nerves. As the days passed, I was told by the detectives that my son was in fact, going to be charged with this crime because they didn't believe him and felt he was covering up for someone. The next time I saw my son, I reminded him that if he didn't cooperate and tell what he knew, it was going to cost us in the long run. As the weeks passed, I fell into a deep depression. I finally told my family about what had happened. My closest sister, Klu, stuck by me daily and began to attend the juvenile court hearings with me. It was such an ordeal to attend and listen to what was being said. I thought I would lose my mind and not survive the overwhelming pain but somehow I did. In between, I never missed any of his visits so as to give him support from his family. It never failed after our visits; I would fall apart and break down in the parking lot. I always braced myself before saying goodbye and pretended everything would be fine and encouraged him to do well, do what he was told, not to get involved with the gangs inside there and not to get any tattoos. He never did like the gang scene. Visiting him was an emotional roller coaster.

My 30 days of disability with the job turned into six months. But eventually decided I needed to secure my job, keep busy and return to work. Not really sure if God would listen to my prayer, I asked God to forgive me for my blunders and give me direction on what to do. I wondered if God even still heard my prayers or if I was even worthy enough to come to Him in prayer as I knew I had broken my covenant with Him. Things seemed to go from bad to worse. My son's case wasn't progressing in his favor and I was feeling more hopeless. Most of my family stood by me during this unbearable, incredibly horrendous time of our lives. I felt a bit shameful for my son's involvement no matter how small in this incident. I slowly started to withdraw from everyone. The whole ordeal, including the trial, lasted about two years. I couldn't bear to attend the hearing. My sister went for me. We met later and she reluctantly gave me the news that he had been found guilty. I broke up into a million tiny pieces that day and felt like God had let me down. I don't know why I blamed God but I did. I felt he had let me down after so many years of serving him. I had lost my young son to what for me felt like a death sentence. I took more time off from work to try to pull myself together.

Every day I felt sick to my stomach. I continued losing weight each week and I was having trouble concentrating on simple little daily things. I wasn't sleeping well nights either. I couldn't believe this had actually happened. Every morning I'd wake up thinking it was just a bad dream. A bit of me died along with his verdict. His father was eventually found but unfortunately, never made it to any of our son's hearings. This embittered me even more.

Several months later, he was to be formally sentenced. I wasn't emotionally stable enough to attend and again, my sister attended for me while I waited at another location. Later, as Klu approached me, the look on her face said it all. I could tell she had been crying. She told me he was given twenty five years to life. I remember thinking I was going be sick, faint or just lose it. I sat speechless for a long while. As I thought about the verdict, anger came over me at the thought that he never said anything. It had now cost him and our little family because we would do the time with him. There was no way to remedy this. I remembered telling him that this could happen. I was furious with God for not coming through for us AGAIN! In my mind, he had he failed us. I thought of all the twenty plus years of my life that I had served in ministry and yet at the time I needed God the most, He was nowhere to be found. I somehow felt He would come through at the end and rule in my son's favor. After all, He had said in His Word that He would give me the desires of my heart and this child belonged to God. Hadn't I dedicated him to the Lord as a baby? Everything came crashing down that day when my sister spoke those horrible words, "***twenty five years to life***." The harshness of this sentence completely took me by surprise. As a mother, it's an excruciating pain that goes through your heart. It was as though someone had told me that he had died. The agonizing thought of twenty five years to life was unbearable I could hardly breathe. I kept wondering if my son would be able to cope and endure this. It was hard to balance my emotions at the thought of losing my son this way and yet at the same time knowing someone lost their life too.

Somewhere another mother had forever lost her son. I felt sorrow for that family and grieving my own loss as well.

As my son began his time at juvenile hall, I never missed any visits and would bring him food from his favorite places. They would allow you to bring outside food in. I kept as close to him as I possibly could. He began to complain about his restless nights with trouble sleeping and experiencing constant nightmares. Staff began to ask me if they could medicate him because he was having trouble adapting. They asked if he had ever been away from home because he was severely depressed, having trouble eating and wasn't interacting with the other wards. I always refused their requests to medicate.

As time went on, I was finally able to locate his father. He didn't have a car and only for the sake of my son I volunteered to make the two hour drive from one county to another to bring him to visit our son and then drive him back. God knows what sacrifices a mother will do for her children! It was difficult to balance my emotions of anger, frustration and resentment towards Carlos for abandoning our children when they were little and the fact that he never chose to look for his kids or support them. I didn't want anything to interfere with any future visits with his father so I suppressed my personal feelings. I felt my son needed what little bit of a father he could get at this time and so I tried to create a family atmosphere for my son.

I was becoming more and more embittered against God. I suppose I was inwardly angry that God did nothing (*at least so it seemed to me*) to help us in our time of dire need. I was angry that his father did not make himself available for any of the children. It took everything within me to suppress it all so I could finish raising the other two children. They were grieving the loss of their brother in their own way. I became a walking time bomb. I was inwardly disappointed, angry and resentful. My sister Klu, continued to be my only support system. I knew my family was still disappointed in me for leaving the ministry. I can't remember all the times I woke up and wished this was all just a bad dream and my son would be asleep in his room. Eventually, it was time to pack my son's personal things away. It was one of the most difficult things I had to do. Once again, it was as though he had died because he was suddenly just gone! I couldn't bear to see his things everyday and smell his scent in the room. And so I finally did what I knew had to be done. I packed his things away. Nothing or no one can prepare a mother for such a thing in life as this and there is no remedy to help us get through it. We do our best one day at a time. I no longer wanted to live in the same house either. The good thing was that I had somehow managed to remain gainfully employed and still made a good salary so I could afford to move. I bumped into a friend who was in real estate and I was able to qualify to purchase my first home not far from the detention facility where my son was. Moving into our home took some of the stress off me because I threw myself into the project of moving, fixing things up and making a fresh start in our new home. The kids really liked it. They made friends right away with other neighborhood kids and went to a new school. I had returned to work and was doing everything I could to properly balance my home life. Every day when we prayed for our meals, we included my son. We did the best we knew how to keep his memory alive in spite of knowing he was going to be gone for a very long time.

During the time of the move, my ex-husband Carlos began earnest efforts to be more involved with the other two kids and communicated with me more. He continued working with his band performing here and there but he wanted to try reconciliation with us. At first, I told him he must have bumped his head to think I would ever seriously consider that. Perhaps because he realized he had failed our son; he started visiting the kids saying he was sorry and wanted a chance with us again. About a year later, that's exactly what happened. He came to stay with us. He made more efforts to visit which made me very happy. I thought he was really sorry this time and maybe he really had changed? I suppose it was me that must have "*bumped my head*" this time because a few weeks after he had moved in I began to see the old familiar red flags from his past. He frequently appeared to be under the influence of something.

The thought sickened me that he would be using drugs under my roof with the kids around. I was hoping against all hope that I was wrong but one day while he was out, I saw his jacket hanging and had a strong urge to look in his pockets; something I had never done before. I found some drugs *(crack cocaine)* along with a pipe. I decided to look through his things in the room and found even more drugs and drug paraphernalia. I packed his belongings and when he came back *(probably from the connection)* I told him to leave the house immediately. Of course, once again he said he was sorry and would try harder. As he was talking, it was obvious that he was high. I told him how sorry and stupid I felt even thinking he had changed. He left the house that evening. This new reconciliation plan of his didn't last one month. I was relieved that he was finally gone and I could grieve with my family alone and honorably instead of with his drugs and all the drama and the careless way he was caring for the kids. As time went by, I learned of so many things he had been doing in the house while I was away at work. I was so glad he was gone yet disappointed that I even given him another opportunity. The kids and I continued our visits.

Not long after, I met and began dating a man who claimed to be a good Christian. Ironically, his parent's were pastors of a Spanish church too. He had grown up in church and we had so much in common. We dated for a while and within a year's time; we began having intimate relations. I felt so bad because I had never been with anyone else but my ex-husband which by now we had been divorced for thirteen years. More than anything, I felt I had offended God. Two years later, my son turned eighteen and was transferred to another county that was closer to my job.

I contacted my real estate agent friend and she found me a location closer to my son and my job. The house was bigger and nicer. During the school break, we moved into this house. It had all the makings of a better life as well because of the schools and shorter distance to my job. I was very happy about this house and things seemed to be looking better and better for my family. I wasn't crying as much and I felt like I was moving ahead. I continued to date this gentleman. Although he proclaimed to be a Christian, I never saw him pray, read his bible or live what I knew to be a spiritual life. None of his fruit bore any witness to me as a Christian man and it should have been a big red flag for me to see; I should have known better. It is said desperate women do desperate things. Well, it's true because within a year's time in my new location, he moved in with us. I will never forget the spiritual offense I felt I had committed towards God by allowing this man to move in. It was so out of character for me and my upbringing. I figured I had already fallen into sin. To make matters worse, I did something even more stupid in hopes of making things right before God. I wanted to legalize our sex life and not live in sin. So I agreed to marry him. By this time, my family had completely cut me loose anyway. It was a stupid thing to do but I thought things would get better if we weren't living in sin. I never would have believed it if someone would have told me this was going to happen because I was always on fire for God and now I had allowed myself to wax cold. I was miserable the whole time.

We got married which was a disaster from day one! He became insanely jealous of everything and everyone. He began to exhibit serious psychotic controlling behavior towards me and the kids. I saw his real colors. It was as though I was in prison in my own home. There was no turning back now. In hopes of making things right, I had made a huge and painful mistake. I could not possibly have made it any worse! God definitely was not in this decision and I didn't know how to remedy it. Out of the mouths of babes they speak and one day my daughter told me how she didn't like him and he was scary. She was truly afraid of him. I should have listened to her. I had successfully alienated myself and my kids from everyone and it felt terrible. And since my family didn't talk to me anymore, this worked perfectly for him because he didn't want me interacting with my family anyway. I was quiet and submissive for the most part. I believe he actually broke my spirit. I was of a mindset that I would do my time with this beast in my personal prison and make the best of my morbid situation. After all, I had brought this upon myself. I couldn't see a way out and my mind was on overdrive every day. My only relief was going to work and getting out of the house. My co-workers noticed the changes in me and would ask if everything was okay? I was a newlywed but I wasn't acting like one.

One day out of nowhere, my sister, Klu, showed up at my house. It was so refreshing and I was so excited to see her! It seemed like forever since I had seen or talked to her. She had a strange look on her face as she stared at me. She asked what was wrong with me because she didn't like the way I looked. I told her I was fine and pretended to be normal. Sisters know sisters and she knew something was terribly wrong. She humored me for a while but after, she asked again what was wrong with me because I looked terrible. I broke down and confessed to her how things really were. I told her how insanely jealous he was and how he was punishing me around. While we visited, he suddenly showed up unexpectedly and I panicked. I didn't know what to do or say. She never liked him at all. She continued talking with me and expressed how this was definitely not me and I had to do something to get away from him. I continued to tell her how he treated me and how I was afraid of him. She was surprised how much I had changed to allow this man to completely control all I did. He didn't say much when she left. He simply asked why she had come over and what she wanted. I explained how she was just passing through and stopped by to say hello.

My sister began to visit me more often and he didn't like this. She kept coming to see me anyway. Eventually, I began to give things a second thought. Not long after, my sister brought my mother and she was surprised at my appearance too. This time he was home. I wasn't allowed to wear much make up, pluck my eye brows, shave my legs, or comb my hair like before. After several visits with my sister, I began to feel a spark of hope. My mother had a long talk with me and it surprised me to hear her say she had been praying for me and that she loved me. She reminded me how I had helped her out of her valley and how it hurt her to see me this way so defeated when I used to be so strong in the faith. It felt so good to hear those words. It was like a cool, soothing ointment on a deep raw wound. Later I paid the price with him because he questioned me about what we had talked about and what was said. He reminded me how he had told me he didn't want my sister or family coming over.

Eventually the marriage grew much worse and more violent. There were many times I would lock myself in the bathroom and cry for long periods of time because I felt so far away from who I used to be. I wanted to feel God again but I didn't believe He would forgive me. I couldn't seem to find my way back to the cross and I lost all hope. I considered suicide, what I would say in my suicide letter and how I would ask my sister, Klu, to care for my kids. I could actually see myself driving up to the mountains and driving off a cliff to show him he couldn't have me and how this would pay him back. I continued to emotionally wear down on a path of self-destruction with pills and hunger strikes.

One day I thought about something my mother had said to me the last time I had seen her. She said she would be praying for me so I decided I would begin fighting back because my other son who was now 15 years old had begun physically trying to defend me when my husband was abusive to me. Although I wasn't sure God would hear my cries, I continued to pray for help anyway. I wanted out of this situation and so I began communicating with my sister again. Slowly I began to wake up out of my stupor I was in. I saw myself and the kids in a cage with no privileges for anything unless he said so. This was completely contrary to my nature but it had become that way out of my own self-condemnation and guilt for how I believe I had failed God, myself, my kids and my family. The worst part of it was what I was doing to my children. I was growing tired of this and realized I had to make a choice to lie down and die a slow death, take myself out by suicide, or fight back and escape this animal. With the help of my sister, I began to think of ways to escape. Something in me began to wake up. I know now that it had to be the prayers of my mother.

One day I told him I wanted to reconcile our marriage because I was tired of fighting. I wanted to give him a tangible show of good faith by putting his name on my house title deed. We went to see an attorney to have it done but I actually tricked him into signing other papers. Earlier that day I had taken the kids to my sister in case he got violent. When we were on our way back home from the attorney's office, we had been n another argument. I confessed to him that he had just signed marriage annulment papers and boldly told him I was throwing him out and he was no longer welcome in my home. I threatened him with what would happen to him if he dared to bother or harass us again. I told him that I had told my family and especially my brothers about what he was doing to me and the kids. He was dumb-founded when he found out that he had actually signed annulment papers. He cursed me out and threatened me but I bluffed and told him my brothers were on their way to the house even as we spoke and if he even thought about laying a hand on me again, he better think twice. Ultimately, he got all his things and left. I was so relieved and startled that it worked! My bluff actually worked! Of course, I didn't think it would be that easy and I was always looking around to see if he was parked down the street. I changed all the locks of the doors and sealed all windows in case he came to the house when I was not home.

One would think that I had finally learned from this experience and perhaps I would get right with God and run back to Him. But sadly, I did quite the opposite. I continued working at my job to stay busy but struggled to forgive myself and lived such incredible guilt and self-condemnation. I know now that my spirit had been broken and I had mixed emotions. I longed to forgive myself and move on but didn't know how. I felt dirty and unworthy. My mother spoke with me but it still wasn't like before. After all, they had a ministry and a reputation to uphold. I walked around feeling like a loser. I beat myself up over all of it trying to heal myself but as time went on I only continued to withdraw from people even more. I was now doing what my mother had done for so long. I was still talking to my mother and for that I was grateful. Daughters always seem to want the approval and blessings of our mothers. It meant a lot to me for her to forgive me but on the other hand, I had not judged her or dad when they fell but encouraged them both back to God.

It wasn't long after that I began going to *Happy Hour* after work with my co-workers. I met some new friends and began the club scene with them. It was funny how I found myself looking around wherever I was to see if this beast of my ex-husband might be stalking me. It was a creepy feeling. I met a lot of nice working-class people and I made a lot of new friends, both male and female. It felt different to go out and not be harassed. I worked on my self-esteem which was completely shot by my past abusive relationship. It was hard to accept a compliment from anyone. By this time, my sister slowly began going out with me too. I felt really bad to think that we used to minister together singing for the Lord and now here she was with me in nightclubs. My family was completely devastated and embarrassed that we were both out in the world now. It was hard enough when I left but now my sister had left too. I was the pianist/singer and music arranger and she was our lead singer. She had a powerful anointed voice.

One of the hardest things about entering a club was wondering if we would bump into anyone who would recognize us from ministry or knew we were once Christians. I would smoke pot out in the parking lot before entering a club so I could feel relaxed. It was crazy because my conviction would actually begin as I was getting dressed to go out. When out on the parking lot, several times I can remember praying within myself, *"please God, don't come tonight"*. There were those times I was in a club dancing a slow song with a gentleman when for some reason the music sounded like an old altar call hymn and I would get so choked up. I would leave my partner there on the dance floor to go to the ladies room where I quietly locked myself in the stall sobbed and prayed to God, *"Please God, help me, forgive me, don't come tonight, be patient and wait for me"*. I'd sit there thinking about how I used to serve God with peace and joy and help my family through the most tragic difficult time of their lives and now the shoe was on the other foot. I beat myself up and hated what I had become. Looking back, it must have been the prayers of my mother. This convicting experience happened a few times. I hated when this happened and I would try and think of something else to distract me so I wouldn't feel like crying. There were a few times that I did run into someone I knew but since it was usually dark inside these places, I would make my way out and go elsewhere. I always knew I was running from God and my calling. It was the saddest, loneliest feeling ever because I knew I didn't belong there. I had no business at these places of hopelessness and ugliness that the world called fun.

Once again, you would think that I had learned my lesson but I guess not because I seemed to get worse. I graduated to experimenting with drugs along with my usual daily pot smoking and drinking. Smoking pot always seemed to take the edge off and calm my nerves. I couldn't believe my own self either. I know that no one would believe me but I actually prayed every single day! Even so, I just got worse. I truly did feel shame and guilt for letting God and everyone else down. I would run into pastors who knew me in public and invariably they reminded me what a blessing I was to them. It always made me feel so uncomfortable and undeserving. They always concluded by telling me they would be praying for me. I ran and ran from God. It was a difficult thing to have been in ministry for so many years and now to be out of fellowship with my God and my family. It tore me up inside every day! It was the absolute worse time of my life. I asked God to supernaturally touch and deliver me. The worst part was having my little sister with me.

My Lowest Point

I was still an emotional wreck. I had more wreckage than I could handle. I was crying in the middle of my day for no apparent reason and at times it felt like I would lose my mind. The slightest little thing would trigger a river of tears. One day, I went to see my doctor about getting more anxiety pills. She had previously prescribed Zanax for anxiety and sleeplessness during the time of my son's ordeal. She had continued prescribing them for a long time. After she spoke with me about what was going on, she felt I should see a specialist and strongly urged me to take some time off from work. She didn't want to give me anymore pills and expressed concerns about my emotional fragile state of mind. I agreed to talk to the psychologist she referred me to.

I kept my appointment with the psychologist. She sat and listened while I did all the talking. She was amazed at what I had been through and felt I needed to go into a facility where I could get some high-quality, intense treatment. She recommended a minimum stay of thirty days. She explained how this was a very nice, private facility and the kind of insurance I had would cover all my expenses. She actually wanted me to go directly from her office that very same day! I was blown away and thought about my kids and what I would do to arrange for their care. She insisted I was unable to continue like this for very long and said I stood a very good chance of having a complete nervous breakdown. I asked for a week to get my personal life in order before having myself admitted and she agreed.

The week flew by and I went to have myself admitted at the facility. It was an upscale sanitarium where I was allowed to wear my own clothes. I had a very nice, large, private room. It was actually a lovely facility. My room had a balcony overlooking the beautifully manicured garden and lake area. As the days went by, I cautiously tried to let my guard down while I talked to my therapist about all the things that had been going on in my life for the past several years. I did a lot of talking and crying while she listened. I was given medications for anxiety. I didn't like being medicated but she felt I was overly agitated and wanted me to be relaxed during my stay there. I had several counseling sessions with her in the days that passed as part of my treatment.

Two weeks passed and I was allowed to have limited visits. I had a visit from a personal friend and a family member. I was embarrassed for being an emotionally wreck. But in my heart I knew I was a strong person and that this was only temporary and I would in fact, get through it. I also had physical therapy. I remember the therapist telling me how I had so many big knot nerves on my back and neck. One day during my third week of counseling, I had been crying and was very upset when suddenly at the height of my session, the therapist interrupted me and commented *"Awe, I'm sorry, times up, we can finish this next time."* I literally felt as though she had taken me to the twenty fifth floor of a building and pushed me over. I didn't know how to come back down to the first floor in a hurry and land safe. I struggled to bring my emotions under control. It was as though what I had to say wasn't important to her because *"my time was up"* and this was just her job. It was devastating and I felt totally disrespected because it had taken me so long to get comfortable and trust this lady. It was all about time to her and not at all about me getting well (*so I thought*). I guess that was the reality but I didn't know how to bounce back. She simply apologized and stood her ground that we would finish this up at our next session in a couple of days. I immediately shut down, run to my room and sob my heart out. I was in a meltdown mode and felt myself having an emotional breakdown. I could hardly breathe and my head hurt so badly. I began thinking about all my failures and how my life had come to this in an asylum full of broken people. I felt like my life was over and I would never recover from this. Oh, how I regretted being there. I couldn't even stand on my feet. I had snuck in several Zanax pills with me during the admissions process *"just in case"* I had a bad day or couldn't sleep. They were hidden under my facial compact. At that moment I definitely was having a bad day. I took several pills to quickly calm myself down. I still couldn't seem to catch my breath and felt like I was dying. The pills didn't appear to be working fast enough. I lay on my bed and sobbed. Time went by and still there was no change. I got up and took three more pills, turned on the television and tried to wait it out. I tried walking around my room but my legs kept buckling. I prayed, *"Oh God help me."* I was so angry at the therapist and wanted to go tell her off. In desperation, I filled the tub with hot water and decided to relax in a bubble bath. Sometime during the bubble bath the pills must have kicked in and I fell asleep. Staff noticed I hadn't checked in for a few hours, nor had I come down for dinner. Later that night staff came to check up on me. They found me submerged under water in the tub. When I awoke, I was on my bed with a machine over me pumping water out of me. I didn't remember what had happened until the next day.

Unfortunately, after this experience they had me on suicide watch. Someone was in my room at all times, even when I used the restroom and showered. I explained I wasn't trying to die, but only wanted a quick relief from my last counseling session that had gone bad. This went on for the rest of the week until they finally believed me and I was left on my own. In between this time, I had a visit from my very close friend, Julie Amaya. Oh, how nice it was to see her! It was as though I just received a fresh glass of water after being so thirsty for what seemed like forever. She spent the day walking around the grounds with me while I shared my heart. She reminded me how hopeless her suicidal life had been until I told her how much Jesus loved her and could give her peace, strength and joy if she received Him into her life. She spoke kind, hopeful, life-giving words and promised to continue praying for me. She told me to fight hard to get over this and reminded me that the same God that delivered her was going to get me through this too. Before she left, she prayed for me. When she left, I sat alone with my thoughts of our visit. It was funny because I had sort of lost track of time and happy memories while I was in this facility. A few days after Julie's visit my mother came to see me. I remember the perplexed look on her face that day as she walked into my room. She didn't do much talking. She mostly listened to me throughout our visit. It wasn't until the end of our visit that she began to speak words of encouragement into my life. Just like my dear friend, Julie, mom jogged my memory of how I had the power and the will all *within me* to get through this and get out of this place. She reminded me how I had been so strong for her when she was in her backslidden anguish and that I needed to pray to God to reveal Himself to me once again and pray myself through this. She warned me that if I didn't, I would lose everything I had. She said, *"God isn't finished with you and you don't belong in this facility."* She anointed me and prayed a long dynamic prayer over me before she left that day. The next day, the reality of my mother's visit and words hit me very profoundly as I awoke and lay in my bed thinking. It was as though what she had said to me went through my entire being. I kept thinking about her powerful words she had spoken over me and how *"the strength was within me."* I remember feeling so alert, strong and in a great mood as though I had an awakening of some sort. Miraculously, the darkness and sadness had lifted! I thought to myself, *"What the heck have I got myself into? What am I doing here all crushed and defeated?, I really don't belong here."* I began to see things differently, clearly and positively. I felt the urgency to get out of this place after three and a half weeks of the sheer madness believing I was too frail and weak to be normal anymore. I suddenly realized that I had in fact, given up on myself and my kids. I needed to get back to my normal life. I prayed for God to give me the strength to do what I knew had to be done next.

That afternoon as I talked to the therapist, my story completely changed. I told her I didn't know what had come over me, I was neither crazy nor helpless as I had thought and furthermore, I realized I didn't belong there anymore. I told her I was checking myself out just as soon as I got my things together and reminded her that they could not hold me against my will. She asked what I was going to do when I got out. I told her I would be returning to work. She sat and looked at me in amazement! She asked me what had changed, what had happened and if I had thought this through. I didn't think she'd understand if I told her I had been anointed, prayed for, touched by God and had experienced a powerful awakening. I simply thanked her for listening to me when she did. I agreed I had a lot of unfortunate, regrettable experiences but I felt I was done here and needed to go back to work, my children and what was left of my life. That afternoon, I left the facility and to my amazement, I never had any more episodes of depression. Miraculously, I was able to return to work. My job actually helped me stay busy. I worked locally again but not long after, I began to travel as before. I was back to my investigative work and travel. It felt good to be my normal self again. I slowly picked up my pace of job locations, reports and everything else that came with the job. My boss was delighted with my work and began to use me on several local big contracts. It was challenging work that kept me happily busy. I was feeling productive, confident again and had a feeling I was on my way to total recovery. I didn't forget to thank the Lord.

The Sky Towers
(Enjoy the Ride)

It was now the mid-eighties and I still had my good-paying job and a home. I was driving a nice company car with carte blanche on a generous expense account. My sister continued to be a big part of my life. She had been my only support system all this time while I was still running from God.

One day I was with a very close family friend who unfortunately, was also a PK running from God. He was a phenomenal guitar player. He and several of his other brothers used to play guitars in some of the biggest tent revivals our parents conducted. We had a special bond of understanding as PKs because of our parents' ministries and the similarities of our upbringing that other people would not be able to relate to. His name was David and we both would meet for drinks after work. We used to tell people we were cousins. It really felt like it since we had grown up together. We had many discussions about our upbringings, our mutual regrets, our parents, the struggles, and all those legalistic religious, sanctimonious people that were always interfering in our family lives and criticizing us as PK's. Sometimes we would be at a party and we would be off to ourselves having drinks and talking about what ever happened to so and so and where they were today? We would laugh at the craziness of us drinking and talking about God and exchanging stories about our church experiences both good and bad. Sometimes we would see someone we thought was from church and we would crack up laughing. One day while I was still at work, David called and wanted me to meet him at the Sky Towers which was our usual meeting place. He wanted me to go with him and some friends to a special party. I agreed and met him later. It was a private upscale party of some friends he worked for. I had been there at the Towers before and I really liked it. It was located on a high top floor overlooking downtown. We could see everything from the balcony and the view was breathtaking at night. We met and he introduced me to a few other acquaintances. Everyone at the Towers was either hanging out having drinks, playing cards, getting high or just hanging out. There were always people there. About a half hour later, another really handsome distinguished looking gentleman with salt and pepper graying hair walked out from another room dressed very nicely and looking really sharp. David introduced me to him as Roland. I remember thinking how very striking and attractive he was. This guy walked around and asking everyone if they needed anything. A while later, David and I took the elevator downstairs and walked over to an upscale Italian restaurant establishment to get some quietness and something to eat. As David and I had dinner, I inquired as to who this Roland guy was. He commented "*Snow White*" and laughed. I figured it was an inside joke. He said Roland was one of the fellows they all partied with and was no one I wanted to get to know anyway. I told him I thought he was very handsome and asked if he was married or had a girlfriend. He said no but that he was a "*ladies' man*" and laughed. We later returned to the Sky Towers to hang out. About 10:30 pm, this guy, Roland announced it was time to leave. He called for the car up front and a few minutes later, several of us took the elevator down to the parking area. There sat this beautiful extra-stretch cream-colored limousine. I remember thinking that it was already 10:30 pm and we were barely heading to this party. I heard one of the fellows saying that it was a "*divorce party*" for some high rollers. We were a group of seven that all got into the limousine. I was the only female in the group but I felt safe because of David and the other fellows I already knew from hanging out. I noticed that these gentlemen were all dressed very nicely. While in the limousine, I was attracted to Roland. I liked his soft-spoken voice and perfectly polite mannerisms. He was the most handsome of them all. As we were on the way to the party, Roland began to pass around a mirror with some "snow" (*cocaine*) and everyone in the limousine began to snort some lines. When it was approaching my turn, I noticed they were snorting with a one hundred dollar bill. David was next to me. He had introduced me to cocaine some time back but it had just been the two of us. When my turn came I passed and jokingly stated, *"No thank you but I'll take the piece of paper when you guys are done."* Roland asked me if I was sure I didn't want any? I thanked him and told him I was good. He asked me if he could get me anything else. I took a drink instead. Well, we finally arrived at the party. It was definitely a high rolling party! There were a lot of very expensive sport cars, professionally well dressed business people of all ethnic backgrounds. The place was a beautiful mansion located in the hills of a wealthy location. Everyone seemed to know Roland. It was clear he was popular with all the ladies too. One of them said, *"The candy man is here."* I observed him, everyone and everything going on around me. I noticed Roland kept going in and out of the restroom accompanied by different people, especially the ladies. As some guests went in, others were coming out. This went on for the first couple of hours. There was a band playing. David and I hung out, drank and danced. We were having a great time. While dancing with David, I commented how Roland was a busy boy with everyone in the restroom. He laughed and commented that he was powdering people's noses letting them sample his product to make money later and that's why he was known as the candy man. Everyone had been waiting for him to arrive. Throughout this party, I noticed Roland looking our way and watching us. At one point, David had to use the bathroom so he excused himself. As I was taking my glass over to the bar, Roland abruptly walked up next to me, took my drink and got me another. He began making small talk. He asked if he would be intruding on David if we danced. I accepted and as we danced, I chuckled and told him that David wasn't my boyfriend and was actually my cousin. He laughed out loud and said *"Is that right? I've been watching you two since we got into the limo and thought you guys were a couple. I thought how lucky he was to be with such a beautiful woman. I couldn't keep my eyes off of you."* I thanked him and told him that David had called me at work and invited me to go with him to this party. He laughed again as though relieved. He told me he thought I was very beautiful from the moment he laid eyes on me at The Towers. After the song was over, we stood on the dance floor and danced a slow dance. Later, we went over and sat to talk for a while. He asked how come he had never seen me before. I told him I had been at The Towers many times before with David but never saw him either. He continued small talk about how glad he was that I came and that he was able to meet me, then we were interrupted by his candy man duties to the restroom. As he walked away, he told me, *"Don't go far."* I laughed and flagged David over. I told him what his friend Roland had said about him and I being a couple. He thought it was funny too. Turns out Roland had also asked him how he knew me. David commented that he began to tell Roland that we'd known each other for years when they were interrupted by someone who needed to talk to Roland and they never finished their conversation. He never got to tell Roland that we were cousins. About an hour later, Roland came over and asked me to dance with him again. We talked some more. He was curious why I wasn't getting my nose powdered with the rest. I told him that it just wasn't my thing tonight. He wanted to know how I felt about drugs. I told him I really didn't knock anyone else doing it and I was just particular who and where I got high at. He asked why? I laughed and jokingly commented I felt like I was being interviewed for a job. He laughed and said that it wasn't often he bumped into a beautiful woman that didn't enjoy getting high. I told him *"I didn't say I didn't get high at all,*

I just didn't care to do it with others in public with people I didn't know". He said he liked my responses. I just smiled and kept dancing. I felt nervous dancing with him for some reason. I think he was too because he stepped on my foot a couple times while we were dancing. Well, one slow song led to another. He asked me where I was going after the party. I said *"Home, it's already three o'clock in the morning."* He asked me where home was. I laughed it off and told him *"For a candy man, you ask a lot of questions."* I never did answer him and just kept dancing. Shortly after that, we all returned to The Towers. Everyone was walking towards the elevators. David was going to walk me back to my car when Roland walked over to us and started some small talk. David realized he left his jacket in the limousine and went back to get it. Roland wasted no time in talking to me. He expressed how much of a pleasure it was to meet a true lady. He asked if I was married or had a "Sancho" (*Spanish slang for boyfriend*) waiting for me somewhere because he had hopes of seeing me again. I told him I wasn't married nor did I have a sancho. Once again I said that he sure asked a lot of questions. I told him I had a great time myself. He shook my hand, kissed me on the cheek and I felt a piece of paper between our hands. He just looked at me as though to see my reaction. I couldn't help but chuckle and opened my hand to see what it was. Well to my amazement, it was the hundred dollar bill they used in the limousine to snort their cocaine with. It was now folded and he had written his telephone number on it. He said *"I remembered what you said about wanting the piece of paper when we were finished with our business"*. I shook my head and smiled. He commented that he had wiped it clean too. David was on his way back. Roland asked if he could see me again. I said *"We'll see."* David walked me to my car and we decided to go for breakfast ourselves.

While at breakfast, we talked about the party and his friend Roland. He said how he thought Roland liked me a because he hadn't seen him pursue a woman as much as he done with me and how Roland doesn't usually dance because he pretty much conducted business all night. I asked what kind of business Roland was in. He said *"DRUGS"*. Suddenly I remembered at the condo when he told me, *"Snow White"*. The light went on and I snapped to what he meant (Duh!). He told me that Roland was a cool guy but he didn't think I should get involved with him. He suggested I simply have fun with him, party and hang out. He commented I should not fall for him because he wasn't my type. I asked why because he actually did seem like my type. He said *"looks are deceiving, that's why"*. He commented to me *"just as guys use women, I should do the same, just have fun, enjoy the ride but guard my heart"*. He discouraged me from giving Roland any personal information about me like where I worked, lived, hung out or any phone numbers. He made me promise him I wouldn't give Roland any information at all. I thought nothing of it accept that he wanted to protect me as a brother would a sister so I promised him I wouldn't.

As we ate breakfast, David reminded me of the times when our family would go visit his parents and they went to special church services in his city. Our parents left us in charge of supervising all the kids: his eight brothers and my six siblings. It was so much fun. One time we attempted to make a spaghetti dinner to feed the troops (*kids*). We cooked dinner but as we were about to serve, he accidentally dropped a few noodles on me so I picked them off me and threw them back at him and they stuck to his neck. It wasn't long before it turned into a full blown noodle fight all over the kitchen. By the time we fed the kids, there were noodles hanging from the ceiling, stuck on the walls and sauce all over our clothes and face. It was so funny. We had so much fun that we lost track of the time when it seemed like suddenly, our parents got home. We saw the headlights of the car and everyone scrambled to clean the mess and then ran to pretend they were asleep. He and I continued to clean up as fast as we could, never able to get to all the noodles hanging from the ceiling or off the walls. We were both reprimanded for being irresponsible and acting like kids ourselves. All our brothers and sisters by now were laying down on their beds and couch, under the blankets pretending to be asleep but secretly laughing. We talked and laughed about that night and many other good times we had with our families in the ministry and how much our lives had changed to where we were today. He shared some personal secrets that he had never told anyone about his parents. I remember feeling so bad for him and his brothers. He really spilled his guts that early morning. Maybe because he was partly still drunk and feeling vulnerable. That's when he said he began to hate the things of God and wondered if there was really a God at all to have allowed so much sadness to happen to him and family while in the ministry. I asked why he never told anyone or talked to his parents about how he felt all these years. He just explained how there was no real communication with people or his family. It was all about ministry and saving souls but no honest communication or love felt at home. There was no one he could think of that would understand or believe him anyway. That's why they just loved when our family went to visit because we were family to them. He said he would take all his secrets to his grave. I remember feeling bad for him and how familiar his story was to mine but after hearing him spill his guts; I felt I had nothing to complain about. What struck me the most was that he felt his innocence had been taken from him and how they all felt cheated from having a normal family life because of his parent's were pastors. He told me about a married woman in his dad's church that was about 28 years old. He said he thought she was such a pig, I laughed. He told me a story about when he was fifteen. This woman twice inappropriately grabbed him in his groin area and whispered what she would like to do to him. He didn't know what to do. He felt scared and embarrassed. He didn't know who he could trust and tell or if anyone would believe him because she was a "*hermana*" (*Spanish for sister in the Lord*). He shared how he simply would hide from her every time he saw her coming to church. She had done this twice to him. He explained how he used to see her in church with her hands raised up praising the Lord. He thought she was such a nasty woman. He wanted to tell his brothers but he felt they wouldn't understand because they were much younger than him. One of the most startling of his stories was how he explained the cracked bathroom door in his house and how he had seen his father a few times through the crack of the bathroom door injecting heroin into his arm. He said he was so blown away that he wanted to cry. I just stared at him and listened in disbelief. I thought I had horror stories of my own but his took the cake! I shared with him about my similar experience with one of my father's church elders who molested me in my dad's car as my father was giving several church members rides home from church. David shook his head and asked me where I thought God was during these times. He asked me if I thought it still went on in churches today. We both agreed that it probably did. We wondered what kind of stories other PK's had like ours and how the average person probably wouldn't believe things like this really happened in churches.

It was such a sobering conversation. He said playing his guitar in his dad's church was like a hobby and something social to do because (*like me*) everything he wanted to do was either wrong or sinful. It was no picnic being a PK. He didn't mind going to church because he hoped to meet girls there. When their family got home from church, it was always a cold atmosphere, never a warm and loving one. His parents were not the same as they were at home either. He too shared thoughts like I used to with my brother, about getting old enough to leave the house, never look back or step into a church again. We talked about our lives since Sunday school, growing up in our teens as PK's and how we both were musicians playing instruments and singing. We chuckled at our lives right now. He was such an awesome guitar player and I played piano and sang. We reminisced about the revivals our parents held, the awesome music all done by PKs and how the power of God would really touch and heal people despite what went on in the background. We remembered how people were healed right on the spot from their illnesses and/or delivered from demonic spirits. It blew us away how now we were out behaving like demons ourselves. We both agreed how we would have never in a million years believed it if someone would have told us that our lives and our parents' lives would turned out the way they did. We talked about the divorce of both our parents and how it affected us. We shared the silent pain we felt as a result of their divorces and what it meant for us. It would be the cross all us kids had to bear. We were taught that divorce was wrong and voila! Both sets of our parents were now divorced. We thought it was pretty crazy. I asked him if he thought we would ever come back to God and ever get back in ministry. He said he knew he would NEVER, ever have anything to do with Christianity again. He liked playing the music and singing but as far as ever going back to a church or having a relationship with God, he was done and had his own way of beliefs. Going to church just wasn't him anymore. I remember how grieved I felt as he expressed his views of Christianity and how bad things had changed in his life. I told him I had hopes to return some day. I didn't know how, where and when I'd do it but I still felt a call to go back because I felt I was called to do a new kind of work in a new anointing and not the way we were taught. I didn't see God in the same way anymore because of our experiences. He didn't feel the same way and wasn't interested in finding out. He just repeated that he was done with church. I told him *"You know, some day I'm going to write a book about us PK's."* He laughed and said it would either be a real hit or no one would care. I told him if I ever got my life together, I was going to look him up and maybe we could start a band together and call it "**Jamming PK's**". We laughed it off. After our long breakfast I took him back to the Towers and went home. I cried that morning for David. I suppose it brought back bittersweet memories of when we were in ministry with our parents. It was such a wakeup call in my spirit. I wondered how many other PK's were out there like us. I mean, good kids at one time, gifted kids that could sing, play instruments and could have really be used by God. I know now that my heart was grieved tremendously for PK's. I thought about what I'd share in a book someday. Perhaps it was something that just dropped and rooted into my spirit on that morning. The feeling never left me. Tonight I felt so extraordinarily lonely and empty inside. Needless to say, after this day I continued to go out with David and or meet up with his group at other social gatherings. Ironically, Roland began to appear at places David and I were at too. David would continue to remind me to be cool and just have a good time, *NOTHING MORE*! Sometimes as we were dancing slow songs, he would whisper in my ear, *"Guard your heart, mija, and just enjoy the ride."* It all seemed perfectly normal and innocent. Roland told me he looked forward to my company and enjoyed it when we would go out together but he wanted to spend some alone time to get to know me better. He would tell me he didn't know what it was about me that brought him comfort and peace that he had not felt before with anyone else. I wanted to believe it was God's favor over me. He felt I would bring him good luck. I told him I didn't believe in luck. The funny thing is we always traveled with other people in a group, including David who by now Roland believed he was my cousin.

Months quickly passed that we all hung out and traveled together. Roland and I began to go out more, alone. David was comfortable because he always went along so he would be close by me where he could watch out for me. I asked David why we always traveled in a group. He simply said, *"It's a long story, babe, don't trip, just enjoy the ride."* There were a few times Roland asked me not to dance with certain people. I didn't know why and I never asked. I figured it was a guy thing. There were other times that Roland and I went out to dinner and other places and these guys not only came with us in the limousine but waited for us both inside and outside the establishment including David. I remember one time asking Roland if David could join us for dinner. He smiled and very nicely said he wanted it to be just the two of us and David was fine where he was. I sort of thought it was rude of him but figured he brought these guys because he sold cocaine at different places and never knew if some knuckleheads would start trouble. I wasn't really sure. I was just observant and figured things out on my own. There were a couple times I questioned David about what I saw. He would tell me that it wasn't good for me to ask too many questions and that I should just enjoy the ride and not take Roland seriously. There was this one other time when Roland and I were out at a very nice restaurant. The staff already knew him by name. They went out of their way to accommodate and cater to us. I didn't give it much thought and figured maybe them too, were some of his customers. Dinner was nice and after we finished, I excused myself to go to the ladies room. On my way there I noticed David and another gentleman sitting at the bar. He motioned to me where I was going. I pointed to the ladies room. He and his partner thought nothing of it. A while later, as I was leaving the ladies room to return to my table an intoxicated gentleman standing at the side of the bar by the ladies room got my arm, leaned very close to me and said *"Hello there."* As he did this, his drink spilled along the side of my black silk sleeve down my arm to my hand. I quickly began to wipe it. The drunken man was trying to wipe me off too. I tried to excuse him and get away so Roland wouldn't see any of it. David and his partner quickly came over and began to reprimand him. Before I knew it, Roland caught the action and walked up abruptly and quickly figured out what had happened. Suddenly, the restaurant manager was behind Roland apologizing and stated our dinner was on the house. Roland told the drunken man that he owed the lady (*me*) an apology. To my shocking amazement, this man told Roland he could go blank, blank himself. I was gently pulling on Roland to just let it go because the man was drunk. This man then turned to me and said *"Ok beautiful, I'm sorry."* I took Roland by the arm to head for our table. As we started walking back towards our table, I heard Roland tell the guys in Spanish to make sure they take him outside and teach him some manners. It seemed everyone was looking at us by now. It was embarrassing. We could hear management telling the guy he had to leave the establishment. As we sat at our table, Roland still looked flushed, with a stiff jaw and in a subtle sort of way. I could see he was trying hard not to let this incident bother him. I had butterflies in my stomach. I reminded him the guy was drunk and not in his right mind. He said he couldn't stand people who were loud, couldn't hold their liquor and or made public scenes. About fifteen long minutes later, David came up and whispered something in Roland's ear. All Roland said was *"Okay."* I was thinking that once the dancing music started, he would cool off. He asked if I didn't mind if we didn't stay for the music because he wanted to leave. I was about to answer when he told me to get my things because we were leaving. I told him I really didn't mind and that we should just try and enjoy the rest of the evening. He again calmly (*yet firmly*) said *"We need to leave NOW, get your things."* So we got up and walked out front where the limousine was waiting. We left quickly. We headed back to The Tower. All the way back everyone was very quiet. Only the music was playing. He apologized again and offered to pay for my dress. I was trying to just play it down like it was cool and told him it was not a big deal. I looked over to David and he just rolled his eyes and slowly shook his head then looked out the window. It was like he wanted to tell me something but didn't. It seemed like forever but we finally arrived. As we entered the elevator, everyone remained quiet with stoic faces. As soon as the doors opened and we began walking down the hallway, we could hear the loud music coming from the condo where there was always a party and the sales of cocaine going on. Roland told me to go into the other restroom and clean off my sleeve while he went into the room to talk to the guys. The guys went left into the bedroom and closed the door. I went the opposite way into the other room to wash my sleeve. I found a blow dryer in one of the drawers and dried it off. When I came out Roland and the rest had just walked out too. I wanted to leave and was trying to catch David's attention to walk me out. As I was looking around for him, Roland caught my eye and motioned me to go out to the balcony with him. There was another couple out there sitting and talking. He asked them if they didn't mind going inside because we had some business to take care of. Roland closed the sliding door. He again apologized for tonight because he wanted it to be a special night and it turned out disastrous. I told him how it really didn't bother me. We talked for what seemed like hours while the party went on. We were totally oblivious to anything going on around us. Time seemed to stop as we talked. For the first time he expressed how he enjoyed my company and felt he was falling for me. He continued to express how he had not stopped thinking of me since the time we met which by now was nine months. He told me how much I occupied his thoughts and how it was starting to bother him when I danced with other guys. I really didn't know what to say and just stood quiet through it all. I was thinking about what David had told me, how I should not allow myself to get involved with him because he was no good for me and he didn't want me to get hurt by him. Although I was looking at Roland, I was having my own private thoughts. He continued talking and sounded so sincere. I felt his words penetrating my heart. He said he wanted to see me more and begin a relationship except he hardly knew anything about me and he needed to. I asked why? He said it was important for the kind of business he was in. He needed to know he could trust me. I asked if he meant he could trust that I wouldn't tell anyone about his cocaine business. He just smiled. I asked what kind of business he was in that he needed to know more about me. He said import/export. I pretty much figured out what his business was by now but I asked questions as though I didn't know what he was talking about just to see if he would come clean and level with me about what he was doing. I didn't want him to know David had already briefed me in on what they did. Again, I asked what my personal information had to do with his business. He didn't really elaborate much except to say that so far, he liked how I carried myself in public and that he had been observing me carefully all this time. He liked what he saw and didn't know what it was about me but he felt good around me like he could talk to me. He began to ask me personal questions about my life. He asked where I came from because he had never met or seen me in his circles. I told him it was because I definitely wasn't a part of his circle. He asked if he would know my circle of people because he pretty much knew everyone. I laughed and commented that I was positive! Of course I was thinking about my fellowship friends at church that I once hung out with in ministry. They had nothing to do with his world of drugs, parties and this lifestyle. I really didn't want to discuss my backslidden life right there that night. I was sure he wouldn't understand anyway. I could sense that he was thinking I was hiding something because of the way he looked at me. He was very observant and keen on discerning of people. I knew he'd never understand even if I tried to explain so I jokingly told him that I was a *"fallen angel"*. Now he laughed. I know he had no idea what I meant. I never elaborated much and simply asked if we could change the subject. He apologized for making me feel uncomfortable but asked me to consider dating him exclusively. I told him I would think about it. He asked very politely for my home number. As long as we had known each other I hadn't given it to him. Against David's advice and instruction, I gave him my phone number that night. It was a long night into the morning. We continued to see each other and we were quickly coming up on a year of hanging out together. It worked out good for me because of my traveling. I didn't feel the need to commit to anyone or anything. Every time he brought up the issue of a relationship, I changed the subject and he knew it. I kept telling him to give me time. He began to think it was because I had a "sancho" (*Spanish for a boyfriend on the side*). I always remembered David's words telling me to just *"enjoy the ride and guard my heart"* but it was too late. My feelings for Roland had grown much deeper than I wanted to.

One day, I called David to invite him over the house to talk. He was on his way out of town on some sudden business. I confessed about giving Roland my phone. I asked what was so important about Roland that I should know. He didn't care to discuss it over the phone and told me to wait before making a commitment to him until he got back from his trip in a couple of days. He was upset that I gave him my number. He emphatically told me not to make any decisions until he got back in town. He made me promise to wait until he got back and he would come tell me what I needed to know about Roland. He commented that what he needed to tell me couldn't be said over the phone and it would take some time to explain. He needed to sit down and explain and he didn't have the time because he was already leaving out of town. I promised to wait for him. Laughing, he told me Roland had asked him to be honest with him and tell him if I had a sancho at home. He said he laughed it off and told Roland he was tripping too hard and no I did not have a sancho.

I continued to see Roland and talk to him on the phone all the while David was out of town. At that time we didn't have cell phones. We used pagers. Roland wanted to know if he could come and see me at my home. I remembered David telling me not to tell him where I lived or anything personal about me until he got back. I told Roland I didn't entertain at home because of my children but agreed to see him the following Friday after work. We agreed to a given time and location. The Friday came and we were set to meet. As usual, he was on time and was there before me. He was with three other associates. Off we went to dine at one of his favorite places. I thought of everything he had shared the other day and how very charming he was. My heart said "*Give it a go.*" I was very glad to see him, I missed him too. Of course I wasn't going to tell him that. We were sitting in a cozy fireplace setting relaxing and talking. Once again he began to share from his heart about how he felt I was the woman for him. As he was talking, I remembered what David had said about waiting and I wondered what in the world could be so important that I had to wait? I figured the worst thing that David would say is that Roland was already married or he was a fugitive. I already knew he wasn't gay. Good grief! What could be worse? I just couldn't figure what was so important that David had to tell me. I trusted David with my life so I was going to wait as promised. Roland asked why I needed time to think about what he had shared with me the other day. Either I wanted to be with him or not! He admitted to putting feelers out there to find out where I came from, what I did, what I was all about, and who was in my circle. He said no one knew anything about me. I thought it was kind of funny and chuckled that he would make such a big deal about something that was really nothing. I thought to myself, had he asked around my church circle, it would have been a different story. So he sells drugs, big deal! I figured I'd throw him off with what I did for a living, about State job and what I did in saving tax payers billions of dollars. I told him how I purposely was careful not to put my personal business out there especially concerning my family. He agreed and understood a bit more why I was so careful. He said that it was a smart practice in my life and it obviously worked because no one really knew me or anything about me. I couldn't help but laugh inwardly. He said he practiced the same in that he didn't give out a lot of information to people he didn't know either. He commented that everyone that inquired about me only knew me as David's cousin and basically that was it! I asked if we could change the subject. I promised to give him an answer in a week. Shortly after, we got a table and had our dinner. We hung out all night as he also conducted business. As David; just have fun, enjoy the ride but just guard my heart. That's exactly what I was doing until he got back. This night would be just another night of enjoyment and David would be here soon to clear things up.

Fallen Angel

On the day David was to return, he called to tell me he would be gone an extra two days due to some unforeseen problem. I told Roland I would was out of town for few days on business. That would kill some time for my cousin to return. That following Saturday night, Roland and I along with the regulars went out to a Cuban restaurant. There was a long line to enter but when we walked up, we were immediately waved in. It felt really cool that we didn't have to wait but then again, it was about "business". Roland was taking care of some business upstairs as the rest of us partied and danced to the music. It was a typical night of drinking and dancing but as I looked around, I had this brief moment as I was dancing; what I would do if something went wrong upstairs with Roland. Eventually, Roland walked out and I watched his facial expression to see what I could discern, good or bad. As the music was finishing, I made my way to our table just as Roland was approaching. Roland ordered something to eat and he whispered (*in code*) that everything went great! Later, in the hours of the morning, we all started making our way out to the limousine waiting. We were all talking and walking towards the open door awaiting us, I heard a person yell out; *"Judy, Judy is that you*?" I just about died a thousand deaths that someone from my church would be there and know me by that name. I was hoping it was another

Judy and thought it was highly unlikely that anyone there would know me anyway. After all, what would someone from church be doing there too? So I just kept walking. The only people who knew me by that name had to be from church or my family. Just as we were about to approach the door and get in, this guy yelled out again *"Judy"*! He had caught up to us and attempted to nudge me. My heart sank! As I took a quick second to compose myself, Roland stepped between us and said *"Excuse me, sir, but I think you have her mixed up with someone else, her name isn't Judy."* I slowly turned around to look at him and unfortunately I did recognize him from the *"Chapel"* church long ago. I thought to myself *"Oh no, not him"*. I quietly told Roland that it was okay, I knew him. I attempted to introduce him to Roland who was just standing there dumbfounded, speechless with that stoic look to his face. He didn't care to respond when I introduced him to my friend. This guy wanted to talk and catch up. I just wanted the ground to open up and swallow me of embarrassment. I was speechless too and couldn't think of what to say quickly to get rid of him. He kept saying things like, "It's so nice to see you," and "You look great!" But I was horrified that he saw me dressed the way I was. I certainly was not dressed like the *"Sister Judy"* he once knew. We made quick small talk and then I told him we were holding up traffic and I couldn't talk but that I'd call his sister during the week and we would all catch up. He looked somewhat troubled. I'm sure he couldn't believe I was just cutting him off this way. I quickly excused myself, got in the limousine and off we went. All the way back I didn't know what to say. It was embarrassing to say the least and it so dampened my night. Neither Roland nor any of the guys said anything about this *"Judy"* incident. Usually all the way home, they discussed business, laughed about certain things or just talked about how things had gone. But tonight it was quite the opposite. All I could hear was the music playing. I could tell by looking at all the guys that they too were a bit perplexed at what had just taken place but no one said a word. Roland was especially quiet and distant. He wasn't even sitting close by me as usual. I was thinking about all the people this guy would tell that he had seen me at this club. Somehow I had banked on never running into anyone I knew from church because of this new crowd of people I now ran with. I was sure no one would ever recognize me as I had lost a lot of weight and dressed differently now. How embarrassing.

When we got back to The Towers, the usual partying was going on and the place was packed. The music was loud and Roland asked me to wait a couple of minutes while he did his usual briefing of the meeting with the guys. I thought about simply slipping out and just leaving but I knew it would look awkward. He came out few minutes later and told me to meet him on the balcony to have some privacy. I knew he was dying of curiosity to bring up this *"Judy"* incident and wanted to talk about it. As we walked onto the balcony, he ordered everyone inside. Everyone went in and he closed the door. There was an awkward, uneasy silence. Shortly after, he walked up to me and sternly (*in my face*) asked me if this guy was one of the guys from my circle that I never wanted to talk about. I lied and explained that he was the brother of a friend of mine that I used to work with. With a rigid look to his face, he got up close and asked me why he called me *"Judy"* and wanted me to explain why I was using this alias. He didn't give me a chance to explain and began to question me more about who I really was because he was now very uncomfortable with me around his business. I told him he was making a big deal out of nothing, it was complicated and I really didn't want to talk about all this right now. By now he was livid and demanded to know who I was connected with because everyone is connected to someone. His face was stern and he looked like he was about to explode. He demanded me to stop the excuses tonight and just explain why the heck this guy knew me as "Judy." He wanted me to clear it up with him before I left. He confessed to feeling that maybe I was a law enforcement plant and he insisted that he had to know right here, right now and tonight! I explained it was simply a childhood name given to me by family and anyone that knew me when I was younger. It's what personal friends who know my family call me. He continued with that stoic look as though he didn't believe me. I don't know why I just didn't tell him about *"Sister Judy"* from church. I just couldn't get myself to explain that I was a backslidden Christian and that's how everyone knew me at church. I was still somewhat buzzed from drinking and smoking at the club and didn't want to talk about God stuff either. Man, talk about something ruining my high and sobering me up quick! He walked away from me and was just looking out to the city below. I could tell he still didn't quite believe me. He just kept quiet and glared at me from a distance. After a while, he dropped the subject and agreed we would finish this later. He walked me to my car and I went home.

The next morning, David called me and told me how Roland had called him early in the morning and explained to him what happened at that club. He said Roland asked him very seriously who the "blank...blank" I really was and why this guy called me *"Judy"*. David simply laughed and told him he was acting paranoid. He explained to Roland that it was a childhood name (*just as I had told him*) that only few people knew me by that name because it was a family name given to me years ago and it's just what close family and friends called me. He told him it was my nickname and that I came from a good family and I wasn't the average snake (*woman*) and he didn't have anything to worry about with me. He reassured Roland that I could, in fact, be trusted and vouched for me that day. He gave Roland his word that I was good, (*meaning I wasn't a rat, a snitch*). Roland seemed to calm down and said that I just seem too good to be true. David says he tried to discourage Roland from seeing me anymore and suggested he look elsewhere for a lady because I actually wasn't his type anyway. Roland told him that he wanted to stay with me but had to be sure who I was and that I could be trusted. David laughed again at him and told him to calm down, quit being so paranoid and chill. Little did Roland know that it was David himself who told me not to share any personal information with him.

The next day, David called to let me know he was on his way back and would be stopping by my house before he checked in with Roland. He wasn't sure what time as it was an eight hour drive.

The Bombshell

Finally, David arrived. I had made a pot of coffee and snacks. He began by asking me how I really felt about Roland. I told him how much I had come to love him and really wanted to continue our relationship. I told David how I promised to be honest with him before giving Roland an answer.

David reiterated the fact that he had warned me for a good reason. He slowly began to explain some things and I couldn't help but interrupt him and ask if Roland was married or a fugitive from the law? David said no and continued talking. I started to ask "If he is this or that? but he told me to just be quiet and listen because it was far worse than anything I could imagine. Well, I couldn't imagine what could be worse. He asked me not to interrupt him and just listen until he was completely done. He began by telling me that Roland was a very powerful man. He wasn't who or what I thought he was at all. He is basically a business man in organized crime, "a criminal businessman." I thought to myself well, I already knew that. He sells drugs and it's not so bad. David continued to explain how Roland pretty much ran a lot of illegal businesses, not just drugs! He says "It gets worse! He is also a parolee and was a major, big-time shot caller with a prison Mafia gang. He explained how Roland is known to be ruthless with people and that his nickname is "Boss".

David could see that I was speechless and blown away by now. He continued to tell me that he himself (*along with the other guys we travel with*) all serve as personal body guards when Roland comes out from prison. He says, "*This is why we all travel together in the limousine because business is explosive right now, things are very busy and unpredictable*". We are all body guards that put out fires (*take care of things or problems*) that may arise when he's out and about taking care of business. He says this is why Roland never travels alone and moves in circles he knows or is in control of because of the enormous drugs he is supplying to many people and businesses. He was a big drug dealer controlling a lot of the drug industry through his ties to the underground world here locally and throughout the United States. He further explained that when we go to parties, most of the time it isn't all about partying but really has to do with consummating drug deals or big transactions taking place under the guise of a party, celebrations or dinners. Sometimes there will be people in these places that know him or know of him and may want to harm him due to past business deals gone sour, or deaths, etc. He doesn't take any chances. He repeated the fact that Roland and his associates can be ruthless without warning. "*I don't want you hurt in all this*" he said. We never know when something is going to go down. We are all always 'packing' (*carrying guns*) and ready for anything. There are times we have to be brutal with someone who is uncooperative or out of line and I worry when you are with us that something could happen. He reminded me of the incident not long ago when we were all out and that drunken man spilled his drink on my arm and disrespected Roland. This man had to be taken out back and taught a lesson. "*We don't even know how this man is today or if we left him alive or not. That's why we left as soon as we did.*" Instantly, I remembered that night and everything made sense now about how everyone was so quiet all the way home and the look on David's face when I looked over at him. It all came together for me. I wondered if they had just shot and killed him but didn't want to ask. I thought about the first party we went to when we first met and the constant traffic in and out of the bathroom and the fact that they called him *"the candy man."* I thought of that couple and others on the balcony at The Towers and how quickly they did what he asked of them. It suddenly all made so much sense. When David finished talking, I stood quiet for a long while. All I could say was *"Wow, you were right, I had no idea it would be all this."* He said he knew I would be blown away because I didn't come from this lifestyle and because of our church upbringing. He warned that I had nothing in common with this guy and said *"Rita, you're not criminal material and I don't want to be responsible if something happens. I don't know what I would say to the familia (family) if something happen to you".* He explained how he was sure in time, all this would surely wreck my life even if I was innocent because I'd have a hard time in court explaining or having to prove I knew nothing. He pleaded with me to dump Roland. He commented; *"This world isn't for you, mija."* David went on to admit that unfortunately, he could see Roland really cared for me too because he had changed so many of his ways. He usually never got hooked on a chick. With him, it was either business or just an evening of pleasure but the guys had begun cracking jokes on how they think he was sprung on me. He normally doesn't ever dance or date chicks as long as he had with me. David shouldn't have mentioned Roland's feelings for me because suddenly I had a flood of nonstop tears running down my face. I honestly felt I was feeling love for this man. David reached for my hand and said how very sorry he was that this had hurt me. He reminded me that he would be around as long as he could to protect me but unfortunately, he could see this was getting serious and out of his control. He knew Roland pretty well and he had been so sure he wouldn't get serious like this. He regretted he had ever introduced us. He really didn't want me pulled into something I couldn't or wouldn't be able to get out of later. He reiterated the fact that eventually I would get hurt. I continued to quietly sob. I felt deceived. I thought of how Roland didn't look anything like I thought he would. I had heard about him. He was smart, intelligent, charming and such a true gentleman.

He didn't look anything like a criminal, let alone a ruthless one. In fact, he could pass for any professional, even an attorney. David explained that this was partly how he would infiltrate himself through business dealings with so many professionals, doctors, people in the entertainment industry, attorney's, restaurant/club owners, etc. Roland had the gift of gab coupled with diplomacy and had a way of talking professionally with all levels of people. He usually got whatever he set out to get. He explained that although he was a true gentleman, he had no problems calling out a death warrant or having someone disposed of for disrespect, lying, stealing, or anything else he was displeased about. As we continued talking, Roland continued paging me. It was awkward now that I knew what I did and I had totally mixed emotions. I'm not sure if I was hurt, sad or just angry. I felt love for him and now it seemed the right thing to do was dump him and cut off the whole relationship as soon as possible! I thought about how I would let him down slowly so as not to tick him off either and of course I wasn't going to let him know that David was the one to tell me. David said *"Well, now you know. It's up to you if you still want to see him again."* He said he wasn't sure how I wanted to handle all because if Roland found out that he (*David*) had told me all this, it would definitely put a strain on their friendship but his first loyalty was to me as (*familia*) family. He also said that later tonight he had to go check in and he was sure Roland would ask him if he'd heard from me since I hadn't responded to his pages. I told David that my game plan was to tell Roland that I myself inquired around about him and was given the 411 by someone else. I told David not to tell Roland we had met or talked.

David left and I sat in disbelief. He was right; I would have never guessed it was what he had to tell me. I thought about the kids, my immediate family in prison ministry and how all this would cause so many problems. The worst would come if and when law enforcement got a hold of this. They would think the ministry was connected all along and end the access to the prisons for them. I couldn't do this to my family. Thank God I had dropped out of ministry when I did but unfortunately, we were still family. Roland continued paging. The next day (Saturday), I slept in. Roland had left several messages on the answering machine. Later that afternoon, I called him to tell him I was sick and since I had cried so much, I really sounded like I had a cold or flu. I told him I'd give him a call later. He had hopes I would feel well enough to see him for a while that night. I needed time to think and strategize how I was going to resolve my relationship and cut him loose in a way he'd never find out that I knew about his little secret life. The next day, David called to see how I was doing and I told him I was still in disbelief but thankful for his honesty. He said that Roland had spilled his guts to him last night about how he felt about me and that his gut told him I was the woman for him. David said he couldn't help but laugh and told Roland *"Come on, you never fall for these broads."* Roland commented to David, he felt that for some reason Rita was different and felt in his heart she was the one for him. David said he didn't know what to tell him because he was so serious so he just stood quiet. He never told Roland about our little meeting prior to reporting in that night. I thought about what David said; the part that Roland cared for me a great deal really stood with me because I felt the same way. I was running from God and now I was also going to run from this unhealthy relationship. Finally after a few days, I took one of Roland's call and spoke with him for a while. I told him I had been sick and later busy traveling with my job. He asked if I would tell him where I lived so he could come to the house and perhaps bring me some soup or anything else I needed to feel better. Of course, I made some excuses as to why I couldn't meet. He was sure something was wrong. I reassured him that everything was cool. We talked some more but before we hung up he asked if everything was okay with me. I asked why? He said he didn't know why but I sounded different, somewhat cold, distant and superficial in our conversation. Funny how he picked that up because it's exactly the way I was feeling. I told him it was because I didn't feel good. He seemed to be sensitive and precise in reading people's vibes. He was so right on.

The inevitable day came and we met. He was always on time. We went to one of our favorite restaurants out by the beach. It was so nice to see him again. I really wanted to throw my arms around him and hold him. He looked so handsome and charming. As usual, he wasn't alone and David wasn't with him but we went off by ourselves. They sat us at our table. It was a difficult time because I needed to be as normal as possible before I told him what I needed to tell him. We had our dinner and afterwards we were driven to the pier where we got off to walk around. At one point he stopped to ask if everything was really okay or was it that he just hadn't seen me in a while. He took my hand and said he needed to see me more and asked if I had an answer for him about dating him exclusively now. I paused a minute and we walked over to sit down to look out towards the ocean. I looked into his face and told him I actually did have something to talk to him about. His demeanor changed and he said, *"I knew it, I knew something was wrong since the last time we spoke on the phone"*. He immediately asked if there was another man in my life. I laughed and commented how I wished that it was that simple. I told him I too was curious about him before making an *"exclusive"* commitment. I told him I got the information on him too. The look on his face and mannerism slowly began to change and he looked a bit perplexed! He asked what I was talking about. I told him I knew who **"Boss"** was and that I wasn't sure we couldn't do this anymore. His expression changed, he firmly set his jaw and I could see he was completely taken aback by the bombshell I had just dropped on him. He wanted to know who told me. I told him I did my own homework and someone filled me in on him and that I now knew what he was all about. He told me that he used to wonder how I would react if and when he told me about his real life. He said he was just surprised I had found out on my own. It was quiet for a minute and he asked *"What now?"* Before I could answer, he began to reassure me it didn't change anything about his feelings for me and he was still very sure we were meant for each other. I told him I didn't think we had enough in common for a relationship.

It wasn't anything personal but neither was it anything I wanted to deal with in my life, with my family and my children. He asked me to be totally honest with what he was going to ask. He promised he would be a gentleman and simply walk away and never bother me again. He asked me to look him in the face and tell him that I didn't love him at all and he would walk away. I calmly began to express what I felt but then the tears filled my eyes as I shared how I did love him but unfortunately, there was no way we stood a fair chance of building a healthy relationship. He asked if we could try and work at it because he could see himself in a good, honest, loving life with someone like me. He tried to assure me that he was in a position where he didn't have to get his hands dirty in the mix of business as much anymore other than giving verbal orders. He could work things out differently to look like an honest working man and that he would even get a regular, working job. I asked what the heck he meant by that? I reminded him that no matter how he tried to paint the picture or how he put things, we could never have a private or a good life with the eyes and ears of the world upon every move we made, especially law enforcement. He went on to say that he had asked God this last time when he was getting out of the penitentiary to send him a good woman so he could settle down and not long after that was when we met. I asked him *(jokingly as I was still in tears)* if he actually even believed in God and prayed. He said he never had before but since we had met, he had started talking to God. He said he wasn't a religious man but he did acknowledge a *"higher power"*. He looked so sincere and pleaded with me not to give up. He said he knew my family was religious because David had told him all about our parents. He asked if I still believed or if I prayed. I told him he had no idea how much I believed in God at one time but I wasn't a praying woman anymore. He asked me to start talking to God about this and he said he would too. He commented that he would make a deal with God about us. I told him he couldn't just bargain and make deals with God. He said that he was desperate and didn't want to lose me and would even begin lighting a candle every day until he got his answer. It sort of blew me away that he was thinking like this. I felt like I was caving in to him and I wanted to stay with him that night. We stayed a while longer before we went back to the car and then he took me back to my car. He got quiet, held me for a minute and kissed me on the cheek as we said our goodbyes. I could see his eyes were watery. He said he couldn't bear the thought of not seeing me anymore and all this sounded like it was the end for us. It was so very, very sad because I really didn't want to let him go but I knew I needed to. As he was reminding me to talk to God about us and talking very fast, I was thinking about what my family would say when they found out who he was and what he was about. I was sure they would never accept him; especially my parents that were in prison ministry. All this could turn into a huge scandal.

I cried all the way home. I knew God knew my heart. I asked God to help me get over Roland. I honestly felt pain in my heart that this would have to end. I wasn't even sure God would listen to a prayer like this asking God to help me with a decision concerning a criminal. How crazy was this? What was I asking for any way? I just knew in my heart that I loved this man. I went home and tried to forget all this mess and decided I would try to get on with my life.

The next day David called to ask what had happened. He said Roland was not himself and was ticked off at everyone. I told him that I told Roland I did my homework and got the information from a friend who told me who "Boss" was all about. He asked if I was okay and I said, "No!" and began to cry again. Later that afternoon, David came over and I cooked dinner. We talked about this situation for hours over dinner. He commented how miserable both Roland and I were. He jokingly said that Roland had been quiet and distant from everyone and drinking more than his usual self. He joked and said how funny it was to watch us both acting like kids in love. I asked him if he thought I had done the right thing by cutting him loose. He said that as painful as it was, yes! He also knew the power of love because he chased after his wife for six years before he finally won her heart. Then he went off to Viet Nam and in the end, he still lost her. He said that it was his love for her that kept him going during combat. I confessed to David how much I loved Roland but there was too much at stake to compromise.

The next few weeks passed painfully slow. There were a few times I met some friends for happy hour but it wasn't the same anymore. I was miserable because I wanted to be with him. Roland continued to page and call at home leaving messages but they went unanswered. I continued to ignore most of his calls. Sometimes I would take one of his calls and we talked for long periods of time. He had even asked David to intervene on his behalf but he wouldn't. Little did Roland know David was the one who had enlightened me about "Boss".

One day I was out of town working. I didn't feel like dining alone so I bought got some snacks to take back to my room for my dinner. I was in my room writing reports and listening to the radio. Roland continued paging. On one of those pages, I returned his call. We talked for a long time. It was the same kind of conversation as before and he pleaded with me to reconsider. He wanted to drive out to join me in my room that night but I told him I was there with my supervisor for a meeting at a military base which wasn't true.

He told me about a big business deal he had going the next day (afternoon) at a big Hotel out of town by an airport. This meeting was set for noon and he was meeting with some heavy-duty, high rollers from afar off country. He asked me to wish him luck. I reminded him I didn't believe in luck and that he should be careful with whom he was dealing with because things are not always as they appear. He was sure everything would be fine because he had done business with these people before. We eventually hung up. That night I had a dream in which I saw him getting arrested. In my dream I could see undercover agents handcuffing him. It felt so real. The next day I was bothered by that dream. By that afternoon, I called to talk to him but he didn't answer. I called David and he said Roland was out taking care of business. I asked why he wasn't with him. He said two others went with him and he was supposed to stay back by the phones. I told David about my dream and how much I wanted to warn Roland. Maybe he could cancel the meeting for another time because I felt it wasn't a good thing. He told me everything was already in motion but he would tell Roland I had called. While at work that day, the dream I had was heavy on my heart most of the day and I felt uneasiness about it all. That afternoon I drove back home. I hadn't heard from Roland all day which was kind of weird because he usually paged just to let me know he was thinking of me. I figured he didn't get my message and I didn't want to chase him down. I waited for his page but he never made contact. I simply went about my day and figured he knew how to get a hold of me after he finished his business. I said a prayer for him that day and asked God take care of him. I was uncomfortable all day and had a bad feeling about his meeting. I prayed that God would protect him. He never did call.

12

Gone But Not Forgotten

The next day, I was working out of my home and David called and asked if I was working at the office or at home. When I told him I was at home, he said he was nearby and wanted to stop by for a cup of coffee. I asked him if he had heard from Roland. He said he did but would tell me about it when he got to the house. I was somewhat relieved. I started a pot of coffee and something to eat. He got there a while later. It had been raining outside. I served him a hot cup of coffee and as I was pouring myself a cup, he put his hand on my hand and asked me to sit down because he had something to tell me. My heart sank. I just knew it had something to do with Roland. When I asked if it was about Roland, he said the dream I had was right on because Roland had been, in fact, set up by agents. They were waiting for him and had the lobby surrounded. He was arrested on drug trafficking charges. The third guy that had gone with him in a separate car as an observer watched from a distance as the agents moved in on him and his partner and they were taken into custody. His bail was over two million dollars. It was a lot of money in the early eighties. My heart sank in disbelief. I asked a few questions before I broke down in tears. I couldn't believe that my dream had actually come true! It was an eerie feeling like suddenly there was a big gaping hole in the ground and Roland along with all our memories had fallen right in it as though "*we*" had never happened. All of a sudden, poof! He was gone! I wondered if this was my sign from God. David hugged me for comfort and said how sorry he was but maybe it had happened for a good reason. He explained how Roland had done business with these guys before and everything was fine but this second time around, he had been set up. He was going to be looking at some serious prison time. David reminded me how this was the kind of stuff he had been trying to spare me from and how I would always be wrapped up in this if I continued my life with Roland. The next time, it could be me involved and I would be incarcerated for a very long time. Also, my record and reputation would be tarnished forever! I didn't really know what to feel. I certainly wasn't ready to make any decisions over anything.

As time passed, David and I continued going out on weekends. About ninety days went by before I received a message from Roland through another contact. He was trying to communicate and wanted an address where he could write to me. I sent him my post office box address that I used for business. A few weeks later, I received his first letter. I was parked outside the post office. It seemed like a very long walk to the car and I couldn't get my car door opened fast enough to get inside and read the letter. I know it was probably silly but that's how I felt and my heart sank.

The first sentence of the letter brought me immediately to tears. He went straight to the heart as he expressed how in all his years of meeting women, he'd never met someone like me and how there was something different about my person. He said he still felt strong about feeling somehow God has brought us together. I was thinking it was either a snow job to keep me on the hook, or perhaps the Holy Spirit in me that he felt. He proceeded to say he should have listened to me when I told him there was no such thing as good luck the night before his bogus business deal and how he should have followed my instincts. The letter was five pages long, double-sided. He was asking if I would consider visiting him. He had included in this thick envelope a visiting request form for me to complete.

When I got home, I read it once again. My daughter asked who had written. I told her it was Roland. She was already familiar with him from before although she had never personally met him. She knew how much I cared for him and that he had gone to jail for a while. In such an innocent tone, she asked how someone could love another person who is in a jail, can't be seen and isn't not around? With tears in my eyes I tried to explain. I don't think she understood but she hugged me as though to comfort me without even having any idea how I hurt inside for a man I rationally knew was no good for me. I was a backslider and he was a gangster whom I knew didn't really believe in God the way I did. He saw religious people as weak. What kind of chance was this for me to ever come back to my faith and ministry? I always knew I had a call on my life and needed to wind down what I was doing so as to make a Godly commitment once and for all. I continued trying to live my life simple, going out with my friends and dating casually. I still wrote Roland now and then. David kept in contact with me. In time, Roland's trial was over and he was given a sentence of fifteen years to life. David asked if I thought I would wait for Roland. I told him I didn't really know and even if he did the fifteen years or more, it seemed like an eternity and I had my family to think about and take care of. I had lost my son who was given a 25 to life sentence and now Roland received 15 to life. That was two in a row and more than I could handle.

Several months later, David called to ask me to meet him for what he said was a very important dinner. I was thinking it had something to do with Roland. We met at one of our favorite hangouts. After a couple of drinks and some small talk, he began to talk about our childhood again and how much we had all been through in church with our families. We had talked about this before but somehow this time he wasn't quite making a whole lot of sense. To my amazement and shock, he said he had been thinking and wondering why he and I didn't consider hooking up as a couple and begin to actually date. He explained why he thought it could work because of our family similarities of ministerial background. Whew! Talk about a sobering moment! Once again, I sat there speechless as I listened to him rationalizing all this. He was sure our families would embrace the idea of us being together. He told me how he wanted to take care of me and the kids. What an explosive dinner date! I never would have thought this was what he would have to say. He expressed how he felt that together we could actually have a good life, stay sober and go straight. He never mentioned serving the Lord together. He reminded me of all the times I had written to him and encouraged him while he was in Viet Nam and then still kept in contact after he was discharged and was emotionally shipwreck. He talked about all the years he spent in San Quentin prison after Viet Nam and the times I encouraged him to go to college and get his degree using his veterans' benefits when he got out of prison. He confessed to having feelings for me for years now and even more so when we were all partying together, and how heartbroken he was as he watched Roland and I falling in love right before his eyes. He was so sorry he had ever introduced us. It was out of respect for both Roland and I that he never got between us only to discourage me from a relationship with Roland because he didn't want to see me hurt. He felt I was safe with him when we all partied because he could watch out for me. It was just recently when Roland was arrested that he realized just how tired he was of everything and needed me to know how he felt because he was in the midst of making some major decisions in his life. He wanted me to be a part of his new plans. I expressed how I didn't and couldn't feel the same for him intimately because of our family bonds. He didn't care and was sure that with a good life love would follow later. I was still in disbelief the whole time that we talked. Again I told him how sorry I was that I didn't share the same feelings for him. Of course, he was disappointed but he said he wanted me to think about it after tonight because he was going forward with his plans with or without me. He said since Roland would be gone for a long time, he was going to take advantage of the situation and move on with his life. On one hand, I was happy about his decision to quit his drinking, doing drugs and get out of the drug business but felt sad about what he had just shared with me. I never knew he felt this way about me.

I continued to see David off and on as friends in the months that followed as he went forward with his plans to move away and start a whole new life. The day finally came when he was about to leave. He came to the house and asked me once more if I would reconsider. I reminded him that although our families were close, I still couldn't see us in a romantic relationship. My answer unfortunately, was still *"No."* He told me the last time he was in his town (*which was this last time he was out of town*) he had inquired about college at his local university there. He already had college credits from before. I was happy for him that he was really serious this time about changing. He urged me to gather my family and move away with him while I could. He promised to help me until I could get on my feet if I still wanted to leave. It was a bittersweet moment. I was happy for him but sad that I couldn't feel love for him enough to live with him like he wanted. I had always trusted him with my life. He discouraged me again about thinking I could ever have a life with Roland because he wasn't going to get out of prison for a long, long time and I would just be wasting my time not to mention the challenging politics I'd be getting mixed up with in his world if I chose to stay with him. He reaffirmed that I could never have a normal life with Roland and reminded me there would be no getting out once I was in the mix as his "senora" (*Spanish for woman/wife*). Once again, he expressed how he regretted introducing Roland to me years ago. We ended our last night out on that note because he was leaving in the morning. I cried as we hugged and said our goodbyes. He went his way, I went mine.

From time to time, he still called, wrote, sent me cards, poems and songs that he had written for me. Sometimes, our families saw each other at funerals here and there. It was awkward to see him again when I was with my family. He was now sober and doing very well. We would talk and he would ask how I was doing, etc and asked if I was happy. Of course he always asked if I had heard from Roland. I told him we wrote each other periodically.

A short four years later, another one of David's brothers died and my family and I drove out to attend the funeral services. During this visit, we had a time when we sat and talked. He shared how well he was doing for himself and that his offer still stood if I wanted to come live with him and get away. Not only had he enrolled in college like he said he would but he had graduated with a degree in Social Services. He had a great job and making good money. He had bought a new convertible sports car and had his own place by now. I was so very proud of him and his accomplishments. Sad to admit it but I never would have thought he would actually succeed because he had been a raging alcoholic heavily hooked on his daily cocaine use! He reminded me that his place was always open if I ever needed to get away. Now he had new sober friends from his support group that he hung out with. He was a different person and I liked the new him. After all, it was because of him that I met Roland who was now, *"Gone, but not forgotten."*

My First Visit

Against my better judgment, several months later I decided I would visit Roland for the first time. He was being held in a local facility. All the way up to the day it was time to go visit, I had mixed emotions and uncertainties about whether or not I should go. I had butterflies in my stomach all the way up there and even worse when I pulled into the parking lot. I just wanted to see him one more time before he was transferred out of state and give closure to the fact that we would never be together again. I arrived at the facility and the procedure was all too familiar for me because of all my years of experience with prison ministry. We had ministered at this facility a few times before. It was awkward being there to visit an inmate. My heart sank to my ankles as I waited for him to come out. Lots of things went through my mind. I wasn't sure what to expect and what I would say when I saw him. I wondered if my heart would tell me to stay with him. I thought what I would say first when we sat down. Should I or should I not kiss him so as not to lead him on since we wouldn't be together anymore? My mind raced in a whirlwind of thoughts the whole time I was getting cleared to go in. I hadn't seen him since our last evening at The Towers. I thought about how crazy the whole visit idea was but it was too late, I was already there. Common sense told me to get out while I still could then suddenly, the metal doors swung open and there he stood getting patted down and scanned with a metal detector one more time before he walked out. Man, this was all happening so fast. We couldn't keep our eyes off each other as he was being processed. I wanted to cry and didn't know why. Security finished with him and he was escorted across the room to where I was. We weren't allowed to visit with the regular population because he was in "high power", maximum security status and wore different clothing. I watched as he was greeted by several inmates as he walked through the visiting area. He appeared to know quite a lot of them. Several made comments to him from a distance. Roland just smiled and kept walking. I could tell security wasn't at all pleased with it. It seemed like a long, long walk before he got to my table. I stood up, we hugged and my heart melted. I couldn't hold back my tears until security came over and asked us to sit down. This didn't seem to bother him one bit. There was only one other couple in this visiting area so it wasn't as loud. We were both at a loss for words and just stared at each other for few seconds. He began first and expressed how happy he was to see me and thanked me for making the effort to come see him. He said he had waited a long time for this moment. I still said nothing and slowly composed myself. He was very talkative and twitchy. He reminded me that up until the night before his arrest, he lit a candle for us in hopes that we would stay together. He expressed how he knew beyond anything he had ever known in life, that he loved me. He didn't want to lose me and expressed how he felt he needed me in his life to have a normal life someday. He was so sure I was the one for him. He stated he talked to God and expressed how much he cared for me and wanted God to help bring me back into his life. He promised God he would give a substantial donation to the poor or a church as an act of good faith. As he went on and on, I was thinking about what David told me that "*the brothers*" didn't believe in religion and didn't pray to God because they saw this as a sign of weakness. He continued talking, expressing and trying to convince me of his feelings as though time would run out. It was an hour into our visit when he seemed to catch his breath and asked, "*Why haven't you said much*?" I laughed and told him he was talking so fast he hadn't given me a chance to respond. I commented about his prayers to God, and how I wasn't sure he could bargain with God like this and just make his substantial financial donation as a plea bargain. He said he had never asked God for anything before and felt if he made this donation, God would honor his good faith gesture and bring me back into his life. He felt God knew he was sincere. As he continued talking, I was beside myself and just listened to his rationalization on how he communicated and negotiated with God as though it were a business deal. I told him that God was to be revered and I wasn't sure he could do this because God didn't need money. He asked me if I believed in God and if so; what was my choice of religion and how often did I go to mass. I told him "yes" to all the above but what he referred to as "*mass*" we referred to as church services. Before I could elaborate any further, he interrupted me and began to apologize that he wasn't the one to tell me who he was and what he was all about. He was sorry I had to see him like this behind prison walls and apologized for thinking I might had been a "*plant*" by law enforcement because of the "*Judy*" incident. He apologized for talking so much but felt like he had so much to tell me before I left and wanted me to know what he was thinking and what he felt before I left. I asked him how he could suspect me as an Informant. I laughed at the thought of the whole idea. He reminded me of that night we were at that Cuban club when that man walked up and called me "*Judy.*" He explained how this had bothered him even though David had explained it was a childhood name. He asked if I could finally explain why I used two names. He still wanted to know what I was all about when I was away from him or what my life was before knowing him. He said the only reason he still hung on to hope about getting involved with me was because of my cousin David who had reassured him I was good and he didn't need to worry about me. He said again, he let it go but it still always bothered him not knowing about who "*Judy*" was. I sort of chuckled about it all (*Man, if he only knew*!). It was at this point that I told him

I'd tell him all about me and my life but he needed to listen and not interrupt me. He appeared to brace himself. I began by telling him that before I met him, I was just a typical working woman who came from a good Christian family. In fact, my parents had been pastors of a church for years! He interrupted to ask what the position of a pastor was. Since he only knew the Catholic faith, I explained it was a minister like a priest of a church and how through the years my parents ended up in a divorce but later remarried. I told him how I myself was a Christian for several years, playing the piano and singing. He looked floored! His eyes opened wide and stared. I continued to tell him how I sang with a group called *"Judy & The Chapel Singers"* and how we had traveled to different churches and prisons for years singing gospel music and my stepfather preached the Word. I explained how people in my circle knew me as *"Sister Judy"*. Judy was a family name given to me as a little girl or from church. I clarified how the guy at the club knew me from church as *"Sister Judy"* and that's why he called me by that name. I also explained that my step-father was an ex-drug addict from a local neighborhood and was converted through a small Chapel some years ago and how my mom and stepfather moved out of state to start a new life together. He and my mother were volunteers at the local prison but had relocated back. By this time Roland just sat quietly with a puzzled look. I further explained how later "Judy and *the Chapel Singers"* joined forces with my stepfather and my mother that headed up a prison ministry. We ministered together for years. I shared how I had gone through some discouraging times and had taken a leave of absence from ministry (*my Christian life*). Unfortunately, I ended up backsliding. He asked what backsliding was about and what it had to do with religion because it sounded like a dance move. I explained what it actually meant and told him that this was what I had meant when I told him long ago that I was a *"fallen angel."* I explained how I was running from God when I met up with him and my cousin, David. Then I explained how David and I weren't actually blood cousins but our families considered ourselves as close as family and always told people we were family because we had grown up in church together and both of our parents (my *biological parents*) were pastors back in the day. Roland still looked startled as I kept talking about myself, where I'd been, where I was today; it's who I was, am and that's why I believe we could never be a couple. I told him I felt there was absolutely nothing good about the two of us staying together and besides all this, we had nothing in common. He didn't understand what I meant by "*ministry*". I explained and he tried hard to understand. I expressed how I also understood his position with his prison gang stuff and what he did. I could not see him fitting into my world and I definitely wasn't going to join his. I knew he could never serve the Lord and still do what he did for all the "*brothers.*" He seemed to be surprised how I knew so much about his world. I never told him how it had been David who enlightened me as to who he was and how the brotherhood ran their business.

By the time I finished, Roland could hardly say a word. He just looked at me and said "*Wow, I talked to God when I got out this last time about maybe finding a God-fearing woman to help change my life and it seems everything I just heard you explain is what I need*". Now he was more convinced than ever that I had been sent by God. I told him there was nothing Christian about me and my life right now and I hadn't been for many years. I explained how I've been lost for years partying, drinking and living a crazy life disconnected from God. I wanted to be honest with him and express how I couldn't see his life and mine ever come together because we were both on such extreme opposites. I felt like we only stood about a five percent chance of succeeding together, if that much. He said he didn't care and wanted to gamble on working out the other ninety-five percent. He was very determined about "us" and was thoroughly convinced that it could in fact work! By the time our visit was coming to an end, we had covered so much territory and said he finally had clarity about all his questions and curiosity about me. He said it all made sense now and he was so glad to know who Judy/Rita was. He asked if I would consider coming back to see him again? I told him I honestly wasn't sure. He said they would be transferring him out of state somewhere soon and didn't know where due to security. He was adamant that he was in love and wanted to marry me someday when he got out; maybe I could show him how to do the God thing like some of the *"brothers"* he had heard had changed through God. He only knew the Catholic ways; being brought up in Catholic schools. He thought maybe it was his old age creeping in (*now in his fifties*) that he was thinking about change. He said he would continue to talk to God about us and believe in his own way since he couldn't light candles anymore.

All the way home, I thought about the visit and the look on his face as I explained who I was and how he expressed his feelings about God. I know my heart wanted to believe him but I just couldn't be certain and wondered if it was a snow job to get me to keep coming back. I do remember feeling even more sure that I loved this man in a way I had never felt before.

I continued working and traveling on my job and keeping busy with my children.

After several months, I was casually dating this friend of mine named Rick. He was a county employee in another county I worked in. I thought to myself that perhaps this was what I needed; an honest, simple and legitimate man who had no hidden agenda and who was just who he said he was. I figured this would help me get over Roland easier. One day I received a communication through another friend of mine that Roland had been transferred to a facility in another state. He wanted to communicate with me. Months past and I continued dating this nice gentleman and in touch with Roland who lived in a complete criminal world of drugs and prison politics. It was somewhat awkward. Not long after, I received a letter from Roland once again pleading with me to come see him. As the months past I eventually wrote back and told him I didn't want to give him false hope but I was dating someone and in a relationship. I explained to Roland how I wanted him to understand the reality that he had a lot of years to do (*at least fifteen*) and I had my future, children and life to think about but I would agree to write him periodically just to keep him company.

A few weeks later, Roland wrote and said he really needed to talk to me. He wanted to send me a round-trip ticket to go on whatever weekend I could and he would cover my room and car rental. He explained the process to go see him. Once again, I had to be cleared to visit him in another state. The day finally came when I received confirmation about my clearance. Roland had been advised also and was ready to put me on a plane to go see him. The weekend came and I was on a plane to visit him. I suppose it was a good thing my boyfriend at the time lived in another county because I told him I had something to do that weekend. I didn't volunteer any information just that I would be busy. I felt a bit uncomfortable about going to visit Roland and knew it wasn't a cool thing to do if I wanted to rid of him but I went anyway. I visited him that weekend, Saturday and Sunday. We had a great visit and it felt good visiting him and again told him the reality was, I couldn't or wouldn't be faithful nor would I wait for him. To my surprise he said he understood but only asked me to "*guard my heart*" and save it for him. Boy did I ever remember hearing those words before except at that time it was my cousin David who would always tell me, "*Guard your heart*" and now it was Roland who was telling the same. He didn't like that I was in a relationship with someone else but he understood the reality of the fifteen years as a long time to wait. He reminded me that he had not stopped talking to God about us and was still asking God to show me his heart and keep love in my heart for him. He said he wouldn't worry about this guy as long as he didn't penetrate my heart. He also asked me to do him a couple of favors by making some phone calls and asked if I could forward a letter to someone else that would be sent to my mailing address. I didn't see any harm in that; it was the least I could do since he was in a restricted environment.

I continued to periodically visit Roland as he always sent the finances and it cost me nothing. During these visits, he began introducing me to some of the "fellows" and/or his "brothers" as his "senora" (*his woman*). Everyone seemed to have a lot of respect for him and pretty much did whatever he asked of them. We always took pictures on visits either alone, with another couple and/or with some of his associates. He was very selective who he took photos with. Roland explained the process of how prison officials never let them have the photos because they wanted to make copies first for their records. Roland would send the photos to me later. The prison always had a tight leash on our visits. I never gave it much thought and figured it was just prison protocol. He told me they wanted to make sure I wasn't bringing in drugs or other contraband. He explained that a lot of "transas" (*Spanish slang for transactions*) took place during these visits. He asked me how I felt about that. I told him, that I would never be anybody's mule to risk bringing in drugs. Somehow, I wasn't comfortable with his comments and became suspicious about his motives. After all, David had warned me not to ever let him "*use me*" to bring in drugs or other favors because of who he was; I would always be targeted and watched. He continued sending finances to cover all my travel expenses and then some. We had lots of discussions about beliefs, values, traditions, family and life in general. We shared many of the same values of "*old school*" ways. I was amazed at how well informed he was about all aspects of life in and out of prison. He read a lot and subscribed to numerous magazines and it was how he kept informed of so much in the "*free world*". He was a very intelligent man and very keen on issues like politics, sports, making money and so much more. Looking back now, I see how cleverly he had orchestrated various events in the visiting room and outside the small yard to integrate me with various people from other countries. He wanted me to slowly cultivate relationships with other inmate's wives. I didn't like this and I let him know I didn't want to meet people; especially females because I didn't trust them. He felt that there could be a time when we wouldn't be able to visit in the visiting room and he wanted me to know key inmates and what their wives/girlfriends looked like. He said there was no pressure; he only wanted to school me in certain areas so I would always be a step ahead of anything that took place, whatever that meant.

Moving ahead three years, he had begun trusting me with important and sensitive information. According to him, he was also schooling me about certain things so as to stay ahead of other people in business, politics and the psychology of how people think, especially law enforcement. He was always interesting to have discussions with because he was so clever, intelligent and up to date on all technology. I always learned things from him. He pretty much already had me figured out including my strengths and weaknesses. Roland was well versed in life and kept up with the changing times with regards to technology and the latest in cars, jobs, fashions, and even men's cologne to mention just a few. It was amazing how he accomplished all this through magazines. He was an avid reader. He was also a vegetarian. He did not eat any kind of meats. He felt I was a strong balanced woman and appreciated the fact that although I used drugs and alcohol modestly, I didn't seem to have a problem with drugs like other women he knew. He commented how he noticed I wasn't loud, flamboyant and always dressed professionally. Little did he know, it had a lot to do first of all because of my Christian upbringing and my professional job. He commented how he saw that I appeared to have strong good values in life and expressed how he felt they were my strongest assets. He reiterated again how he would be honored to someday say I was his wife. I laughed. He couldn't believe how we could have met the way we did coming from such extremely opposite lifestyles. This was why he felt God was in our meeting one another. He asked me what the odds of meeting each other the way we did were. He felt it was fate that we met. I still thought this was all just so silly and didn't give it much thought. Deep inside me I felt that it was all just a "worldly/secular" accident that happened due to my disobedience and bad choices and nothing more! Visiting him was entertaining and I enjoyed the traveling I got to do from state to state. It was a good way to pass time and it was costing me nothing in return, or so I thought.

Small Favors, Not So Bad

I continued living my carefree single lifestyle without any real pressure and/or abuse from any man. I continued visiting Roland from time to time as the finances came in. He was aware I was dating and I was making some profit doing him some simple "favors." On these visits Roland continued to ask me for small favors to meet with certain people and relate messages. I didn't feel there was any harm in simply delivering messages, sometimes I received packages and made phone calls for him. Amazingly, a lot of these business were prominent and established in society like restaurants, sport centers, limousine services, clothing stores, travel agencies, entertainment, and car dealerships, just to name a few. It was all new to me and I found it amazing and intriguing how much activity went on in society under "business as usual". I was learning a lot in a small amount of time. Many times I played things by ear or simply followed my gut instincts. I can say today that I believe God gave me favor in a lot of things I didn't know and people in general, just liked me and felt comfortable around me. I want to believe that the Holy Spirit within had never left me and could be felt by others because I never had problems with any of these shady people.

One day I was supposed to go meet another one of Roland's very important contacts. I gave my driver the heads up as to who we were meeting and reminded him to simply go along with whatever I did and to just follow my lead. We drove out to a high end Italian restaurant establishment. The gentleman I met with (*Tony*) looked like someone out of an Italian movie. He was tall, very attractive with silvery white hair and nicely dressed. He had the appearance of just leaving a salon because everything about his a persona was perfect; including his hair and nails. He might have been the owner because he seemed to be in control of this establishment. He had his own area where he conducted his business upstairs. Tony, John and I met briefly in the lounge for a drink and some small talk. A while later, Tony suggested we (*him and I*) go upstairs and talk business. He told my driver, John, he would have to wait here in the lounge and could order whatever he wanted to eat or drink off the menu and it was on the house. I could tell my associate didn't like this arrangement by the way he looked at me but he knew not to ask questions and just go along with the program as we discussed in the car. He agreed and sipped on his drink. His face said it all. My contact also had security of his own around him who followed us up the stairs and stood a far off as we ate and conducted our business. Tony let me know that he knew my associate didn't like the fact that he wasn't invited upstairs to this meeting but it was his policy and just how he conducted his business. He stated he didn't trust anyone and the less people that saw his face, the fewer that could recognize or implicate him down the road sometime. He further advised he no longer wanted to meet anyone else I brought with me in the future and he wanted me to make sure they understood before arriving to this establishment again. He said today he made an exception out of respect for Roland but no more from this day on. He said he actually liked my associate and he understood that I needed my security too but he didn't care to meet anymore strangers. Although he was polite about this, he was also very stern. I simply agreed and told him it wouldn't be a problem.

As we began our meeting and he began talking, it occurred to me that this deal could be something other than diamonds but I simply listened and did as Roland said. He just didn't seem the type to be bothered with something as trivial as a few diamonds. He appeared to be too much of a prominent businessman to be going out of his way for something like diamonds. I just had a gut feeling that night that something was not right and I assumed Roland had lied to me about the merchandise in this business deal. For the sake of business and embarrassment to Roland, I didn't ask for clarification of what it was we were moving and simply went along with it all as though I already knew. I figured I'd take it up with Roland the next time I saw him. Tony spoke highly of Roland; how much he respected and trusted his judgment in business even though this was the first time he had never dealt with a woman. He was sure Roland knew what he was doing. He thanked me for taking the time to have dinner with him and discuss this business deal. It took one more meeting with this gentleman to consummate the deal. Later when I questioned Roland about it, he was adamant it was a diamond deal and thought I shouldn't ask a whole lot of questions because the less I knew the better. Oh, how I could hear David reminding me that this would happen! The day of delivery came and everything went as scheduled. I wasn't involved in the transaction. A couple of weeks later, I flew back East again to let Roland know how everything had gone. Ironically, he already knew before I got there and stated he had received great reports about how smooth everything had gone. He expressed how he felt he had made a very good choice with me handling some business. He made a comment that later bothered me. He stated how he felt I could really go places if I continued with him. I asked how so? His response was rather vague. I told him I wasn't impressed and wasn't sure this was something I wanted to do long term. Besides, I was the one taking all the risks. He said he had received nothing but great reports from his people that I dealt with and they liked doing business with me in our discrete way. I was already used to doing business in this manner due to the nature of my true work assignments, so it wasn't acting any way for me. This was just the way I worked every day. It was second nature to me to be courteous, aggressive and yet professional. Roland of course, liked the fact that I didn't have a criminal record or a tainted past that would alarm law enforcement. By this time, I was enjoying the money, respect and the sheer power I got out of all this and a bit of excitement that went into pulling these business deals off but we all know it doesn't last forever. Sooner or later, something goes wrong. Months down the road, I accidentally found out about our latest big so-called business deal. It was, in fact, what I had suspected. At first, it was just small little favors that led to these business deals. All this business moved behind Roland's name and credibility. I thought about a good message I heard in church one time about the importance of a good name. Wow! Talk about having a spiritual revelation at a time like this. By now, I was getting paid very well so I guess I had no right to an opinion of what we were moving. Not long after, I facilitated another deal together with people from another country. He also was a very charming distinguished gentleman. He said he had never done business with a woman and in his country; women didn't get involved with matters like this. He knew Roland well and was honoring this only because of him. I commented, *"Well, welcome to the American way."* and suggested he take up his sexist issues with Roland because I was here to do a job and that's all it was. I suppose I really shouldn't have put myself in harms way either however, everything went according to schedule on that deal too and we later struck up a friendship as well. I was the only woman in business dealings including the crossing of borders and entering prisons where we held meetings, all in Roland's name. At these prisons, they had weapons, phones and plenty of cash on hand. It was one of the most dangerous things I have ever witnessed or taken part in. Looking back now, I realize I could have very easily been raped and/or killed. The mighty hand of God was truly with me and He gave me favor beyond anything I deserved. It was truly the grace of God stretched out to the fullest that protected my sorry, disobedient, reckless life in these prisons where things are done so differently. We never had to show identifications to get in when we arrived; they simply pressed the button, the gates opened and we all would walk in straight to our meeting place.

I suppose it sort of inflated my pride that I had earned such respect through the years from many of these fellows. Each contact was always very charming, complimentary and professional with me. I know this was out of respect for Roland as he always reminded me to guard my heart and not be charmed by any of these men because of their influence and power in the underground world. He wanted to protect me too, or so he said. I enjoyed the wining, dining, and the special gifts of gratuity, the travel and money this brought me under the name of "*business*". The reality was, everything had its perks and it was probably a matter of time that I'd get caught or killed in one of these dealings. There came a time when I finally began to pray to God to protect and help me get out of this line of work gracefully and peacefully.

About the seventh year, I began to resent Roland and for using me as his mule to secure these deals, meeting with people and putting me in harms way just as David had warned. I was also disappointed in myself for allowing myself to fall for all this. I should have known better. Roland was keen on detection and could begin to feel my uneasiness about business. I felt like he didn't take me seriously and as a retaliation, I didn't go back to visit him for a long time. I simply ignored him. He began to worry about me, sending inquiries through other contacts as to what the heck had happened to me and what was wrong? He wanted me to go see him. This had him going crazy as he continued leaving messages, sending beautiful flower deliveries to my job and had other people contacting me for him. I sent word to him that I was out of town on business for a while. He continued writing for months on end. I purposely distanced myself from him. In between all this, I was going out with friends that had good jobs and were legal decent professional people. It was great to hang out with "*normal*" people without any hidden agendas.

At one point, an associate of Roland made contact with me and strongly suggested I go visit Roland and that it might not be such a good idea to keep avoiding him. He suggested I go see him face to face because avoiding him wasn't a smart thing to do. I wasn't stupid and understood what he was trying to tell me. Meanwhile, Roland had once again been transferred to another State facility and it would take several weeks before I could get cleared again to visit. This bought me more time. The next time he called, I took the call. Although upset that he had been unable to make contact with me all this time, he was just glad to be speaking to me again. We didn't have cell phones at that time, only pagers and house phones. By the time we hung up, he was feeling much better.

During this time away from him and "business", I had begun reflecting strongly on my life and what I had been involved with. I thought about how fast the years had passed me by and I was still not settled as to where my life was and when I was going to get right with God. In the midst of all this, I had run into a few people that I had known in ministry. It was so uncomfortable running into people from ministry because I just didn't know what to say anymore. I hated making excuses as to why I wasn't in church or why I wasn't singing anymore. I would just ask them to pray for me whenever they thought of me. Partying was better when I felt a buzz or just high because it sort of numbed my conscience and convictions. I suppose one would think I had learned my lesson, but again I had decided to go face Roland's wrath and hear what he had to say after all these months. He was continuously transferred around various states, never knowing where or when he would be shipped out due to security. It bothered me that I was going to go see him again but I knew I couldn't mess with him either. The prison system never wanted him to get comfortable at any one location because he would be running things (*the yard*) again and they didn't want him to have that much influence at any given facility. He said he was told by a warden that everywhere he went; he left a trail of chaos and havoc. By the time he was transferred again, his attorney called to let me know he was now in another state. I felt like I wasn't as stressed when I wasn't visiting him and decided I didn't want to go as much anymore. I was reflecting on how I got started with little things and thought, '**Small Favors, Not So Bad**." Boy! Was I ever wrong!! It started off small and innocent but before I knew it, I was caught up in things I truly had no business in but it was too late. It wasn't going to be that easy to just stop either as he was somewhat dependent on me by this time. Oh how I dreaded not listening to David when he had forewarned me this could and would eventually happen. The only good thing was that I hadn't got caught in any of these business transactions. It had to have been the prayers of my mom, family, others in ministry as well as my own prayers when I talked to God that kept me safe. All I knew was that God was showing me far more grace and favor than I ever deserved.

15

Who Was I Kidding?

I finally made it to visit Roland in Chicago. We had so much to talk about. I knew he was worrying about me because we hadn't seen each other for several months. I wanted him to know he didn't ever have to worry about me in regards to information he had given me, the people I had met, the favors I did for him and the brothers. Although he said his concern were more about losing me. I wasn't as convinced as I used to be and I was growing weary of his ulterior motives. A friend of mine whom I trusted and who was also a customer confided in me and told me how he would never put his lady in harm's way as Boss continued to do to me. He sincerely cautioned me to carefully consider his motives. It only reaffirmed what I was already feeling that I was just a mule for him and the brothers. He was in Chicago for a few months and had strong ties to the Italian community there. Everyone seemed to know the same people. There was one evening I was picked up in a limousine from my hotel and brought to this very elegant restaurant. I was escorted upstairs to a small private dining area. The owner joined me for dinner. We were serenaded by an Italian trio. It was actually very nice. He spoke very highly of Roland and glad to have met me. Unfortunately, I really enjoyed myself. It didn't matter what state they transferred Roland to, he always sent for me and had meetings set up over dinners with people he needed to communicate with from all nationalities and countries. Everyone that was connected seemed to know everyone and who was coming to town.

However, after this trip, I began to distant myself more and more from him. It was amazing how much he knew about what I was doing. I suppose he had people following me because a few times he asked about certain details that he could have only known if someone had been in the same place with me. This gave me the creeps. I wouldn't take out "kites" (*notes*) anymore either. I knew I needed to stop what I was doing and was sure even God was getting tired of me and my broken promises. It seemed like the more I tried to pull away, the harder it was. I had by now been rubbing elbows with people in high places like the movie industry. It just blew my mind that there was so many dishonest and shady people in high, supposedly respectable places. I wasn't aware that Roland knew so many people from one end of the continent to the other; from the ghetto to high rollers, in entertainment and a few prominent actors which I had the honor of meeting within my dealings.

There was one experience that stands out in my mind that is worth mentioning. One day I drove to a part of Hollywood Hills to meet a producer that Roland wanted me to connect with. He said I'd be briefed about the details once I got there. Roland had been contacted and visited by this producer a couple of times about a movie they were making and wanted to make a certain part of this movie based on Roland's life experience. It had to do with the challenges of returning out to the free world from prison life and how he and I had met. The (*out of state*) correctional system began to feel like this movie project was causing too much conflict with other inmates also wanting privileges. The prison warden began putting up resistance to accommodate anymore future visits and soon after, the visits were suspended for prison safety reasons. A prison riot broke out a few days later. Roland didn't want to discuss the nature of this movie on the phone and wanted me to personally meet with these people. He was giving them the go ahead to use his story of how he and I met and other questions they had. I was to stand in proxy for him. I arrived on time and this producer was waiting. I was escorted to his private office where two very high-profile actors (*well known for portraying mobster roles*) were already there having drinks. For confidential reasons we'll call them Dave' and John. Everyone at this meeting knew who I was before I arrived and who I was connected to. The film they were working on was going to use our story at the beginning of this movie. Roland had worked out the specifics as to how much they would pay me per hour as they interviewed me for our story. A contract was drafted up and agreed upon. Part of the agreement was that they could not use our real names and we could not discuss the movie with anyone. After the specifics were agreed upon, we made a date and time for them to come to my home and record our story as I narrated and answered questions. They would come out and complete it in two sessions. I signed the contract and was given a copy. We all hung out for a while before I commented that I had to be going. I wished I had taken some photos then but it was a surprise on me too. When I told my children who I met at this meeting, they were dumbfounded and gravely disappointed I didn't get there autographs. When the movie was about to come out, they sent for me to come see it before it hit the theaters. It was a bit emotional and amazing to see our story portrayed on screen. It was a unique experience that I will never forget. Everyone from the ghetto to these movie stars was all somehow connected to Roland's business world in one form or another. All of his contacts were ethnically mixed. It was amazing how favors were done back and forth in the name of "*business*". I found out later that many of my visits to Roland were sponsored by some of these same people who needed to communicate with him concerning their mutual business. Flower deliveries to me were common as well; especially after some of our meetings. I was impressed and I thoroughly enjoyed the ride. Gosh! Who wouldn't? I was treated with respect and associated with a lot of very powerful and important people connected to Roland. I have to admit, I enjoyed the feeling and prestige of associating with these people and the money involved. Roland had his hand in many, many things and it was fascinating for this PK who had grown up in poverty and simplicity. Even after so many years of dealings, I was still amazed at his contacts and the things I was exposed to. Even this Hollywood movie deal was completely legitimate. In the midst of all this, I had somehow lost contact with my God and my yearning to return to my calling. I suppose I thought by numbing it all, it would all just go away. Wrong! He was always there in a still but powerful way.

More years quickly passed. Roland continued to be transferred from one facility and state to another; thinking they would hurt his business and communications. This was far from the truth because it actually helped him quite a bit. We took full advantage of what the Feds thought were strategic tactics working to their benefit. It was a joke. Roland would tell me stories about how some of the staff officers actually treated him very nicely and with respect because he, in turn, showed respect to them. Staff would sometimes do him favors knowing Roland wouldn't expose them. For example, because he was a vegetarian, they would bring him special things to eat or sometimes special drinks. Roland would in turn have things delivered to these officers post office boxes as a thank you. No one ever complained or exposed Roland for this. He said staff would often look the other way to things he did and/or give him special telephone privileges. This was another well thought out reason he treated them all with respect. He cleverly continued to smuggle out kites (*notes*) with coded information through other inmates in the visiting room because I wasn't doing it anymore. It was amazing how he had so much charisma with staff members who would sometimes tip him off on things they heard were going to happen so he would be better prepared. I used to wonder how he got so much information in and out. Again, God truly had his hand of favor upon my life all these years because I didn't get caught, exposed, hurt or killed through so much of these activities.

Back home, I continued working and dating my friend Rick because he was also my contact for public records I needed.

Eventually, the job I was working on in San Diego was completed and I went on to my other job not far from where I used to work. This job lasted several months. In the evening; I occasionally met with some of Roland's contacts to give them messages. Looking back, I never felt scared or intimidated but I should have because in later years I learned whom I was dealing with and how ruthlessly violent these people actually were. They had no qualms about issuing a death warrant whenever they felt it was needed. By the grace of God, I never had any problems with them. Maybe it had to do with them knowing Roland, but I say, it had to do with the great God who had His merciful and powerful hand over my life to put a hedge of protection around me.

Surprise, Surprise!
(Again)

Several years passed. I quit my 15 year job as an investigator. I got a local job working for a different State program. I was no longer traveling up and down the State as before. This job was close to home and didn't involve much travel. I really liked this job because I didn't have to travel anymore. I continued to visit Roland from time to time. Now more years had passed. He knew of my new employment and through the years routinely sent roses to my office. People used to wonder who this person was that always sent floral deliveries. I kept my personal life to myself for obvious reasons.

I was on this job for six years living a double life of working my day job and taking care of business for Roland at night. There was this business transaction Roland wanted me to handle. I finally told him it would be my last and I was done. Roland told me this time it was a large shipment of illegal precious gems but would come in as another product. As harmless as this sounded, I worked with these people of a foreign country to work out the specifics. Dealing with these people of different cultures was difficult, tedious and it took months on end to work out. It was to be a deal of a lifetime. The day came when the shipment arrived. Arrangements were made to have it all picked up and delivered as planned. The next day I get a disturbing call that no one had arrived to pick it up. It was imperative someone go get it. I wasn't about to implicate myself and someone else went at the last minute to get it. The next day I went to access the shipment and was in for a rude awakening because it was far from precious gems and diamonds. A contact met me there and carefully broke open one of the containers. It didn't take long to realize it was in fact a huge shipment of cocaine. My heart sank to the floor and my blood boiled at the fact that I had been lied to and used to facilitate the shipment. I could have been busted and sent to prison for a long time. It was more than I wanted or could handle. Unfortunately, there were some unexpected developments. It was the merciful hand of God that I didn't get busted with it all. Sadly, I kept praying that I wouldn't get caught. I told God that after this, I would just quit! I desperately hoped God hadn't got sick of me yet and once again, begged him to show me His mercy just one more time! I know God doesn't bless drug deals but nevertheless, I asked for His protection and strength. I was exasperated and infuriated to no end that Roland had lied to me about this deal. Oh how (*once again*), I remembered David warning me that this would happen and there would be no way out.

I made reservations to go visit Roland immediately. Meanwhile, I had to deal with this mess. I just tried to stay calm and wait it out. This was extremely complex. An associate took it and buried it somewhere until I knew what to do with it. I didn't make contact with anyone. The day came to go see Roland and develop a plan to quickly execute quickly rid myself of this delivery. I couldn't get there fast enough! As I sat and waited for Roland to come out, several of Roland's associates looked at me and nodded a hello and I did not respond, in fact, just look the other way. I wanted nothing to do with any of them anymore. The moment Roland walked out to greet me, he could tell something was terribly wrong by the look on my face. As we met and embraced, with a smile I cursed him out in his ear as I knew the eyes of the world (*security*) were upon us as usual. As we were sitting down, I commented to him; "*this is going to cost you*".

He looked at me and didn't like the cold welcome I gave him and my threatening words. As we sat and talked, I worked hard to keep my composure knowing security would be alarmed if they detected something was wrong. I continued to smile as though everything was normal! After all, he had taught me oh so well. Smiling and holding his hands, I explained in code what had happened, how our contact was nowhere to be found. Maybe he had been arrested or something. Ironically, Roland already knew about my contact and why he wasn't around. I just hadn't given him a chance to explain. He told me the guy had a heart attack and was in the hospital in (ICU). The contact had sent word to Roland how sorry he was but he was hospitalized and critical condition. He gave the name of the hospital and room number in case Roland wanted to verify it and/or have me go see him.

I began to lay into him that he had once again lied and used me one time too many. He had a look on his face I had never seen before but I didn't care and it was too late. I needed to do something quick! I needed relief and I needed it NOW! I let him know how infuriated I was. We began walking to the vending machines so I could get something cold to drink. I needed to move around. As we walked to the machines, I told him once again, "*This is going to cost you royally,*" His facial demeanor was hard and he asked what I meant by that. I told him not to worry about me saying anything or ranking him out on him about business but him and I were done and that I no longer believed anything he had to say about "*us*" because he had lied and used me for the last time. I told him it was my fault for believing he cared for me. We discussed a remedy and a plan to get the shipment off my hands slowly and discreetly.

He pleaded with me not to use this incident to dissolve our relationship. I told him how he had defecated all over what I "*thought*" we had. Our visit was difficult and emotional. At one point I was so angry I had begun to cry and he quickly told me to stop because it would bring attention to our table and it would alarm security. That only served to make me harder inside as I wiped my tears. It was my future at stake, not his. I took a deep breath and concentrated on something else to stop crying. The visit was extremely difficult and much more strenuous than ever before. The whole time he pleaded with me not to cut him loose and not to put an end to our relationship over this. I didn't want to upset him either so I just listened to him but had my mind made up to dump him as soon as I got home. Again, my cousin David was so right. I should of listened. I could have kicked myself over and over as I looked at him talking and wished I had never met him and I told him so. It was too late; I needed his help to rid of the shipment. I had to sit tight and wait this out somehow. He kept asking me to calm down and chill and saying that he didn't want to deal with our relationship right now. First things first like getting me the relief I so desperately needed!

What I found so incredible about that day was how in tune many of the other inmates in the visiting area were to our table. They detected something was very wrong since the beginning because they had been watching our table. It wasn't long when an inmate walked by our table with his visitor on his way to the vending machines. He greeted us smiling and asked Roland what was going on and if everything was alright? Roland spoke a few words and he continued on his way. Not too long after that, another inmate walked up with his visitor and asked Roland if he needed them to do anything. By the time the third inmate walked up with his visitor, Roland greeted him with a smile and told him to keep walking because security was watching us. He told them in code that they would all talk later. Everyone did as he asked.

During this very difficult visit, he said he didn't like this cold side of me and he knew I was mad but he would take care of it in time. With a firm tone, I told him I didn't have time and how everything was at risk right now at home. He told me what to do and who to contact when I got back home to begin the process. After I said what I wanted to say, I wanted to leave early but he told me not to leave because it would alarm security that something was wrong because I never left early. It would be one of our hardest visits of all time and

I just wanted it over with. I was more focused on what he was going to do to remedy my problem. Eventually, we said our good byes and I left. I returned home with no real answers but with a desperate urgency to get rid of the shipment. I was terrified of the fact that someone would get wind of it and I would be stuck holding the bag. It became a sad reality to me what others had told me in the past about getting pulled into something I wouldn't be able to handle. Now, here I was living out this horrible reality. What a shocking surprise, one I hadn't planned on nor was I ready for. I didn't have the time to waste for someone to come get this out of my hands fast enough.

Meanwhile, at my last doctor's appointment, he had told me I was anemic probably due to so much blood loss and needed to come in for surgery as soon as possible. I kept putting this off because I had to secure this shipment and be available in case we had any more unexpected problems. It was definitely something I couldn't handle alone. I was still working full time and my health continued to deteriorate by the day. I was so stressed out; feeling extremely exhausted and frustrated. One of the hardest things was maintaining my composure at work every day enough to get through my daily schedule and not let anyone know anything was wrong at home. They already knew I was ill and would require surgery soon. Every day was a balancing act. Incredibly, I continued to pray to God to help me out of this. I just kept digging myself in deeper and deeper. I prayed to God to let me be strong enough to get through all this so I could walk away. It seemed everything had caved in at the last minute. As far as I was concerned, I had been used for the last time. I began to pray to God that if He let me live through a successful surgery and let me get through all this, I promised to walk away from it all and do my best to live for Him and serve Him wholeheartedly again. I felt like such a pathetic loser and I only hoped that He had not given up on me for all my years of broken promises.

A Drug Dealer

A couple of weeks passed since my last visit with Roland when I finally got that call from Roland that I was waiting for advising me to call his cousin to wish him a happy birthday. The message was for another guy that would come by to pick up a sample. He kept telling me how sorry he was about my loss (*a fake death in the family*) and how much he loved me. I played it off (*as usual*) because I knew our calls were screened and I gave him a bogus story about going to see him next week. This contact was completely out of the area and he would have to come in from out of town and meet with me. I thought to myself, "***Great, I'm a drug dealer now.***" At this point, I really didn't care. I just wanted to get rid of this stuff before word got out and I got caught. This whole thing was more unsettling by the day. I called this person and agreed to meet him in the lounge of a local hotel close to the airport. We were finally going to meet. I got there early, sat and thought about how simple my life used to be and how much more complete my life was when I was walking with the Lord. I took a look at myself as I sat at the bar looking at the mirror in front of me with a drink in my hand and hated what I had become. I missed my fellowship with God. I continued to ask God to miraculously help me change and walk away from all this before it was too late. I felt so low and tired of all this as I sat there waiting to do this drug deal and yet thinking about my walk with the Lord and having this internal conversation with God. I wondered what God thought of me at this most shameful moment.

My guest finally arrived but had another male with him. This other person looked familiar but I couldn't place him. As we began our meeting he introduced himself and his friend. He began by telling me how he knew and highly respected Roland. I could really care less about all that. I just wanted to get rid of the shipment and get on with my life. I kept looking at his friend and had the feeling he was somehow church related. When we finished discussing the specifics of the deal, I thanked him and commented to him how it was great that he knew and respected Roland because it meant I wouldn't have any problems collecting from him. He assured me I would have no problems at all. I slipped him a small plastic baggie in my napkin with a sample. When they left, I was still puzzled about this other guy he had brought with him he called "Speedy." I figured I was just being paranoid and suspicious of everyone now. To my surprise, three days later, I got a call from this guy raving about how great the product was and ready to make a substantial purchase. He would be back in town in a week. This was good news for me. Although I wasn't happy about having to deal drugs like this but I didn't have the luxury of a choice. I needed to get rid of it. Although this guy was going to make a considerable purchase, it wouldn't even put a dent in the quantity I still had. We met, I took another male with me who was packing (*a gun*) to monitor the transaction in case things went wrong. For a moment, I wondered if he could be a plant set up by the feds or local law enforcement but it was a chance I had to take. I gave him the drugs and reminded him of our process and that he was not to tell anyone. I told him Roland was sending backup that would take over this project and he wouldn't be dealing with me anymore after this. Just before he left I asked for the real name of his partner that he had brought with him the last time we met because he looked familiar. He gave me his name and commented that his partner had said the same thing about me and how familiar I looked. We joked about having a twin somewhere and how I probably didn't know him because he was from up north and never came into this area. This transaction was simple, fast and he was in and out in a few minutes. I too, was out of there as quickly as I could. As I was leaving the parking lot, it suddenly dawned on me where I had remembered this guy's friend and the name was right too. He was the son of a pastor up north I knew many years ago when my dad and another pastor held revivals. I thought about what a small world this was and wondered if he remembered me except he knew me as "Judy" and not Rita. Man, this was crazy! Here was yet another PK lost out in the world of drugs. Out of pure embarrassment, I hoped this guy would never remember me. Who would have ever guessed this guy was also a pastor's son? He looked like someone you didn't want to mess with. He was heavily tattooed and scary looking. All the way home; I kept thinking about how many other PK's were out there like us. It was a chilling realism that day that so saddened me.

The weeks turned into months and unfortunately I was still dealing quite a bit of this merchandise because they kept moving Roland around and it made my communication that much more difficult. I wasn't comfortable and knew that at any moment, I was going to get busted and I'd be looking at some very serious time just as David had warned me about. I felt like such a fool for doing what I was doing not to mention I still had my physical complications and needed surgery that I kept putting off. I continued to lose even more weight and blood. I tried real hard to keep working so as to look as normal as possible in case I was being watched by law enforcement. I kept meeting with the same people to supply them with more and more drugs as needed.

It was a couple long months when I got a page from a number that I didn't recognize however the code at the end of the number was a code I knew. I returned the call. Finally, it was the contact Roland had told me about who would relieve me of the entire shipment. His name was Richard. I agreed to meet with him the following evening. We met at a well populated pizza parlor since I wasn't sure who he was and I needed to get a feel for him. I was burned out with Roland's contacts and becoming more and more agitated meeting with people I didn't know. I was no longer as patient and understanding as before either. I suppose my deteriorating health had something to do with this too. We met, talked and he was, in fact, one of Roland's *"brothers"* who had been released from a State facility after doing fifteen years himself.

We talked and got to know each other I had a good feeling about this guy and knew I'd finally be getting the relief from this shipment. I was still reluctant about trusting the entire shipment to him. He too, had people in mind to give samples to. I reported all the details and told him I would fly to talk to Roland and get the green light about the plan. I hurried to get prison clearance again to visit. The next several weeks passed and I was cleared again for my visit to finalize letting this shipment go.

Meanwhile, business was explosive! The demand had alarmingly increased and I began to feel apprehensive about it. It seemed more and more people were talking about the product wherever we went. People didn't know it was my supply. I just kept to myself. I had always listened to my instincts as though sometimes God would give me warning signs. I know I was way out of line and far from God but he never left my heart. I continued to ask Him to help me get through all this and so I could walk away and start serving him. My health continued to deteriorate. Richard and I spent the next couple of weeks meeting customers and introducing him to them since he would now be in charge. I called my doctor and finally set a date to have my long overdue surgery done.

As sick as I felt, I flew out of state for my last meeting with Roland to update him and all the players. My heart had become hardened too. He was so happy to see me but the feeling was definitely not mutual. I was still very disappointed with myself for being stupid enough to allow him to put me in harm's way like he had. I was going to complete my end of the bargain. I told him about everything that had taken place since our last visit and let him know all the customers I had been dealing with so he knew all the players. He asked my opinion about the product and all our customers. I told him about my concerns that this was spreading like wildfire on the streets and we had the entire market! NOT GOOD! I felt it was very likely things could get unpredictably crazy and it wouldn't take long before law enforcement would be tipped off to this drug on the street. We discussed our first and only problem. It was with a woman up North whose husband was doing time with Roland in the penitentiary. She owed a substantial amount of money and had not turned in any of it yet. Roland knew I was having surgery in a week and would be out of commission for a few months. He asked if I could try and deal with this woman first. If she didn't pay, they were going to make an example out of her husband that no one could burn him. He wanted me to tell her that her husband would be disposed of if she didn't come up with the money she owed. Roland was adamant about this. He felt I was slacking off by not handling her and allowing her to get away with the debt. He was tired of all the excuses and concerned that she was jerking us around. She had stopped visiting her husband too. He told me to drive up North and get more aggressive with her. The product had made its way all the way up there too. I strongly suggested we sell the whole project for a lucrative amount and let someone else handle this headache. He said he valued my opinion and would think about it. He felt it was just too risky and no one carried that amount of money. He reminded me that his friend Richard had heart, was dependable and able to handle any problems that would arise, including this woman. He suggested that I should take him with me. Roland felt he had kept his end of the bargain to send relief to get this out of my hands so I no longer would be in harm's way. My concern was that people already knew I was involved and they kept coming back for more and more. It was like we couldn't keep up with the demand. At any rate, he gave me the green light to hand it all over to Richard but reminded us to keep tight records. He noticed that I was looking pale and had lost a significant amount of weight since the last time he had seen me. I told him this

Rita Rangel

would be our last visit in a long time so I could rest and get healthy. He wanted to also discuss *"us"* again. I quickly stopped and reminded him there wasn't any *"us"* anymore because he couldn't be trusted. He became apologetic and made excuses as to why he didn't tell me about the delivery because I probably wouldn't have agreed to complete a deal of this magnitude so he took a chance. I reminded him, *"No, I was the one who took the chance."* He hadn't anticipated all these problems. This only infuriated me even more. He wanted me to wait for him as he only had a few short years left. I could see the anger and desperation on his face and gave him a slight bit of hope by telling him, only time would tell and I wanted all this to cool off before I ever talked about our relationship again. I wasn't stupid; I didn't want to tick him off either. I tried to be as amusing as possible but in my heart, all I wanted was out of there as soon as possible. I had deliberately come later in the afternoon so our visit would be minimized. I was physically and mentally so tired of all this and was finally done! I wanted to head back for home as soon as possible. He wanted me to stay and come back the next day but I told him I didn't feel good and just wanted to get back home to the kids and rest. He told me to write him more and take his calls. I told him I would, but I actually had no intentions of writing or taking any of his calls. I had nothing else to say to him. After the visit, I checked into my room where I slept the rest of the day. My energy was quickly running out. I returned home the next day. Our visit wasn't very good in that it was all business just as David said it would be.

When I got back home, I met with Richard who by now had begun coming to the house regularly. I explained all the specifics of my visit with Roland. He was upset that I had flown all the way up there in my condition. He knew how sick I had been. We had a couple more deliveries to make where I would be telling the customers that Richard would now be in charge. A couple of days later, we drove out to make one of these deliveries to a customer in another county by the beach. The meeting went well. Richard was always packing (*a gun*) which I wasn't the least bit comfortable with.

At any rate, I was going to be getting out soon anyway. After this meeting, we stopped for dinner and drinks. We had a long talk over dinner, mostly about his life, where he'd grown up and had been for the last fifteen years. He expressed how he felt about my dealings with this project and how unsettling it was when he found out it was only me handling it all. He began by expressing how he had pictured a completely different woman handling all this. He was sure there were other players. He applauded me on how well he thought I had managed without anyone's help. He was curious how long I had been doing this because I didn't seem the type to be involved in this sort of business. I remember how polite he was trying to explain himself. This long conversation would continue all the way to the pier later where we walked and sat and talked for a long time. He asked me to be perfectly honest with him about whom I was and where I had come from because he made some inquiries about me earlier (*before meeting me*) and no one had ever heard of me nor did they know where I was from. To this day, I was a mystery he said. They only knew I was Roland's old lady. He also felt I didn't fit the mold of a criminal and noticed I didn't have any hard habits to maintain either. He liked the fact that I didn't party with any of the people we dealt with. I explained that what I did, I always did in private with my own circle of people because I didn't trust people. I felt compelled to be honest with him to explain once and for all who I was. I figured I was on my way out anyway. I began to give him my testimony of how I really came from a Christian background; how my father was the pastor of a church; how I had backslid and fell away from my Christian upbringing and was just partying with David for a couple years when he introduced me to Boss and how I had slowly got involved. I told him I was going to be honest and let him know that as soon as I walked away from all this, I was returning to my Christian walk. He interrupted me to tell me how he had a very close "*brother*" friend who left the brotherhood and turned to the Lord. He said his "brother" now attended a church not far away. He explained how not long ago he had gone to the office a couple of times to leave this "*brother*" a message because he too, wanted to change his life around but his friend still hadn't returned his call. He asked me if I knew his friend and he gave me his name. I told him I'd heard of him and I knew who he was but I didn't personally know him. He mentioned a few other "carnales" (*Spanish street slang for brothers*) who had also turned Christian so he understood about Christianity. He asked if I went to this church. I shared how I used to be involved with Victory Chapel years ago and was even in the prison ministry, playing the piano and singing. He was totally taken aback by what I said. Now he understood why no one knew me on the streets because I wasn't from the streets. I also told him how my family had cut me loose because of all this mess and my involvement with Boss. He said how that didn't surprise him and how it all made sense because I was different from the rest of the women he had met in the past. Richard felt it was the Lord in me that made me different. He said he considered himself a good judge of character and I definitely didn't fit the mold as a hard core criminal. He was surprised I had done as well as I did by myself. He reaffirmed that I was right to just walk away (*while I could*) because I didn't belong in this business and I would only get hurt. He reluctantly commented how he didn't feel I should remain with someone like Boss because he lived a risky life and was always on Federal and State radar. Once Boss got out of prison, he'd always have a tail on him and that was no way for someone like me and my children to live like and I would only be hurt in the end. I felt conviction because here was a hard core gangster giving me advice to save myself. Later I thanked him for his advice, honesty and his kind words. I suggested he too, could change like his "*carnales*" if he would only just take that first step. I reminded him how he had a powerful testimony too, if he gave his life to God. I confessed to feeling stupid talking about God while we were conducting business over drinks too. I told him God could change his life too just like he did for the "*brothers*". I expressed how the happiest years of my life was when I was serving the Lord but I had let myself get discouraged to the point of walking away and never looking back and that was the sorriest decision I had ever made.

I liked this guy. I could discern he had a big heart and was being honest. He was also very respectful and surprised that Boss had a woman like me doing his dirty work for him. My kids had met Richard and liked him a lot too. They used to like when he came over, especially my fifteen year old son because they would hang out and had fun times. I think Richard enjoyed acting like a kid himself. I was scheduled for surgery in a few days on a Monday morning.

I worked up until the Friday before and was scheduled to take three weeks off to recuperate. Right before I left from work that Friday afternoon I heard from Roland on a three-way conference call. He wanted to press me to go deal with that lady up North that still owed that money and how she was avoiding everyone. I told him how I had called her (*several times*) when I got home from the visit and she kept putting me off saying "next week." He was very upset and told me to just go deal with her and that they had already beat her husband real good to teach him a lesson. She still wasn't going for visits anymore either. He insisted I handle this as soon as possible. I came home a little early from work frustrated as heck! I knew I had to remedy this problem before Monday because I'd be in the hospital for few days and off my feet for three weeks after that. Oh, how I hated Roland that day. Meanwhile, Richard had paged me several times but I didn't want to be bothered with him or what he had to say until I took care of this stupid lady. I got home from work and took the kids over to my sister's house. I told her I needed to take a real quick trip up north and I would be back late tonight or early in the morning. I returned home to pack an overnight bag. I locked up the house and was putting things in my car when Richard drove up and rushed me asking why the heck I wasn't answering him? He was worried that maybe something was wrong! He saw my bag and asked where was I going? I told him I needed to handle some business once and for all because Monday I was going into the hospital. He asked again, where I was going. I told him *"up north for a quick trip to handle some business*". He thought I was crazy and told me to wait a minute. He ran to his car, got his bag, jumped in the car; and said "*Let's go.*" We left together. He thought I was insane to take this trip alone in my condition. I explained how I needed to handle this before I went into the hospital and get Boss off my back. I told him how I heard from Boss today and that the fellows had beat her man down because of this debt. The first part of the trip we argued about why I had to go all the way up there. Richard was ticked off and thought I shouldn't be putting myself out there like this and mad that if he hadn't pulled up when he did, I would have gone alone! I told him I was tired of this lying witch. Ironically, she didn't live far from a church area my parents used to have services at when we were kids so I knew the area and had been there before.

Half way up there, we stopped to get some alcohol to drink on the way up. I wanted to numb the pain I was feeling and calm my nerves as I was completely agitated that I had to take this trip. We got there about 8 pm. The plan was that I would knock on the door while he waited on the side and when she answered, I'd ask if we could talk. When she invited me in, he would follow right behind me and assess if there were other people or kids in the house. We were going to just play this by ear; get in there and out in minutes. We were both somewhat intoxicated thanks to Mr. Jose Cuervo, (*tequila*). Thankfully, she answered the door, shocked to see me but invited me in. As I walked in, Richard followed right behind me. By the time she turned around, he was already in and closed the door. She was upset and asked who he was. I told her he was my driver and we needed to talk. There were two little boys sitting on the kitchen table. I felt bad that they were there. I asked Richard to take the boys to the other room where they could play. He got the boys and took them to the room. We were standing in the kitchen when I told her how I was actually there to pick up the money she owned us, how I was under pressure from Roland and the guys to collect and that I was tired of her lying stories. She began to give me more of her excuses why she couldn't pay. Richard walked back in and stood there as she was talking. I asked her how much of it she had because I would take whatever she had. She stated she didn't have any of it because she had an emergency and used the money. I became even more agitated with her and told her how I had people on my back about that money and I was going to get it one way or another. I told her to take off that rock (*diamond ring*) she had on her finger. I used to see it on her and always admired it. She flatly refused and said no because the ring was a sentimental gift given to her by her grandmother. I made it clear to her how sentimental the business was to me and I really didn't care what was sentimental to her right now. I told her I didn't feel well, came a very long distance and how she was wearing my patience down. Once again, I ordered her to take the ring off. We had been in her apartment long enough already. We were standing in the kitchen area and I walked over to where she kept all her knives and grabbed the biggest one. I told Richard to hold her down and I was going to cut her finger off to get it myself. I could not believe myself as this was so out of character for me. She kept saying "No, no!" I told Richard to just hold her down. I was hoping she would cooperate because I really didn't want to do this. I was feeling sick, agitated, somewhat scared and nervous. Just as he had her in a firm grip, she cried out "*Okay, okay. I'll give it to you.*" She pulled the ring off and threw it at me. Now this really infuriated me. I reminded her that when I gave her what I gave her, I handed it to her. I gave her a piece of my mind and ordered her to pick up the ring off the floor and hand it to me. She walked over crying quietly, picked it up and firmly handed it to me. I told Richard to go get pillow cases off her bed and I would take the rest in merchandise. As she sat and cried, we helped ourselves to whatever we thought we could sell from a stereo system, antiques, doll collection and more jewelry. I went through her purse to take her driver's license, employment I.D and just over $83.00 cash which I told her would help cover some of my gas to come collect her debt. I reminded her she was still obligated to come up with the rest. I reminded her that I knew where she lived, worked and if she decided to call the police, she and her family would regret it and would feel Boss's wrath because I was reporting all this to him in the morning. She just sat there crying. I reminded her that her husband's life was at stake and that he had been badly beaten this week because of her. I suggested she hurry and reorder another identification card so she could go visit him and see for herself. During this time one of the little boys came out and wanted something to drink. She held him and distracted him as Richard had loaded up the car with her things. As we quietly headed for the door, Richard commented to her how she better keep all this quiet and we left. I had never done anything like this before and it was truly out of my natural character. I was also tired of Boss thinking I wasn't effectively dealing with business matters. I actually felt bad inside doing what I was doing but I had to numb it so I wouldn't get emotional and weak because the money she owed which was substantial. I was exhausted and needed to rest. We headed back home in the morning. We talked about what had transpired the night before as we headed home which took us just over four hours. Richard commented how surprised he was to see this side of me. I actually felt embarrassed. I thought about her on the way home the next day but at least I had tried and came home with something which was better than nothing. I knew we could get several thousand for the diamond ring. I went to get the kids and hurry home to bed. It was awkward switching from what I'd just done the night before and coming home to my children.

The Sunday night before my surgery, Richard, my sister, and a few of my associates met at a Reggae club to celebrate one of the guy's birthdays. It was nice to be out enjoying the time without any pressure of business. I still didn't like the fact that Richard was always packing. I would always tell him, "**You live by the gun, you die by the gun.**" He would laugh it off saying he would rather always be prepared and not need it than need it and regret not having it. We partied until two o'clock in the morning. I had to go home and shower because in a few hours, I would be going under the knife.

I went home to shower and get ready to go to the hospital. My sister, kids and Richard went with me to the hospital. I was a little scared and prayed that everything would be okay. I had lost so much blood that I had to sign consent form for a blood transfusion if I needed it during surgery. Thankfully, surgery went well. I didn't need the blood transfusion after all but I was very weak. I was hooked up to an intravenous line of morphine so when the pain was unbearable, I could push a button and I would get a dosage of morphine injected into me immediately. When I awoke Richard was standing and my sister there and speaking softly to me. I thought I was dreaming and I went out again. A couple of hours later, I awoke again; he was sitting and reading a magazine. We were talking quietly when suddenly, the curtain opened and it was my mother and one of my other sisters. Although heavily sedated, I thought *"Oh no, not them."* Richard already knew my family didn't talk to me. He politely excused himself and stated he was going to the cafeteria to get some coffee and would be back. I remember my mother having a strange look on her face and asked who he was? I told her he was just a friend. It would be the first time my family saw Richard. I could tell my mother wasn't exactly happy about him being there but then no one in my family had been talking to me but my sister, Klu. I had been in broken fellowship with my family for years. I figured no one would come and at least Richard, my sister Klu and my children would be there in support. I remained in the hospital for several days until I was finally released to go home and recuperate for three weeks.

You Can't Pray

(You're a backslider)

In the weeks after surgery I continued to recuperate and regain my strength once again. Richard continued hanging out with us at the house. It wasn't long after my surgery that he moved in and was actually very helpful during my recovery. Richard, my kids and I and began going on outings spending some restful time together as I slowly recuperated which was nice because I was tired of my previous busy schedule that had me running around and keeping various appointments at different hours of the day and night. I had done this for such a long time that I had begun neglecting my health and my kids.

One day not long after that, we stopped by that church again so Richard could leave his friend (Art) one last note because he wanted to talk to him about changing his life. We had also talked about going to church together sometime. I reassured him that if God could change his other *"brothers"*, God could change him too. I thought this would be a good time for me to try and make my way back to the Lord too. Unfortunately, he never heard from his friend at the church and wondered if he even got his other messages at all. He didn't leave anymore messages after that. As more time went on, Richard had pretty much taken over the business for months with no problems. I was finally completely out of the picture and so glad. I eventually returned to work and I was back on track. I was feeling much more rested and healthier too as I was no longer bleeding, run down or traveling like crazy anymore.

One day, several months later, Richard got a call from one of the fellows that he dealt with because there was a discrepancy in one of their deals. He said the guy sounded upset. I immediately had a bad feeling about this and told him I wasn't comfortable with it at all. I was still at work and offered to drive him to the given location (*since his car was broken*). He didn't want me to go. I reminded him how these guys were friends of mine and we were all cool. Again, he didn't want me to get involved or possibly hurt in the process. When I got to where he was, I noted he and these other guys had been drinking. I insisted that he reschedule this meeting for another time because I had a very bad feeling. As I stood there looking at them, I got this sick feeling in the pit of my stomach and once again whispered to Richard how I wasn't comfortable about the whole thing. We argued there back and forth about canceling. He asked me to just give him the ride to the location, leave him off and he'd get a ride back. We finally agreed it's what we would do, leave him off.

We arrived. Everything appeared to be normal, everyone greeted me well as I had not seen these associates in quite some time. We were all outdoors on this beautiful Friday afternoon. After a few minutes of small talk, they began their meeting. I stood there and listened. It started smooth then gradually things began to escalate. One by one some of the attendees (*not part of this meeting*) began arguing with someone else about some unfinished old business they had from some time ago. I told them all to please just shut up and calm down because there was a meeting taking place and they couldn't hear clearly. It was calm for a brief time and shortly after, they started up again and this time, they began yelling obscenities at each other when suddenly, someone reached for their gun. One thing led to another and there were shots fired in all directions. Everyone began shooting at each other. I stood there in shock at first because of what was going on and then realized this was not going to end well; and this would probably be my last day on earth. Many thoughts rushed through my mind. I thought of my kids that were waiting for me. I realized how my life wasn't in order to die either and I didn't want to go out like this. It was very loud like cannons going off at close range. It was like a violent dream in slow motion. My ears were muffled out by now. I told God I didn't want to finish this way. I pleaded with God to please help me get through this. I remembered trying to warn Richard how this could happen but he wouldn't listen. I wondered where I would get hit first, in the head, chest or heart and whether or not I would feel a lot of pain or would it burn. In these final seconds, I asked God for forgiveness and told him how much I loved Him and if He would spare me from this and give me another chance, I would serve Him the rest of my days. Oh how I remembered sharing in ministry that we are never guaranteed tomorrow and now here I was in that moment. Oh how I dreaded what was to happen next. I kept praying within me; ***"Oh God, Oh God I don't want to go out like this. Please make a way out of no way."*** When the shooting finally stopped, I was in complete amazement that I was still standing there looking around in the middle of all the smoke from the guns. I couldn't see anything or anyone anymore. For a long time I couldn't hear either. My ears were muffled. The silence was incredibly loud! By the time I sort of came to my senses, everyone was gone! Not a soul was around except for me standing there looking around. I was in shock. Sadly, there were several bodies lying around on the ground all around me. Some had died immediately from their wounds and others later would die as they lie there but they would barely survive later. Richard was hit hard and was just lying there! I knelt down next to him in shock not really knowing what to do and still in disbelief of what just happened. It was obvious he didn't have much time. As I attempted to pray, I heard a powerful inner voice say to me *"You hypocrite. YOU CAN'T PRAY! You're a backslider and can't pray for a dying man. You don't have any right to pray for a soul. God isn't going to hear your prayer. You're a backslider."*

I suddenly remembered I wasn't a Christian anymore and thought to myself, *"That's right, I can't pray."* I looked at him and still wanted to pray. I felt powerless and fear gripped me that he would die without God. I felt sick to my stomach to a point I wanted to throw up. I didn't know what to do or if I could in fact, pray for his salvation in my backslidden condition. I was speechless and couldn't get the words out. I was going to pray anyway. I still kept hearing this voice tell me, *"YOU CAN'T PRAY"*. Richard had been hit badly and I was in such shock! He kept quiet as I just watched life leave him. I looked around and saw everyone else laid out. There seem to be bodies everywhere. I looked at everyone lying on the ground and couldn't bear the loud silence. The air was still filled with smoke. There was so much blood everywhere that it had the scent of rust. I guess I went into shock. I kept staring at Richard's lifeless body. I was still on my knees trying to catch my breath and think of what to do next! I noticed my white blouse and chest was heavily blood splattered all over it. It made me nauseous. I could hear someone making moaning sounds. It was one of Richard's friends lying nearby. He had just been released from prison two weeks earlier after doing fifteen years. I crawled on my knees over to him. I wasn't sure where he was hit but he was also covered in blood and mumbling something. I kept asking him if he could hear me. He turned his head around to see me and shortly after, he took his last breath. He wasn't moaning or moving anymore. I continued looking around which seemed forever and saw several bodies laid out everywhere on the grass. It seemed like a long time that I was alone there with all this dead silence. I just kept looking around, still feeling sick to my stomach and felt like my heart was going to stop. I stumbled into the house and looked around to see if anyone was there and then sat on a chair nearby. I thought about running to my car and leaving but just wasn't sure what to do. I thought of Richard lying there. The silence was still and deafening. I felt so scared and alone. I just sat in shock and did nothing. I remember feeling very thirsty. I could see Richard's legs from where I sat. The front door of this house was wide open. I remember thinking how this felt like a bad dream and maybe it really didn't happen. I had mixed emotions and scattered thoughts as I realized I was the only survivor. I was grateful to God but sad that so many hadn't made it. After a while, I could hear sirens in a distance and wondered if it was coming this way since we'd always hear sirens. By now I was out of time because the sirens got closer and closer and louder. and it was too late to try and make a run for it. Not long after, through the front room window I began to see police cars racing towards the property. There was a big dining room table with a large table cloth draped over and around it. I climbed down under the table to wait it out. I wasn't feeling good either. I pulled all the chairs in and under the table where I sat and waited. One by one several detectives walked into the house, identified themselves and asked if anyone was in the house. I remained quiet. I could see them with guns drawn. I just sat quietly and said nothing. I heard them talking and trying to piece together everything they perceived had happened. I continued to sit under this table for over two hours and there were a couple of times I had to sneeze but I held it in. Finally, there was a moment I really had to use the bathroom and I just couldn't hold it anymore. I didn't want to soil myself and by now my stomach hurt from holding it in for so long time coupled with the shock I was in. I had been dealing with a urinary tract infection and was taking medication. Besides, I had time to think and calm down too. Reluctantly, I decided I was going to have to come out or wet my pants. There were officers sitting around this table by now. I didn't know how to tell them I was underneath. Finally, I cleared my throat real loud and suddenly it all got quiet and I said *"I'm under the table and I need to use the restroom."* Every one of them jumped up and drew their guns. Someone ordered me to crawl very slowly with my hand in front of me. They asked if I was alone. I told them it was only me. They were frantic that I had been down there as long as I was. Next thing I know, they attempting to question me aggressively and not allowing me to use the bathroom. I told them that I was not talking to them until I was allowed to use the bathroom. They sent a female officer with me. Upon coming out, I was advised that they were taking me into custody for questioning and possibly charged for several murders. Someone in charge suggested they take me down to the station for questioning before all the media arrived. I was handcuffed and walked to a waiting police. I was rushed out of there and taken to a local hospital infirmary to get physically checked out. They confirmed I had a serious urinary tract infection and was badly dehydrated. Next I was taken to a police station whereby I was interrogated for hours on end. I was accused of killing these people and detectives wanted me to confirm if it was a "*Mafia*" hit of some sort. During this interrogation, I realized how I wasn't afraid but just angry. It was like a strong spirit of anger had possessed me that was foreign to me. Maybe it was because Richard didn't make it and I was still processing it all but I was just feeling such anger and rage. They moved me around several times so no one knew my whereabouts. I was still angry that Richard didn't listen to my gut feeling when I told him something didn't feel right and he shouldn't go. If only he would have listened to me. Maybe it was something I had discerned ahead and I knew something just wasn't right. But it was too late now. He was dead along with others. I wasn't sure at the time just how many others had actually died. My family didn't know where I was and I wasn't sure what to do next. Unbeknownst to me, Roland had already heard what happened by that evening. Law enforcement wasn't giving out any information about the incident to the media. Roland didn't know what to think either because no one knew my whereabouts. He had everyone he knew aggressively looking for me. Meanwhile, I sat quietly and waited this out. I was finger and palm printed but of course, I had no gun powder on my hands. They knew I hadn't or couldn't have shot all those people by myself but they figured I would tell them something, anything! It was truly one of the most horrific experiences I had ever gone through in my entire life. This was my breaking point. I felt my life was now officially over and there was no way out of this. I was going down for many years to come just because I was there. I knew I didn't even have a prayer of a chance at freedom and I felt like a complete loser. My thoughts went to my family and my children and I felt such shame and hopeless despair. The detectives told me they were charging me with several counts of murder and several attempted murders for the ones that didn't die. I boldly told them I didn't care but I continued to pray within me and ask God to vindicate me. I pleaded for Him to show Himself and His mercy and swore I would make it up to Him. I didn't know if I was wasting my time except that one thing was clear, I had made it out alive! What were the chances of this happening? So many bullets and not one had hit me!

I was eventually given my one phone call. I called my sister, Klu. I told her how I was in jail, Richard was dead and she should go to Phase I of our pre-arranged emergency plan. That meant she should get my kids, move my things out of my condo, put them in storage and simply wait this out until she heard from me again. She was also in shock but she did just as we had always talked about in case anything (*like this*) an emergency should ever happen. I spent the first day of my arrest transferred to various places so the media couldn't find out anything and start printing their stories. But the detectives said they were moving me around for my own protection. The word had leaked to the media and this was now a high profile case because it involved organized crime and how this might have been a *"hit"* of several people and now Roland (*Boss*) was wanted for questioning even though he was in custody; out of state. Several men had lost their lives, others were hospitalized and in critical condition. The media wasted no time in sensationalizing this story and how this was possibly being a drug deal gone bad. Every day the newspapers were having a field day printing their version of what they perceived had happened. The whole ordeal was dramatized far more than it needed to be. Every day, the media was printing story after story while I sat in jail trying to wait out my seventy two hours that seemed to pass so slowly. On the second day while in custody I was finally put in a cell with several other female inmates who were curious as to who I was and why I was in jail. They asked me several times what I was in there for. Finally I sarcastically told them I didn't care to discuss my business with anyone and it wasn't any of their business. I took a bunk on the top and tried to just sleep it off. From then on I stayed to myself. I was familiar with jail politics and knew to keep my mouth shut. I asked for the newspaper several times but it wouldn't come until later. I finally fell to sleep out of sheer exhaustion. When I awoke to use the bathroom, no one was around. They had all gone to eat but the newspaper had been placed next to me. I had slept for hours. All the other girls had already read the newspaper. The media continued to have a field day with this case. Unfortunately, my name was splattered all over the story in an extremely incriminating way. I had been asking for the newspaper for so long that it didn't take these women very long to figure out why I was so eager to read it. They knew I was the one they were talking about in the newspaper. The paper wrote all sorts of stories of what they perceived had happened since they had no witnesses. I was amazed at how they could print what they did without any solid facts. They reported how I was in custody and charged with numerous homicides. I really didn't care as much as I was feeling mortified that every one of my friends, family and co-workers would soon be reading about this if they hadn't already done so. I could not even imagine what everyone was going to think or say. I thought about my little family (*the kids*) and how embarrassing all this was going to be for my extended family. I was humiliated to the fullest extent. The women came back from chow and stopped asking questions; instead they were now offering anything I needed.

On the third day, I was awoken in the early morning hours to prepare for my court arraignment. I was taken from my cell, put in chain restraints from my waist down to my ankles and put on a bus that was filled with other male inmates also headed to court. I was the only female on the bus. I was put in the small cage they have on the bus. On the way to the courthouse it was somewhat intimidating as they all just stared at me. Several inmates were talking out loud making sexual, trashy, tasteless and inappropriate comments to me as we were on our way to court. The guards said nothing. It infuriated me to the point where I slowly struggled to stand up in this small cage while the bus was moving. I turned myself around to face them and told them all both in Spanish and English that they all lacked respect, I wasn't a bit impressed by any of them and told them all to shut their traps (*using profanity*). I figured I would use my ace card of politics and told them **"by the way, my senor (husband) is "Boss"** *from* (*gave them his neighborhood*)". I then turned back around and sat down. The bus suddenly went quiet, real quiet. No one said a word anymore. A while passed and I heard one inmate yell out his nick name and say he wanted to apologize for his disrespect. A moment went by and another inmate also blurted out his nick name and apologized too. After that several other inmates did the same. I never turned around to acknowledge any of them but simply sat there quietly as tears were streaming down my face in disbelief that all this was actually happening to me. All I could think of was how I once was minister of the gospel and look at me now. I sat there thinking how I was going to remember this day forever. I wondered what all my family and people were thinking about when they would ready all this garbage. I knew I would never be able to live this down and I would be doing a lot of years for something I didn't do. I wasn't about to say anything either. Murder was murder! I continued to pray there in my cage for God's mercy. I felt such shame to be asking God for help in my circumstances. This was the end of my road and here I was trying to ask God for help, again!

When we arrived to the court, they let all the men out first. I kept looking the other way as they all passed my cage. They were in a line against the wall. Then they opened up my cage and brought me out last. As I passed each inmate, several stated they were sorry again. At this point, I really didn't care anymore. I took a deep breath and held my head up high. It was almost time for me to face the music in front of the judge and I needed to be focused on that. I was escorted by several officers; one in front, one in back and one to each side. I asked why so much security? An officer told me that it was for my own safety. I thought about what he meant with that comment and wondered if I was in danger because that's how he made it sound. At any rate, I was finally put in a cell alone to wait until I was called. I sat there still shackled and looking at my pathetic self. I couldn't believe how low my life had turned out and how disgraceful I looked. I thought about when the enemy is done with someone, we are left feeling helpless, hopeless, and filled with all the guilt and self-condemnation that comes from being a backslider and having failed God. There was a time when I swore, nothing and no one would ever separate me from my God. I had even written a song about the love of God. And yet, here I was living out my failures with my life in total shambles. I was so messed up and broken; nothing or no one would be able to repair this mess, only an act of God! I always wondered about people who were in my shoes and called out to God in desperate need. Now it was me wearing those same shoes. I didn't feel worthy to call on God after serving Him with his anointing on me when I ministered in song and shared the Word. It was in this cell that I prayed to God to help keep my sanity and give me the strength to endure whatever was about to happen in court. I asked God to not let me fall apart when the time came and to please show up on my behalf. I was once again reminded that God wouldn't listen to my prayers because I was backslidden. I had no idea what was going to happen to me or who would show up in court and who would let my family know the outcome. There was so much running through my mind on this day and I felt so exhausted. They began getting inmates from their cells and taking them to court. It was finally my turn. They called my name. It felt like Judgment Day in every sense of the word and I was sick to my stomach. They came to my cell and again, several security officers walked with me. I was walked down the hall alone with no other inmates. When the door to the courtroom opened, I was escorted to the area where the jurors sit and told to stand still, keep quiet and wait. I looked out to the courtroom and saw my father, mother, step-father, sister, a co-worker and several others there in court. Although happy to see familiar faces, I was also feeling so mortified and humiliated. I wanted the ground to open up and swallow me. Funny, because the thing that caught my eye was how I could see they were praying. It felt like a long time sitting there but the lawyers for both the prosecutor and my public defender were all huddled around with the judge. They were having their own meeting as I sat there watching and waiting. I kept looking at the audience then to the judge's area, then to the security that stood by. I wasn't sure what was going on up there with the judge and I didn't know what to think but kept praying within me for God to show up. Everyone looked so serious, even my family. No one smiled or seemed to have any emotion. I was sick to my stomach and very thirsty.

Suddenly, they called out my name. Security helped me up. I was never asked how I pleaded. The judge began to cite various references from the law and talking very legalistically about my charges. The district attorney and public defender also made legal references I didn't understand and suddenly, all I heard and processed was when the judge said I was a *"D.A. reject,"* and ordered security to *"get her out of here."* I was so humiliated and embarrassed. As security was taking me out, I looked back at my family and friends with the brokenness and embarrassment of being called a "D.A. Reject." I thought to myself, *"Great, now I'm a reject."* I had no idea what that meant because I had never been in trouble with the law before. As they were taking me back, I asked one of the officers next to me, *"What is a 'D.A Reject'?"* Using profanity he abruptly told me to shut up and not to ask questions. I told him I didn't understand what had just happened in court. Again, using profanity he told me to *"shut up and don't speak."* Finally, we got to another door at the end of a long hallway. There was this very large African-American female officer. They handed me over to her. She walked me back to the holding tank. As she was removing my shackles from my wrists, I asked if I could ask her a question. To my surprise she said yes. She bent down to remove my ankle shackles. I asked what a *"D.A. Reject"* was because that's what they had called me in court a few minutes ago and I didn't understand what had just happened and wasn't allowed to ask any questions. She commented, *"**Girl, you better count your lucky stars above or maybe you have a praying mother because you're going home today. They aren't charging you with anything.**"* I asked again, what she meant by I was going home today? She said I would be taken back to jail and released from there because obviously, the district attorney didn't have enough evidence to charge me with anything and they were releasing me. She finished taking off my shackles and as she began walking away, she yelled back, *"Don't come back here again."* I couldn't believe what I had just heard. I was startled and sat speechless, relieved, shocked and just plain blown away all at the same time. I thought how could this be? Again, I was trying to catch my breath. They must have made a mistake and then it occurred to me that I had prayed to God and others were in court praying too! It suddenly hit me that God had shown up in my defense, parted the waters and made a way out of no way for me. He heard this backslider's prayer. I was free to go in a few hours; I'd be with my kids again. I cried tears of relief and joy. I thought of Richard and the cruel reality that he was permanently gone from us! It definitely was a bittersweet moment in life for me. Late that night, I was finally able to begin getting processed out. They gave me the same bloody clothes I was wearing when I was arrested which included my white blouse that was stained with dried blood. It gave me a sick feeling to put it back on. I asked if they had a t-Shirt available someplace that I could wear out. They rudely said no and told me to put on the clothes I came in with if I wanted to go home. I couldn't believe verbally assaultive these people were everyone. I knew I just needed to get out as soon as I could before I blew.

I called my sister to come get me and bring a clean t-Shirt. It seemed like hours before she arrived and she brought me the t-Shirt. As she handed me the clean shirt, I pulled my blouse off there in the waiting room and threw it in the trash. After all I had been through, I really didn't care who saw me. I was just glad to finally be out of there. It was hard to sleep that night. My sister and I talked into the early morning hours about so much. The next morning she took me up the mountains to a church youth retreat. My daughter was on a camping trip with the church youth. She had found salvation and was so happy. She was more excited about her conversion than anything (*even seeing me*). I was very happy for her. This couldn't have come at a better time. I expected to see her broken, tearful and very happy to see me but in fact, she was so excited about her conversion and just kept trying to explain to me what had happened and how very happy she felt. I was relieved as well to see her this way. She kissed me and went running with the other youth that she was with. I was totally blown away and surprised! After all, I had prayed for God to camp his angels around my kids and protect them. I asked God to give them peace. Not only had God given her peace but salvation and an explosion of joy too. What more could I ask for? We went to see my son next. He was staying at my father's house and so happy to visit with me as well. He expressed how he was scared and worried for me. We visited for the day and I explained I was leaving the area in the morning for a while until things cooled down. The next morning, my sister took me to the airport to catch a flight out of town. I really didn't have any specific plans. I just needed to get out of dodge as quickly as I could. I had made arrangements to stay with some contacts I had in Las Vegas area. I was on a mission to nowhere and was just going to play it by ear one day at a time.

Back In the Wilderness

I stayed in Las Vegas for a while to let things calm down. I fully realized even more than ever before how important my children and family were to me during this time; but I knew I was no good to them right now with the way I was feeling. Due to the magnitude of this case, I knew the best thing to do was to stay clear from everyone and I planned to stay away indefinitely.

I began drinking a great deal every day to cope and maintain my emotions because I was so broken inside. I was angry that Richard hadn't listened to me and as a result, he and others were dead. I knew that it would be in the newspapers for a while and everyone would be talking about this for a long time. I thought of what my immediate family was going to go through because people everywhere would be reading this and following the story. By now my face and name were plastered in all the papers. I didn't need to see or talk to anyone for a while. Oh, how I remembered David warning me that this sort of insanity would happen and my life would be tarnished forever if I even lived to tell. He was so right! I should have walked away when he first told me. Without a doubt I would have to pay the price now. I told myself I had to suck it up and just deal with it because it wasn't going to get any easier from this day on. I needed to move on but not sure how because I really didn't have a plan except to simply lay low, be cool and wait things out. I didn't know what Roland or the others were thinking or what the plan was' if there even was one. I didn't want to communicate with because I knew law enforcement would be watching closely just to get a break in this case.

Several weeks passed and I sent word to Roland (*via another person*) that I was okay but was temporarily away and wouldn't make any contact for a while. He had sent word to me earlier through this same contact that he was offering assistance, or anything I needed. I didn't want to deal with anything related to him and the *"brothers"* right now. I knew eventually, the time would come that I'd have to clear the air, just not now. During this time I was perpetually angry at everything but especially at myself. I trusted no one! Every day I was feeling more emotionally and mentally fatigued and like a homeless drifter that didn't belong anywhere. I didn't have a home, family or a real place to be. I was drifting from place to place, one day at a time. Money wasn't an object at this point so I suppose that helped. I took enough cash with me so I wouldn't have to use my credit cards and tip off law enforcement as to my whereabouts. I had heard they were looking to question me about another incident.

Still out of town, one day I drove to the mountains and spent the day just thinking, drinking and crying for what felt like hours. I was also grieving Richard's loss and wishing he had listened to me. I had always told him, ***"You live by the gun, you die by the gun."*** and voila! Here we were living that reality! I was saying goodbye to so many things in my life and trying to dismiss all the thoughts of all the *"what if's, I should of', or I could of."* I knew things would never be normal again either and now I had to make the best of where I was. The thought of suicide crossed my mind several times that day. I knew no one wanted anything to do with me for fear of the ramifications of association with me and how it would cost them later. I was feeling shame at the thought of being around my children. And my poor sister! My family strongly advised her to stay away from me because I had a lot of "heat" on me. I was too much of a liability. God bless her heart. She never stopped loving, helping or supporting my efforts nor did she ever judge me. At times she let me know she didn't like something but continued being my loving sister no matter what. I knew as much as I didn't want to think of it, this was something only God was going to be able to work out and mend.

After a few weeks on the road, I returned home just long enough to get my car out of police impound and visit with my kids. I came back into town, got my car out of impound and left that night again. I stayed away and kept limited contact with my sister so as not to put her on the bad side of the family or law enforcement in case her phone was being tapped. We were close and she was in contact with me the whole time. I drove north headed toward the Reno area for a while. It took me a couple days to get there because of exhaustion. I would stop in small towns to rest overnight. When I finally arrived at my location, I was greeted by some friends. They all had good jobs and were stable people. They liked to get high as well. We would all get together and hang out or have Bar-B-Q's. I realized being around people seemed to help my nerves. I was smoking a lot of pot and drinking to help take calm my nerves and feel normal around people again. Everyone knew why I was there and what had happened back home and they gave me space. There were times I felt like I would emotionally lose it! I did a lot of superficial things like going shopping, and out to the movies. I would get manicures and pedicures so as not let myself go but I was still a walking time bomb and an emotional wreck.

I worked hard in front of people to remain normal. I wondered what normal even was anymore. Every time I saw a police car or a detective car pass, I felt my skin crawl and I froze up inside. Whenever I heard sirens, I would get a sick feeling in the pit of my stomach again. It took a long time for this feeling to pass. Every time I heard loud noises or helicopters above, I would practically jump out of my skin! I had a lot going on in me that no one had a clue about. I just wanted to be home with my kids in my own house, sleeping in my own bed with everything that was familiar to me. I knew law enforcement would be watching the house too.

Early one afternoon, I said my goodbyes to my friends. I drove into a little town where I had stayed before and decided to walk through the uptown area into all the different little shops and try to relax. I smoked some weed to relax a bit. After couple of hours of walking around, it occurred to me that I hadn't eaten and now it was about dinner time. I saw this Italian restaurant and stopped by to get a bite to eat. It was a warm night so I decided to eat out on the patio in the back which looked so inviting. There was Italian music playing softly in the background. I had a couple glasses of wine and a bite to eat. I had been reading a local paper and towards the end of my meal I began to hear what sounded like church music coming from somewhere nearby. I stopped and listened. I looked around but no one else seemed to hear it. I wondered if it was just me or was it the good wine I had but I was sure it was church music and kept hearing familiar worship songs. It sort of made me sad inside. I felt such conviction and wanted to cry for some reason. I thought I should just get out of there and walk some more. My waiter came around to ask if I needed anything else. I asked him if by chance he could hear some church music or was it just the wine. He smiled, looked at his watch and knew exactly what it was. He said it was in fact a little local church around the corner and on certain nights, (*like tonight*) they had church and sometimes they could hear the music. He pointed towards the area where the church was. I paid my bill, thanked him and left. Curious, I walked in the direction of this church. I could still hear the music as I got closer. But by the time I got to the church parking lot, the music had stopped. The doors were open. It was a distance away. As I got closer, I could hear the minister talking and by the time I reached the door, he had already begun his sermon. I quietly walked in, sat at the back and just listened. I don't know why I felt like crying as I sat there but I did. I guess it had been so long since I'd been in a service and I actually missed going to church. I sat through the whole message then I could tell he was coming to the end. I quietly got my bag and slipped out. As I was walking across the parking lot, a lady came out walking to catch up to me and thanked me for coming and asked why I was leaving so quickly. I told her I had to be somewhere. She asked if I lived close by. I lied to her and said I was from the San Diego area visiting some friends. After some small talk, she asked if I would be offended if she prayed for me before I left. I was startled but I agreed. She prayed such a simple, quiet but powerfully piercing prayer. Funny thing, while she was praying, I was wondering if she could smell the alcohol on me from earlier. She just kept praying peace and direction upon my life. When she finished, she reminded me that no matter where I was in my life, Jesus loved me and was always there with open arms. I began to quietly weep. She hugged me and continued praying. I continued crying telling God how sorry I was for turning my back on Him the way I had and asked Him to be patient with me. I asked Him to make a way out of no way in my wilderness because I was so lost, felt lonely and I really wanted to come home. I asked him to please continue to cover my kids with a hedge of protection while I was away. She asked me if I knew Jesus. Still crying, I said I used to serve Him but had been away for a while. She continued praying. What she said next just blew my mind. She said God had showed her I had a calling on my life, I was a precious gem to him, He hadn't left me and I had no idea what blessings awaited me ahead if I simply totally surrendered to Him. I couldn't stop crying and I remember the loving warmth of her hug. It had been such a long time since I'd had anyone speak to me about the love of God. I was so broken. As she hugged me, she asked my name and said she would write it in the back of her Bible and pray for me that I would run back into the arms of Jesus soon. I thanked her and started walking back to my car. When I got into my car, I continued to cry not sure why but I wanted more than anything, for God to see my hurting heart and help me get through my situation. He visited me in a special way that day so that I would know He was with me. I began to thank him tonight even though it was under these circumstances that I had been drinking. I felt His peace and was completely sober by the time I got back to my room.

I thought it was a pretty good evening until I was approaching the door to my hotel room. I saw what looked like a note on my door. My heart sank! Many thoughts raced through my mind as to who in the world knew this was my room and who could have come to my door in a city where I had just a handful of friends. I thought to myself, this church and prayer was too good to be true. As I was about three doors away from my door, I noticed that the neighbor's door also had a note. I stopped, turned around and looked down the hall. I saw that there were notes on most doors. What a flood of relief when I realized that I was just one of many who received some advertisement. Now I felt so much better. I walked up to my door and retrieved the advertisement. As I walked in and sat on the bed, I began looking at this note. Would you believe it? It was a Christian track. It was entitled *"I will never leave you"*. I smiled and once again tears filled my eyes. I thought *"Okay God, I feel you. I get it."* It struck me how this evening was such a God-ordained divine appointment starting at that restaurant, hearing church music over the Italian music playing, my walking into that small church and hearing the sermon all the way to the prayer out in the parking lot by a lady who didn't even know me and now this gospel track on my door that was right on! To everyone else in that hotel, it might have just been *"religious"* nonsense, but it was clearly meant for me that night, loud and clear. I still knew how to hear from God and He wanted me to know He **WAS** still with me. He sent me what I needed just on time and I continued to thank him for not giving up on me. He showed me how he was forgiving, patient, all-knowing and non-judgmental about all the things I had done. After that night, I felt He was going to see me through this and I slept like a baby. I was in the habit of smoking pot and having a couple of drinks before I went to sleep to relax. That night I forgot to smoke and just went to sleep. I will never forget this unique time alone with Him out *"In My Wilderness."*

The next day I called David to tell him I was in trouble, had been on the run and needed a place to stay for a while. He had already heard what had happened and was worried sick for me. He didn't think I should be alone and urged me to drive to his place. I left early the next morning. It took me several hours to get there but I finally arrived at his place. He was at work but had put the key where he said I would find it and let myself in. Not long after, I went to the market and picked up some things for dinner. He didn't have any groceries in his place. That afternoon I started dinner. It felt so good to cook again. I had a sense normalness. I felt happy, safe and content which I hadn't felt for so long. He called before coming and asked if I needed anything. I told him to bring some ice which I had forgotten. I didn't tell him that I had made dinner. By the time he came home, dinner was ready, the table was set and we were ready to eat. I had lit a candle I found in the cabinet and even cut a few flowers from the neighbor's yard next door to use as a center piece. When he walked in, he was stunned and pleasantly surprised. He thanked me and gave me a hug. I don't know why but I began to weep again. At that moment I realized I had been so cut off from my normal family life. I had not felt this for what seemed like forever. We ate, talked and got caught up with our lives. Later we went into the living room to continue talking. I explained what had happened on the day of my arrest. He was already familiar with all the players involved. He shed tears of remorse for having introduced me to "*Boss*" and everything associated with him. He had hoped this would never happen and I would never be hurt or affected by Roland's lifestyle and "business" matters. He talked to me in depth and gave me some suggestions and ideas on how to handle the rest of this nightmare. He was just so blown away that I had not been killed. He reminded me that this was the kind of stuff he had tried to warn me about years ago. Later in the evening he pulled out his guitar and began to play. Of all things, we began to sing some of the old church songs we knew from years back. It was such a peaceful, relaxing night. Later that night, he had a request that if I wanted to drink or smoke he didn't care but asked me to do it out on the patio for the sake of his sobriety because he just might want to join me and he didn't want to get started again. I told him how proud I was of him and of course, I'd respect his request. I let him know how pleased I was to hear him say that because in years past I had always tried to help him stop drinking. He never wanted to go to any alcoholics support meetings. He always said he wasn't ready for anything like that but now he was very actively pursuing his sober recovery with a whole new circle of like-minded friends that he hung out with. By now, he had also finished his bachelor's degree just as he had said he would and he was working in the social services field. In short, now he was legitimately and gainfully employed, stable and was doing great in his life. This was such an awesome change from the last time I had seen him when he was very much into drugs and alcohol. The next day he took off from work and we spent the day just hanging out together. I also called my sister to let her know where I landed and that I was okay because I had not contacted her in several days and I knew she would be worried. A week quickly passed. And I felt like I was recuperating from the worst part of my ordeal. I also realized that I wasn't smoking and drinking as much either. I was taking it one day at a time.

One Saturday morning after sleeping in, I was up making coffee. I was wearing one of David's big button-shirts and socks when there was a knock on the door. I was sure it was some religious people knocking. He got up and went to answer the door. I heard him greeting someone and invite them in. To my shock and amazement, it was my mother and stepfather Pete. I was floored as well as speechless. They just stood there and looked at me for a few seconds and I quickly told them I'd be right back. David sat and chatted with them and served them coffee. Minutes later I came out dressed more appropriately and we all sat and made small talk. I felt embarrassed and somewhat shameful. David left the room so we could talk I guess. We talked but for some reason I really don't remember everything that we discussed. Pete did most of the talking. He expressed what appeared to be genuine concern for my well-being and that they had only come to see how I was doing. My mother didn't say much. He wanted me to know they had me in prayer and somehow, all this would get worked out. They didn't stay long but in a weird sort of way they made it known that they were there for me. He informed me how the incident and my arrest had been splattered all over the media almost on a daily basis. Some people had even called him at the ministry to confirm if it was in fact me, *"Sister Rita (Judy)?"* He just wanted to know if I was okay or if I needed anything? It was sort of a relief too. My mother was somewhat reluctant but made small talk anyway. I was a little distant and still dumbfounded that they were here in the living room with me. Pete kept talking and I was reflecting on the day the Lord had begun to speak to me at that parking lot when that sister prayed for me. It felt like things would come together somehow. Today was one of those days I was reminded that he was working things out already. They didn't stay long and as they began to get ready to leave, Pete asked if we could have a word of prayer? They called David out, we all held hands as Pete prayed. I couldn't help but quietly weep during this prayer. As Pete was leaving, he gave me a Pentecostal hand shake; in other words, he secretly slipped some money into my hand. My mother shocked me when she reached out to give me a hug. Her words *(for once)* were very few but her body language said she loved me. As they walked away, I began to weep, I'm not sure why. It was actually so good to see them both.

After they left, David apologized for what just happened. He too was taken by surprise when they just showed up at the door. He said he panicked and just didn't know what to say other than to invite them as familia *(family)*. I told him I was sure it was my sister Klu who had told them where I was because absolutely no one else knew my whereabouts. They had come into town, called the family and got the address. It would be another couple of weeks after this visit that I began to make plans to return home. I had a court date with my teen son to attend and I couldn't miss that. By now, I was feeling much better, not as confused about everything and was better focused on what I had to do next. Thanks to God and David that spent many hours and days coaching me, I was ready to begin to deal with my personal life that included my children and rebuilding whatever was left at home.

My belongings were all in storage and I needed to find a place to live again. I knew the Feds weren't going to give up on me and sooner or later, I would have to speak with them. I had my head on better now and could at least talk without falling apart. I began to stress about leaving my comfort zone and safe haven here. I started having trouble sleeping again. He said he was going to miss my home cooking. As a bachelor, he didn't do much cooking, much less full meals. Little did he know how profoundly therapeutic and pleasant it was for me to do these normal things again.

The following weekend would be our last because I would be headed home. He took me to dinner at this really nice place in town. During dinner, wouldn't you know he brought up another memory of our old church days when our parents were in ministry and all the crazy things we did to people's cars while they were in church and the times we got into trouble; I think he missed that part of our life. He used to like reminiscing about how we always looked forward to the weekend revival services when everyone would come into town for revivals. We talked and laughed but when he got to the part where his father had left his mother and the ministry, his expression changed. He knew we had both gone through the same thing and I could identify with what he felt. At that moment, we were two lost PK's who came from the same strong Pentecostal background with the same experiences of our pastor parents with the same regrets in our lives. I reminded him again that if I survived this crazy life of mine, I would one day write the book. He laughed. We went back to his place and watched movies trying to stretch out our days before it would end. We had hot apple pie a la mode waiting for us when we got back. I asked him if he wanted to go find a church tomorrow morning and we would go together like old times. I was hoping he would say yes but he shook his head and said "No". He said he just couldn't stomach churches anymore and he had his own beliefs. It made me sad but I told him it was okay. Sunday morning came and he was up early making our last breakfast. By the time I got up, showered and dressed, he had the table all set up. I don't know where he got the rose, but he had a beautiful pink rose set in the center of the table in a coffee cup. I thought it was sweet that he had gone through so much trouble. We always had so much to talk about and there was never a moment that we weren't laughing but this time was different. It was our final meal and time together. He asked if I would consider relocating to his side of town after I took care of business at home. He promised that he could help me start a new life. I told him I didn't know about any of that at this time because I had unfinished business to take care first. After breakfast, he wanted to take me to a special get away place he knew of. It was up in the mountain which wasn't far from where he lived. He said it was his refuge when he needed time out from all the madness of his world. He grabbed his guitar and off we drove to his getaway place. It was in fact a peaceful naturally sight! We sat by a stream that was as beautiful as a picture postcard. We talked and laughed about so much. He played his guitar; we sang and enjoyed the day. He was really sad to see me go and thanked me for spending time at his house with him because he needed this time away from his usual work routine too. He confessed how he had wanted to beat up one of his supervisors for the crazy things he did to get over on the workers and was a big bully. I shared how being at his house gave me once again; a sense of normalcy and for the most part, a lot of my anger and fear had lifted. As usual, I was in tears but this time they were tears of joy and gratitude. Before we left his special place, I asked him if I could say a prayer over both of our lives and he agreed. I took his hand and began to pray for us and all the baggage in our lives – the hurts and healing needed in both our lives. We both cried as we sealed our prayer "*in the name of Jesus.*" We earnestly prayed that we would both find our way home wherever that would be. He actually thanked me for the prayer. Ironically, it occurred to me that I was a backslider and wondered again if God had even heard my prayer or would He honor it? I knew I sincerely meant it and it was deeply heartfelt. I banked on the fact that God knew my heart. I encouraged David to take time to talk to God every chance he got. I told him I was going to do the same to get my life back to where it used to be with God.

The next day (Monday), he had taken a personal day off from work so he could spend the day with me before I left. We hung out at the house. Later we went to a local nursery to pick out some flowering plants that he wanted to plant in his patio and in the house. He said he wanted to plant them in my honor because for the most part, we had been enjoying fresh flowers throughout his house all those weeks I had been there. He had never given flowers much thought until I came and suddenly he noticed how nice they looked. We picked out several of them and took them back to the house, planted some out on the patio, in front of his place, in the bedroom, on the kitchen table and sink area.. He said he would keep my memory alive by surrounding himself with flowers. I was moved at his sincerity. We sat and had coffee. He read a poem he had written about 2 little kids now grown up. It brought me to tears. He briefed me in on the list of contacts he gave me if I needed back up. Later he helped me pack my car and I finally left. I hadn't even left the city when I was already in tears about the unknown. What would I be facing once I got back? I knew it wouldn't be easy but it was inevitable. Not only that, I had never run from anything before and it was time I faced the music no matter what was out there awaiting me. I did a lot of thinking and crying on the way back. I had just over eight hours to myself with God. Again, my mind raced all the way home. I kept remembering the night I had heard from God in such a precious and personal way and how I felt so strong that everything would work out because God was on my side. I clung to that memory when He showed me that he was still with me and would never leave me alone.

I finally was about an hour away from my sisters and had a big knot in my stomach. I began to feel stressed out. I called my sister to let her know where I was. I finally arrived at her house. I spent time talking to her and getting caught up. I called my son who was at my father's house and told him I would be over to see him the next day. He was glad to hear from me and could hardly wait to see me again. He told me how he had been so worried for me and figured I would probably just forget about this appointment.

The next morning, my sister and I had breakfast. As promised, I called David to let him know I had made it home safe. It was summer so the kids were out of school. I drove over to my father's house to spend some time with my son. It was so good to be together again. Dad said how he had been so worried for me and any dangers I might be facing. I reassured him we were all going to be fine. My son was close to Richard and I could see he was very sad about his death.

After a few days, I sent word to Roland that I needed assistance with a good attorney to represent me. Not long after, we connected by phone and he of course was elated to have finally made contact. He wanted to see me as quickly as possible and had already made arrangements for me to meet with an attorney but had been waiting to hear from me. The assistance would come from a high powered attorney whose office was by the beach. This same attorney had represented a lot of very prestigious individuals in government. Everything had been pre-arranged and they were on standby for my call when I got back into town. My next big step would be to get through the trial that would soon begin. This was going to be my biggest challenge.

Back To Reality

Days later, I called the attorney who had been waiting for my call. We set a date to meet. The following week I kept my appointment. His office was very luxurious to say the least. I was in awe of the surroundings. He was already aware of my case and all the circumstances. I guess his fee had also been worked out because during our meeting, he never mentioned a retainer fee. He also let me know he was a personal friend of an Italian associate friend of mine and mentioned his name. I thought to myself what a small world! Everyone seemed to be connected to each other. I didn't ask any questions and he told me not worry about anything anymore because everything had been worked out and he wrote his private number on back of his card. I was not to give this number out to anyone! We discussed a few more specifics of my case as I was going to be one of their key witnesses. He gave me some extra cards to give out to anyone who wanted to talk to me, interview or any harassment from any law enforcement. He cautioned me about not making any statements to anyone. I thanked him and left.

I called my Italian associate to tell him about my appointment with this attorney. He was glad to finally hear from me and that I had finally gone to see the attorney. He wanted to talk in private and asked me to come over the house. We set a date and time for me to come to his place. I remembered to be on time! This guy had a thing with people who were late in keeping their appointments and I knew it. I was about 10 minutes late one time in bringing an associate to meet him in Vegas and he exploded! He cursed and told us both off and didn't care whose fault it was or what happen to make us late. He wanted to make it clear that we were **NEVER** to be late again and keep him waiting, not even one minute! He made a disturbing comment that sent chills up my body and I never forgot. He said *"I won't even wait for GOD, much less anyone else"*. That was his pet peeve so I drove on as quickly as I could to make it on time. He lived out by the beach so it was a long drive in the traffic. When I arrived, he was in the kitchen cutting up some bread. I glanced over at the table and he had set it up for us to eat. I laughed and asked him what this was? He said in his gruff voice, *"It's a little pasta dinner. We're eating here so sit down."* I chuckled and told him how nice of him to do this. He said he didn't want to be so serious with what we needed to discuss. He was hungry and the best way to handle business was with good food and good wine. He began to talk about a few things that had been troubling him. He knew I knew (through *Roland's contacts*) some contacts in another country that could help him. We discussed his business and I guess Roland had agreed to refer someone to him. We sat, ate and exchanged information. He was always such a serious stoic man. I had never seen this relaxed side of him. It was nice and I told him so. He just smiled. In the past, he always seemed to be on edge, serious, unapproachable, demanding and callous. For some reason, I had favor with him and he liked me. Maybe it was because he was a friend of Roland's and I wasn't trying to get anything from him. I wanted to believe that God, once again in His mercy, had given me favor with him too. He was always respectful with me and never crossed boundaries when we were out and about. We talked about what happened on the dreadful day that I was arrested. He wanted to know all the specifics. We talked until we finished dinner. Then we went over to the living room. As we were about to sit down, I noticed a pistol by the bar area and by the phone. I jokingly asked him what was up with all his toys lying around. He smiled and said one never knew when trouble lurked and he never wanted to be caught unprepared. It sounded like what Richard used to say. He walked over to his bar and fixed us a drink. We continued talking about a lot of things. He gave me the plan and cautioned me about talking to anyone. Meanwhile, he instructed me to call the attorney or him if I had any problems with anyone. He assured me that no one would be bothering me again. We talked about my meeting with the attorney and inquired if the attorney asked for a retainer. I told him I thought it was odd that he never mentioned a retainer. Once again his only comment was, "*Good, good. It's all covered; you have nothing to worry about.*" I thanked him for whatever he did to make this possible. He said that Roland was a very good friend of his and he would help him out anytime with anything he could. We had a long chat about who my attorney was and who the individual in government was that he had represented at one time. I was completely blown away; I couldn't believe it! I was amazed that I was assigned that same attorney.

I watched his expression and entire demeanor change as he expressed grave disappointment over Richard's death. He liked him from the first day they met at one of our meetings. He was very sorry about the whole ordeal. He walked over to the bar again, fixed himself a drink and this time he came back with an envelope. He put it on the table next to me and said this was something for me and the kids to help keep us afloat for a little while. I was taken by surprise. I didn't quite know what to say and just looked at the envelope. He made it clear that it wasn't a loan but rather a gift for us on behalf of Roland. Our meeting went well. He promised me that everything would turn out fine and if there were any problems, there was no need to worry myself because my attorney was getting paid well to handle this case and any unexpected problems. I thanked him for dinner and the envelope. He walked me to my car, gave me a hug and a kiss on my forehead. I thought it was so special. I left there feeling much better about my case and things in general, especially about the cash which turned out to be five thousand dollars. It was going to be helpful in securing a new place to live.

Once again, God extended His favor over me and I had favor with the landlord. He was renting me the house and prompted me to move in as quickly as I could because he didn't want the house vacant for very long. He was giving me two weeks free rent since it was the middle of the month. He just didn't want the house vacant! I was also able to get caught up with bills. It was perfect.

The kids and I got settled in quickly. Everything went well because I had all the money ready to move in and pay a few bills. I felt like I was on my way to a normal life again. I kept thanking God for His favor and direction. Later I called my attorney and my Italian friend to give them my new address. The kids got enrolled in school and things just continued getting better. About a week later, a huge flower arrangement was delivered to the house. I couldn't imagine who they could be from. I knew Roland didn't have my new address yet. It turned out to be from my Italian friend who wanted to thank me for coming out the other day and wish us well in our new location. It was a pleasant surprise. I was starting to feel so much better emotionally. I had been staying with my sister for a while. Miraculously and purely by the merciful grace of God, I was able to find a new job that month. It was a lead given to her but she wasn't comfortable doing that kind of work and gave it to me. I made the interview and I was hired. God was with me as things began to fall back in place for me and my little family.

I continued working my new job and I liked it. I started at 5:30 in the morning and I was out by 2 o'clock in the afternoon. Great hours! I still had time to do other things that needed to be done. I continued visiting my son who was still in custody. He had been so worried for me when he heard what had happened. He was just one year away from his release and he would soon be home again. By now I was home most of the time now due to my work hours. I was able be home when the kids got home from school. I liked this schedule. I hadn't begun going to a church yet. I really couldn't find a church where no knew me but I knew I wanted to go. My father kept inviting me and telling me about this little church in he was visiting. The Pastors were very nice and the church was not too far from where I was living. He said they were a simple, humble couple with a real heart for the community. My Dad knew I didn't want to go where people already knew me. He said he didn't think anyone there knew me at all. That was the best part. I wanted to start fresh somewhere and work on restoring my life once again. Dad said the pastors did a lot outreach ministry in the community which included park rallies, food ministry, youth programs and dramas. I told my Dad I would go visit sometime I just didn't know when. He didn't push or pressure me into going. He only said that was fine; whenever I felt ready, to just go. It was funny how not that long ago, my father was lost, found his way back to God and now was inviting me to go to church. How crazy was that? I was still drinking a bit and smoking in the evenings before I went to sleep to take the edge off my nerves which were still not normal, although not as bad as before. I had good days and bad days. Sometimes the slightest thing would trigger me off and I was an emotional wreck. I did a lot of suppressing in those days. I was still asking God to help me find myself and get through all the self-condemnation I continuously struggled with. I just kept asking Him to be patient with me.

Living My Nightmare Again

I continued working, trying to stay focused and still dealing with so much but I constantly reminded myself of all my current blessings of a fresh new start. I had my two children with me, gainfully employed, a new car and a nice big home to come to at the end of my day. I was grateful to have landed a good job in the midst of my storm. I struggled to keep focused on my comeback and not so much my setback anymore because it just seemed to take so much out of me. It was always a balancing act to keep focused and act normal when I had bad days.

The trial finally would begin and I was subpoenaed to attend. They had someone in custody that had been charged for the entire atrocity. Oh, how I dreaded attending this trial! I tried hard to get out of having to attend. I called my attorney and asked if he could somehow work things out and to get me out of having to be there. He said there was no way. I had to be present and had to take the witness stand. I set my mind on getting through this. The day came for me to go. My sister and father went with me. I was quiet and sick to my stomach the whole time we drove to the courthouse. We arrived and parked. My father prayed that everything would work out. My legs felt weak, my stomach was upset but I knew there was no way out. I just tried to keep focused on my faith in God, and the fact that I wasn't alone because my God and family were with me. My attorney was going to meet me there.

It felt like one of the longest walks I have ever taken. We walked into the courthouse and found some seats. I recognized several people there who gestured a hello. I quietly kept to myself with my family and waited to talk to my attorney. There were several detectives over in a corner. Two of them were the ones that had badgered me on the day of my arrest. There were a lot of security personnel everywhere as well as media. I asked God to please show up, and give me peace and boldness to get up on the stand with confidence and do what I had to do without fear. Not long after, my attorney walked in and boy, did I feel better! I continued silently praying and asking God for inner strength. My attorney called me over and we discussed my case and what would probably happen. He brought me up to date on what was going on. He wanted me to know things weren't going to be as bad as he had originally thought and he just wanted me to be calm through it all. Court got started and the preliminaries began. Soon, I was called to take the stand. My part of questioning lasted for quite some time. They showed me gruesome photos of the crime scene that brought back every detail memories I worked so hard to forget. While on the stand, I could see familiar faces staring at me curious as to what I was going to say. When my questioning was done, I was told I could leave but had to return the next day. My heart sank to the ground with grave disappointment. I did not want to return!

The following day, most of the same people arrived but even more than before. I noticed that there was a lot more press there too. The questioning continued and I was asked difficult questions as to what happened. By the grace of God, I finally got through it all. We left the courthouse and stopped to get some lunch. I was feeling emotionally fragile again and thirsty. I never wanted to look back. I worked hard to avoid reading the newspapers because they kept printing exaggerated stories of the trial and what they perceived had happened. I came home that day and sobbed for the most part. Seems the whole ordeal was triggered in my mind and heart because of those photos. I tried turning off the trial experience when I got home so as to forget all the gruesome details.

22

Rose Hills Cemetary Experience
(A place of life)

A few days later on a Saturday morning; I was driving side streets to my post office box to pick up my mail. My daughter spent the night at my sisters because they were all doing somewhere for the day. I was having a difficult and emotional time again dealing with things. The trial completely threw me backwards and felt like I was having an emotional melt down. I had been hearing and reading the papers about the trial and negative talk about things going on that were not good. I was so sick of it all. I had been drinking and smoking trying to stay emotionally afloat and just ride the wave. I began to feel like I was caving in and reliving this whole ordeal all over again. I couldn't seem to bounce back. I remembered all the gory photos they showed me during the trial and it just sickened me. I really thought this ordeal was behind me but after going to court for those two days, I realized for so many reasons, it wasn't. I suppose I had simply suppressed it all. I'd been crying a lot again, feeling frustrated, angry, stressed out and depressed. I was having severe problems shutting down at the end of my day with painful headaches. I had called David the day before to talk about how I was feeling. He suggested I get out of town, bring the kids to come stay at his place for a while until things blew over. I didn't know what I really wanted to do. I couldn't just leave either because I had just started this job too.

This particular Saturday, I had this overwhelming feeling of despair come over me like I had run out of road in my life. I was feeling like I felt the day I had admitted myself into the mental hospital, at a breaking point. The reality set in of how I had thrown my life and dreams away and I wasn't going to recover from this as easily as I thought. I was exhausted from so many sleepless nights and feeling like such a loser again even though I had been abundantly blessed. I knew the enemy was messing with my emotions too as I was having all these doubts. I continued driving and sobbing. By now, I was on Rose Hills Road by the cemetery. It had been drizzling for days. My past had come back to bite me with a vengeance! The thought that I couldn't save Richard and the way he died had pierced me through the heart that day for some reason. I needed to stop driving. I turned into Rose Hills Cemetery. I drove to the top of the hill that overlooked the city. I parked my car and just sat there looking out over the city below and sobbing with such, profound grief. It was about 10:30 in the morning and I was already an emotional wreck. I don't know what happened as it seemed I was clearly on my way to a normal blessed life again and things appeared to be working out. My mind raced a thousand miles an hour. I thought about what I had put my children, family and ministry through and what they must really think of me. I felt an incredibly overwhelming sense of despair and began to reason with God to forgive me for what I was about to do. It just seemed the right thing to do. This all took me by surprise because I honestly thought it was over and I would be fine. It was scary experiencing all this again. Something was terribly wrong. I was taught that God wouldn't forgive suicide but I also felt like God knew my heart and how much a person can take. I believed this was the best thing to do because I couldn't see myself ever being normal again (*even though I tried*). I knew people would never see me the same anymore. I couldn't breathe right either and felt sick to my stomach. I had a bottle of pills (*downers*) I always carried with me for rainy days. I suppose this was that rainy day. As I was fumbling with the pill bottle, I kept crying and shaking so badly that I couldn't open it. I had some smokes in my ash tray so I lit one up to get a grip of myself as I felt such a sense of panic. Funny how I remembered about a bottle of alcohol I also had in my trunk that I could chase down the pills with. I hadn't slept but a couple hours off and on since the trial began. As I sat there looking down the hill, I began to cry out to God, to forgive me and give me a sign of what to do. There was a furious tug of war going on in my mind: *"Do it! Wait, don't do it."* I remember looking out and thinking to myself, *"Man, this looks like a good day to die."* I felt dead inside anyway, full of regrets, without any purpose. What difference did it make if I just disappeared? No one really wanted me around them either, for obvious reasons. I was nothing but a liability. I figured my kids were better off with my sister anyway. She was a better parent than I was. I suppose I was trying to justify what I wanted to do as the best decision for everyone. I prayed and cried out loud for God to hear me and help me sort my mess. I thought how disrespectful I had lived all the years after serving him so long. He had used my life in ministry for years and how I had wrecked it all. I even thought about the fact that I was brought up in church as a pastor's daughter and wasn't supposed to end up like this; I should have known better. I told God how tired and sorry I was with my miserable life. I asked God to forgive me for all the wrong I had done and please, please come and lift this weight of ugliness off me and give me rest if this was not what I should be doing right now. I couldn't speak anymore because I was exhausted and my head hurt so badly by now. I prayed for His hand to come, touch, deliver and set me free once and for all or just let me die quickly with His forgiveness.

I finished smoking and sat there playing out my life. I walked over to my trunk and got the bottle of alcohol. This spiritual battle went on for what must have been a couple of hours that day because by now it was just after noon time and I was still crying and praying as I sat there. I don't know where the time went. I told God if he restored me, I didn't care if I ever played the piano, sang or ministered again; I just wanted to feel Him in my heart again.

By now it was raining hard, real hard and I just watched it rain. Before I knew it, I fell into a deep sleep sloped over my steering wheel. Hours and hours later I woke up because I was feeling cold. As I awoke and looked out, it was very quiet and I could hear slow drizzling outside. Now as I looked down in front of me, I could see bright city lights below. It was now dark. I was calm and my mind wasn't racing out of control. I had slept for many hours. I suddenly realized something. I wasn't sure what, but *"something"* was different as I sat and looked out. My heart rate had completely calmed down. It was a supernatural sense of rest and calming peace that had come over me. I didn't feel anxious or suicidal anymore. I couldn't explain what I felt except that I wasn't sad, tired, angry or anxious anymore. I remember feeling completely sober and alert. Something supernatural happened to me as I slept because everything about me in that car was different. I felt God had heard my desperate cry and performed spiritual heart and mental surgery on me as I slept. I even felt lighter as if the weight of the world had been lifted off my shoulders. God had touched me while I slept. I just knew it! I still knew how to hear God's voice. It occurred to me that everything about me was not the same inside. I sensed that the power of God had invaded the evilness that was in my car and whatever battle took place as I slept, the power of God had taken over. I don't know what happened when I fell asleep but it was lights out while God fought for me in that car that morning and now evening. I thought to myself, *"This is crazy, could this be real, who would believe what just happened?"* I now began to feel the awesome presence of God in a subtle but powerful way that I just sat there and started to cry in a different way. I felt the spirit of Jesus come over me and I was now feeling thankful and began to praise him for touching me. I hadn't felt this in a very long time. I knew that I knew, something happened while I slept and the evil oppression had lifted. I looked at the seat next to me and saw the pills I was trying to open and the bottle of liquor was on my lap. Miraculously, I was suddenly able to open the pill bottle with no problem. I got the pills and threw all the pills into the bottle of liquor. I shook it so as to dissolve them and poured it all out the window as I wept. It was still very quiet but felt a sense of peace. I continued to cry before his presence and thank Him for what had taken place. He had lifted my pain and settled all my crazy thoughts of confusion. I put my head back on the seat and just pondered on how this place was where we bury the dead and now, it had become a place of life for me. What a crazy moment in time. Somehow I knew God had heard my cry at this cemetery! No one would have believed how this day unfolded. A while later; I heard a tap on my window that scared me. It was the security officer who came and advised that they would be closing in thirty minutes and I should be making my way back down the hill. I still sat in amazement of what had just transpired. I had painlessly been transformed in my sleep.

All the way down from the hilltop it felt like it was taking such a long time. I was in awe the whole time I drove. I kept wondering, what next? I wasn't sure I only knew that something happened, I was feeling different and was ready to start this journey one day at a time. I wanted to call somebody and tell them what had just happened to me but I didn't know who to call. I knew that this would sound really ridiculous and crazy; maybe they'd think I was high or something. I went home and just thanked the Lord all alone. When I got home, I went to my room to pray. For the first time, I knew that I knew, He had heard and touched my life in a very real, way. I was still feeling exhausted and went to sleep like normal that day and didn't need to smoke or drink. The next day I actually slept in which felt weird. Later that afternoon, I went to pick up the kids from my sister's house. I shared with her what had happened to me and I was going to try and make changes in my life. I told her I wouldn't be going out drinking or clubbing anymore. She had a look on her face like she wasn't sure if I was serious or I could actually do this. I told her I was honestly going to try and change my life with God's help one day at a time.

Rita Rangel

A few days later, I called my dad and told him that I was ready to go visit his church. He was excited and happy for me. He told me to go a little early so he could introduce me to pastors Danny and Nadine. The day of church finally came. I was a bit nervous but felt good to be in church and hear gospel music again. Not long after, I finally made my way up to the altar for prayer. I stayed a long time and repented on my own. I felt like God had taken me in His arms and welcomed me back. For some reason, I remembered the lady I had met in Reno, who prayed for me in the church parking lot and told me she would be praying for me that I would run into the arms of Jesus again. That day had finally come. Oh, what a glorious feeling it was! I felt so good and clean. I continued visiting the church on my own for weeks making new friends and getting plugged into activities. They used to sing with cassette tapes for worship. This was new to me. I had been in church for a few months when I began looking at this beautiful baby grand piano that sat in the corner of the church up front. I had noticed it long ago but never really paid much attention to it. They had it covered with a beautiful burgundy cloth. No one ever played it. One Friday night while we were in the middle of worship, the cassette tape got tangled and it stopped working. I felt so bad for them because they had to quickly go put in another tape in. I had never seen tapes used for worship in a service. Somehow it just didn't feel right.

Another Friday evening in church, we were singing worship songs that were very familiar to me. Again, the tape player jammed and stopped but they kept on singing without the music. I felt sorry for them and thought for just a second about the piano in church and how easy it would be for me to just walk up and help with music. As quickly as the thought came, it passed. After church, we were all in the fellowship hall having coffee. My dad sat next to me and quietly asked me what I thought about helping them with music the next time they needed help. He said he had thought of me when the music jammed during the service and how I already knew how to play the piano and all their songs. I was startled and told him I had

216

the same thought too. He suggested I tell the pastor that I knew a little music and maybe I could help them. A few minutes later, the pastor came over and sat at our table. I thought to myself, here's my chance. I waited a while then asked him if I could talk to him for a quick minute. We went off to the side and I explained to him that I play piano and pretty much knew most of their songs and offered to help them with music. I offered to walk over to the sanctuary and play the piano for him so he could hear me play. He responded with, *"Oh great, Praise the Lord!"* As we started walking back to the sanctuary, it suddenly occurred to me that I hadn't put my hands to a piano in over 15 years. I thought to myself, *"Wow! I can't believe I'm going to do this, what if I don't remember the music?"* I began praying as we approached the piano. I was a little nervous. I sat and put my fingers to the piano, closed my eyes and began playing and singing worship songs nonstop. I fought back the tears because I couldn't believe I was doing this. It had been years since I played piano. It was as though I had never stopped playing because it all came back to me. I continued playing and singing several of their worship songs. A while later; I opened my eyes and noticed several people in the church sitting on the pews just looking and listening too. I looked up at the pastor who had a funny look on his face. I stopped and he said he was just blown away that I played the piano with my eyes closed and without any music in front of me. He thought it was awesome. I told him I didn't use sheet music because I only played by ear and didn't read music. He wondered why I had sat in his services as long as I had without ever saying anything about being able to play piano. I tried to explain that I had been lost out in *"Egypt"* away from God for several years and was coming to his church to get restored. He said *"Praise the Lord, I had no idea you played the piano."* He asked if I could play piano beginning the next service which was Sunday morning; I agreed. I had such a warm reception from the people in church. Everyone was happy; they clapped their hands that someone would finally be playing the piano. Many people told me how much they enjoyed my music. I was humbled and so grateful for the opportunity. The door had opened for me to exercise the musical talent God had given me long ago. What amazed me was that the pastor didn't seem to be concerned about my past only that I was coming to his church. He believed I was God sent. This was encouraging to me to say the least. He had no idea where I had been or who I was connected to. He was a man of prayer too. He just praised the Lord that I was able to meet the need for music in his church. It would become part of God's plan for my restoration. Afterwards, all the way home I thanked God for what had just happened. During this time of my life, I cried a lot because I was sensitive to the things the Lord was doing. I felt as though I was going through a cleansing process. I was slowly getting restored. It was like *"WOW!"* I spent a lot of time thanking God for the restoration. I was so grateful for what God was doing in my life. I was walking sober and being delivered from my stinking thinking one day at a time and didn't know it.

There were so many times when I would suffer through terrible doubts of self-condemnation over where my hands had been. I felt like I was putting dirty hands to the plow and I wasn't worthy to play the piano, or to lift my hands or sing praises to Him. I struggled with my past and constant thoughts of worthlessness. No one knew this but God. I just kept going to church and hearing the Word. I had to pray myself through this all the time! Hearing Pastor Danny's sincere preaching gave me the hope and encouragement that I so desperately needed. I just continued going to church and growing spiritual muscles. Playing the piano and singing helped me to walk the straight and narrow. It helped me because I was raised that you shouldn't take the things of God lightly or play with the things of God. I had seen so much of it growing up in church. I don't know how other backsliders ever managed to fall away and get back up and walk right back into ministry. Yes, Jesus forgives but the fall isn't something to be taken lightly. I had seen this for years and I didn't want to be like them. Now I understood what my mother struggled with when she used to talk about feeling condemnation. Now it was my turn to walk in her shoes. If you had told me back then, I never would have believed that I would be in this predicament myself someday. I wanted to just keep it real but I secretly struggled with self-condemnation. I didn't tell anyone what I was feeling, I just stayed plugged in and faithful to this ministry. The pastor had a true burden and vision for the lost. He was so sincere and on fire for God. He was faithful and anyone could see that he loved the Lord. I admired that about him. He had been a drug addict himself in the local streets of another county but was delivered and changed his life from a heroin addiction. I was inspired and encouraged by his sincere spirit to help the lost at any cost and train those who were new in Christ. He also ran a men's recovery home next to the church.

I continued committed to my restoration and severed all my previous carnal relationships. I stopped hanging out at clubs and changed my phone number to avoid hearing from my old party friends and contacts. Helping this ministry play the piano also helped me to curtail smoking marijuana and drinking on the side as well. When I started going to this church, I still struggled off and on with sleepless nights. I asked God to take that nasty habit away so I wouldn't feel like such a hypocrite. I was committed to going to church and staying plugged in. Even though no one at church knew this, God knew my secrets and I was just so grateful to be feeling Him in my life once again. Every time I went to church and heard the Word, I would either get convicted about things that I needed to let go of in my life or, I was encouraged to continue serving Him knowing He would eventually heal my weaknesses and deliver me from whatever was not pleasing to Him. God knew my heart as well as my struggles. I always prayed before I put my hands to the piano keys for God to help me get over my personal demons. This restoration was definitely not easy and it was sometimes hard to get through even one day at a time but I knew I was on my way to getting completely restored. I had been through worse things in my life than this. As I continued attending church, it gave me a sense of purpose. I had no idea how my life was going to turn out or when I would know I was fully restored but I just continued to be faithful. No one in this church knew about me other than my Dad and his family that helped me. I was ashamed of myself and my past but I knew that it was God-orchestrated for me to serve in the music ministry.

My immediate family found out I was in church and I'm sure they wondered how long I would last. I really didn't care because I was going to give it my best shot and try to be faithful in the little things. I knew I had messed everything up royally by backsliding years ago so any criticism was something I had to live with as an ex-leader in ministry. There was nothing more difficult than trying to prove myself to people. Funny how I never cared what people thought before and now I did. I knew I didn't have to prove anything to God, He already knew my heart. It was other people and family that were challenging and had doubts about me. I stayed away from all of them and stayed plugged into my church.

I began to develop a real burden for backsliders like me because of my experience. Now I knew just what a lonely road it was and how next to impossible it was to get back up on your own. No one's experience is ever the same either. Sin is sin, failure is failure. Condemnation destroys and robs us of total victory. Every day was one more day of walking close to God. I didn't want to take any of this for granted either. I thought about all the people in my past that were so lost without the Lord. How I wished I could help them come back to Jesus! I often remembered David and Richard. I remembered sharing with David how I would eventually come back to God and write a book. All I could do was pray for him and others that the Lord would send them an angel to witness to them as He had done for me in Reno in that parking lot. I began to develop a real prayer life. I often thought of many of the lost that I had crossed paths with on the streets. That included the dope drop offs, pickups and collections and those who were dealt with for nonpayment. I was troubled at times by the many faces of lost inmates I had seen in the prisons of Mexico while involved in business deals. I felt shame that I used to go into the prisons with my family to bring the hope of Jesus to the inmates and how later, I was going into these same prisons with dealers who controlled the drugs and laundered money in and out of these same facilities. I could have so easily been raped or killed. No one would have known or even cared. For that I was grateful. I was always reminded about the value and importance of prison ministry such as I had been involved with. My parents continued going into the prisons. I still didn't have much fellowship with my immediate family other than my sister. They were concerned that I still had "heat" from law enforcement and contacts from my past. The joy of the Lord, indeed, was my strength every day during this time and my sister continued to be my only family support system.

On a personal note, should you have a family member, a friend or you know anyone who is backslidden, I encourage you to *NEVER* judge or turn them away despite what they've done or how scandalous it may appear to you. God will judge and deal with them. Not one of us is so spiritual that we can't continue to love on someone who is slowly getting discouraged and slipping away from God. We all know someone that "used to be" a Christian in church and now they are lost out in the world. Some of us know pastors that are no longer ministering. No matter what someone has done, there is no one sin bigger than another. Sin is sin! The best way to restore someone back to God is to practice the true, unconditional love of God with forgiveness. Let them know you are praying for them. Call them! Invite them to church or just to have coffee. Don't let them feel like losers or failures. We already know we failed and we feel like scum. It's such a turn off to run into so-called Christians with their self-righteousness.

Everyone has skeletons in their closets and anyone can fall from grace. Once you have had a true encounter with the Lord Jesus Christ, it is impossible to live a normal life again. We are never happy out there running from God. I have met so many wounded backsliders in my journey. Yes, I said _wounded_ by none other than critical, self-righteous Christians. I'm talking about the walking wounded who have been hurt -- not in the streets but yes, by

Christians in our churches today. It is a turn off and is so destructive! I was so wounded and caught up in a web of unforgiveness, hurt and pain. The only one that suffered was me. Backsliders need to be loved back in to the church with your prayers and sincere, humble demonstration of unconditional love, just the way our Lord Jesus Christ would do. After all, we are called to be His hands and feet.

In all my years out in the world; I never once (*not one*) met a happy backslider that was better off without God in their life. We need your prayers! To this day, I can count on one hand, the people I ran into that invited me to church and sincerely said they would be praying for me. They showed me love and told me what a blessing I was in their lives. There is so much wasted talent out there from people that used to be in church and or in a ministry. The power of prayer does the convicting; the rest is up to you. Follow up on the lost, invite them to your BBQ's, parties and fellowships. You never know, one day they just might put aside their pride and actually come back. Love is a powerful gift that can't be disputed. A judgmental attitude turns people off and away from Christianity. Every week, look around you in church to see who isn't there anymore and go find them. Pray for them; send them a "*thinking of you*" card, a text, or an e-mail. Call them or reach out to them on social media like Facebook or Twitter, anything! Only don't give up on them. You may not know it but believe me when I tell you; it's a matter of life or death. Trust me, I know. It almost killed me. I believe if it had not been for the prayers of the people who never gave up on me, I would be dead today. Thank God for my Rose Hills experience where I found my life again through the supernatural amazing grace of God. Life prevailed over death. I was out there alone and disconnected from any Christians with no one to talk to or help me through my ordeal. I believe it was the power of prayer that ultimately prevailed that day. I became dead to my old self and it was the most appropriate place to leave my past buried once and for all. Rose Hills carries a different meaning for me today.

23

A New Man

Several months passed after my conversion. I was still working on my restoration and being faithful to my piano commitment at church. I was attending all the services and plugged into most of the activities. I had made new friends too. It was such a good feeling hanging out with folks that loved the Lord and were radical about being a Christian and serving Him wholeheartedly. I was still hearing from Roland who continued to write and kept asking me to go visit him. I knew I couldn't just ignore him as if he would just go away. Since my conversion, I found it really difficult to find things to talk about with Roland. It definitely was not like before. Nothing in my new life had anything in common with him. He would never understand my decision to serve the Lord. I felt like I was on a spiritual honeymoon. It had been several months since I had seen him and I rarely wrote anymore. The prison system was moving him around more and more. No one in my new church (*including the pastors*) had any idea about Roland (*Boss*) or anything of my past. No one asked and I didn't volunteer. It had been months since I had any contact with anyone from my past either. It helped that I changed my phone number.

One day I received a communication at my post office box from my Italian friend who had left the country some time ago for a while.

He had recently returned. I had changed my telephone number and forgotten about him too, but I still had my post office address. My heart sank and I wondered what I should do. He wanted me to call him just as soon as I got a chance. I thought about what I would say to him when I heard his voice. He wasn't anyone I could simply avoid and he definitely wasn't one to just go away either. I knew if he really wanted to find me, he certainly would! I had seen him do this before. I began to pray about what to do and what I should say when we did make contact. A few days later, I made that dreadful call. He sounded so happy to hear from me. He asked how the kids and I had been doing and asked if I needed anything. I told him we were all fine and everything was going good. We chatted a while before he asked if I had visited or communicated with Roland lately. I had a feeling he already knew I hadn't. I told him I had been very busy with the new job. I asked if everything was okay with Roland. He said everything was fine but that I should probably make plans to go see him and chat a while because he needed to speak to me. He said he was going to be speaking with him again during the week and wanted to tell him I would be going to see him soon. I agreed to go visit Roland before the month was over. I prayed that night for God to see me through all this, mend my heart, give me favor and help me get rid of this guy in a way that would work out well for both of us. I knew I needed to use wisdom too because cutting Roland loose was not going to be easy because he was convinced I was sent by God. How crazy was this? I could only see the worst of this situation. I even thought that if something should happen to me, at least now I was walking with the Lord in my heart and so I knew where I would be going. I thought of the kids too. I had no one to talk to about all I this. I just figured I should continue to pray to God and trust that somehow He would show me what to do and what to say. I knew that God had a way of making a way; out of no way. He had already parted the waters for me through the most difficult ordeals of my life. I had to just trust him with this last request. I wasn't sure if God actually cared enough about people's relationships but I knew he didn't want me burdened down with stuff from my past and the pressures of the unknown. I knew this situation would take a miracle to work out.

A few weeks passed before I was cleared once again to visit Roland. By this time he was in Kansas. It was going to be a long trip. The day finally arrived and I was on my way to Leavenworth Kansas. I prayed for God to be with me in our visit as I explained to him about my conversion and why I wouldn't be back to see him anymore. I needed to let him know I was now a fully committed Christian and I was done with him, favors, calls and business meetings. I pictured him getting explosive. I arrived at the penitentiary, cleared security and was escorted to a table away from the other visitors which told me he was in segregation status. I sat and waited until he came out. I could see familiar inmate faces looking towards me and on occasion, they would nod their head acknowledging me. When the door finally opened for him, he had to get patted down one more time before walking over to me. He was smiling and appeared to be in good spirits. As he walked towards me, several of the other inmates with their visitors greeted him. He knew people from everywhere! He finally got to our designated visiting area. After we sat down, he kept saying how excited he was to see me and how it had been too long. He explained how he was being housed in the segregation unit since his arrival and unable to mingle with the regular population. He had been placed there since until they could figure out where they were going to put him because he was still under investigation for other things. Roland said we would probably have a lot of surveillance during our visit but he didn't care and wouldn't let it bother him as long as he got to see me. I wondered how happy he would still be once I told him about my conversion and plan to dump him. I just smiled and listened to him waiting for an opportunity to start to tell him what I had come to say. There was no turning back either. I was there on a mission and it was on! Seems he had so much to talk about. I sat and listened for the most part because I honestly didn't know what to say. We had a few hours to visit because I had come from out of state and they gave us an all day visit. Each prison had its own set of rules which the warden could override and or cancel without any notice if he wanted to.

It felt awkward visiting him. Our visit was nothing like before either. There was no pressure about anything or on edge about business explanations of different events. He was in good spirits with no agenda. He finally asked what I had been doing. I talked about my job, the kids and some of the things we had been involved with. He asked about certain contacts (*in code*) that he referred to as my uncles and family members. He said how he had recently spoken to my uncle (*our Italian friend*). He elaborated a while about that. As he was talking, I could sense the moment was coming when he would ask the question that would lead me to tell him what I had to say. I began to pray within myself for courage.

The moment came when he asked what else I had been doing with my life. This opened the door to share with him. I paused and repositioned myself on my chair as I prepared to tell him what I had come to tell him. I began by saying I had something to tell him and it might not be something he wanted to hear but he needed to know. I reminded him how we had always been out front with each other about everything and anyone including who I was dating. He agreed and said he didn't like the tone already and asked what was so important. He asked if it was a new sancho (*boyfriend*). I asked him to just hear me out. I began telling him about some changes in my life. He became serious and his demeanor changed. He positioned himself on his chair too. He took my hands and just stared into my eyes as I began by telling him how very unhappy, problematic and strenuous my life had become since we began our relationship in his crazy world. I reminded that I was just a simple person with a simple life going out here and there with my friends until I met him. I never had done any of the things I eventually learned to do since I hooked up with him. I proceeded to explain how my life was different now. Somehow I couldn't quite get the words out to just tell him straight out that I'd become a born again Christian. I only said I wanted out from our relationship once and for all and I would not be coming back anymore. Before I could continue, he abruptly interrupted me and asked if I had found someone else in my life that had stolen my heart. I was feeling apprehensive and nervous. I thought for a quick second and said, "*Well, actually, yes*" and before I could continue, he unexpectedly pounded on the table with his hand, leaned towards me and said "*I knew it! I knew that's why you weren't writing, visiting and changed your telephone number!*" By this time, everyone heard him pound on the table. You could hear a pin drop in the visiting room. Security yelled out his last name and quickly two security officers headed towards our table. They asked what was going on? They ordered him to quiet down or his visit would be terminated immediately. He didn't move! He sat with a stoic look and just kept staring at me. I couldn't believe what he had just done. I reminded him (*whispering*) that now **he** was bringing heat to our table. I wanted to chuckle at the silliness of it all because he just jumped to conclusions and assumed it was another man. I was embarrassed too that everyone was now looking towards us. He was so angry and furious. I wanted to explain how silly he was acting but just kept quiet and stared back. It was very quiet as no one knew what was going to happen next including me. As security stood standing there, he slowly composed himself. Security asked him if they were going to have any problems from him. He told them "*no.*" We resumed our visit and everyone else in the room carried on with their visits. Slowly, the visiting room went back to normal. His outburst took me totally by surprise and by now I am a bit annoyed. He still wasn't saying anything and just sat quietly with his stiff jaw staring at me. I told him that he should cool off because he hadn't even given me a chance to explain. He said there was nothing to explain because "***another man was another man***". I thought to myself; if he only knew. He demanded to know his name and where he was from. By now, I was a bit agitated and was sure I wasn't going to get anywhere. I picked up my plastic baggie with my money and my car key, and began to stand up. He wouldn't let my hand go and firmly pulled on me to stay sitting down. I commented that we were done and would finish this conversation some other time. He said "no, we're going to finish this today and right now. I told him if he had anymore outbursts, I was walking out. He asked again, what this guy's name was and where is he from. I said (*sarcastically*), *"His name is Jesus and He's from everywhere, where do you think he's from"?* I took advantage of the moment and with spirtual boldness started talking as fast as I could about my breaking point at Rose Hills Cemetery, how my life was touched in a powerful way and I've never been the same since then. I let him have it with both barrels that I was now committed to the Lord once again and was going to live for Jesus. I told him we had nothing in common between us anymore and I wanted him to respect my decision to go back to my Christian walk and live for God. He was still staring at me as I continued talking as fast as I could. Now he looked somewhat perplexed as I shared how I had even began playing the piano and singing at the church where I was attending. Incredibly, with a baffled look he said, *"Wait a minute, wait;* are you saying *you found religion?"* Now, he took me by surprise that he had just got it and the light went on in his head. I thought he totally understood me. I told him that it wasn't religion but more about a personal relationship with the Lord. He stated he didn't really understand how I could go from his/our world to God and change just like that. I told him I knew he wasn't going to understand but I was going to continue in my walk with the Lord anyway! He confessed that he could tell from the beginning of our visit that something was different about me and my countenance but he couldn't pinpoint it and was just waiting to find out what it was during the visit. I told him I was really sorry that it didn't work out for us but that I was in fact very happy to be back with the Lord and I wasn't going to change my mind. I further reminded him how *"we"* had nothing in common anymore and I wanted him to respect the fact that I came to tell him in person where I stood and what my life was like now. I reminded him that I had told him before; that I was a Christian before and today I just wasn't sure what he would say or how he'd feel about losing me to God. He was much calmer now. He said he was happy for me and he was glad that the man I was talking about was really Jesus and not a "vato" (*Spanish slang for "man"*). I reminded him that he hadn't let me explain earlier. He expressed how he now felt kind of silly but still felt very strongly that I was sent to be his soul mate and he continued to ask his higher power (*in his own way*) to help keep me in his life. I told him I was restoring my life right now and wasn't looking for any relationships whatsoever. He said he was glad to hear that because he would be home soon and he would continue to believe I would be his wife someday. I asked him if he even heard anything I said because I wasn't waiting for him and it was over. Security continued to monitor our table. If they were listening (*and they probably were*), they must have been totally blown away at our conversation.

The conversation turned to me talking to him about his own life and how God had a purpose and a plan for his life too. I told him he had a real testimony if he ever considered giving his life over to God himself. He commented, *"testimony" I'm not a 'rat.' I'm nobody's testimony and I don't testify for anyone!"* I chuckled as it was obvious he was thinking in the secular. I tried to explain that it wasn't that kind of testimony. I told him to just forget I had even said it because I already knew he wasn't going to understand. I went on to explain to him how God could use a soldier like him. He asked, *"Use? Use me as a soldier? Nobody uses me, I use them."* He had no clue at all what I was talking about so I tried to break it down as best as I could so he would understand how God could use a soldier like him for His honor and glory. I explained how if he ever decided to give God a chance in his life he would change and he too could share about the power of God in his life, how the Holy Spirit would give him boldness and he would be testifying/sharing very powerfully. He got caught up with the word *"spirit"* and asked what I meant about spirits because that sounded kind of creepy. Again, all this didn't make much sense and I continued to try and break it down for him to understand which was difficult. I asked him if he had a Bible he could read and see for himself. I told him I would write him during the week and give him some scriptures to read. He asked what *"scriptures"* were. Everything in the spiritual sense was literally foreign to him. I had to explain almost every step of the way. He stated he didn't know how to read a Bible even though he went to Catholic school growing up. I explained it was like a regular book that had an index at the beginning. He had to find the name I sent him, go to the page it was on and find the chapter and verse to read. Boy this was a real task to explain. He took everything literally. He asked me to explain again what I did in my church. I explained how I was helping with the music, how I played the piano and sang. He asked if I'd sing him a song. I asked *"Right now, here?"* He pleaded with me to sing. He wanted to hear me sing. He said he never knew I knew how to sing. I felt embarrassed and thanked God we were having a segregated visit away from the crowd and had privacy to ourselves. I decided to sing him something he might know like, *"Amazing Grace"*. He just stared at me as I sang. As I began singing, I was praying for his understanding. After I finished, he said he had never heard it sung so beautifully and he really like it. Shortly after, we walked to the vending machine for some cool drinks. As we walked, I began to explain how he too, needed God in his life and being in the position he was in, he could do more to help his brothers out than bring violence. I talked to him about how someday God would hold him accountable for those whom he had ordered assaults on and even in the future. I explained how God gave life and only God said when their life would stop, not him. I gave him the John 3:16 scripture, *"For God so loved the world that He gave His only begotten son, that whosoever believed on Him should not perish but have eternal life."* I explained how God had an ultimate plan for his life but the devil had lied to him for so many years about what his purpose was. It wasn't to move drugs, make his profits, hurt people, intimidate, have people disposed of or have people fear him, etc, but to live an abundant life that mattered with a real purpose and a plan; a life where he could really organize soldiers for God and take people off the streets and out of prisons to give them a real purpose in life by his own example. I explained how he could turn his current position around since men respected and looked up to him. He listened attentively as I gave him pretty much my testimony. He was a deep thinker anyway. By the end of the visit, he was calmer. He appeared to have taken it all in and said he had never heard about *"God stuff"* this way. He told me about a person he was dealing with that was giving him a bad time and was planning to have him disposed of tomorrow. He asked if it meant he shouldn't do that because of what I just said. I told him absolutely; and reminded him he would be held accountable after hearing what I had just told him about what God had to say about this, *"God gives life and God ends it, not man."* Our time together seemed to fly by fast. I asked him if I could pray before I left and he agreed. I thanked God for our visit and prayed for Roland's understanding of spiritual things. I asked God to speak to Roland after I left and that he would begin to think about what I had shared so that he would make the right decision concerning that inmate giving him a bad time. I prayed for God to open Roland's mind and heart to the spiritual realm and give him understanding and peace in his heart after today. He listened attentively and said amen when I finished. There was nothing normal about this visit. I came to drop a bomb on him about my conversion and our break-up but I ended up witnessing and praying with him. Nothing like I had expected! I was surprised at his lack of knowledge of anything spiritual in spite of the fact that he had attended private Catholic school for years as a young boy. As I left, I thought about our visit and everything we talked about. I believe he returned to his cell and thought long and hard about our conversation because I knew he was a real thinker and he would try and dissect everything he didn't understand. I prayed for him on the flight all the way home. I prayed God would begin a work in him. I could hardly wait to get home and send him more scriptures to read since he appeared interested. I had no idea he would be open to listen to me talk about spiritual things or else I would have brought some scriptures with me. Wow! You never know how God will work. I felt good about going to see him this time. We didn't talk about any business at all! It was all about the work God had done in my life, my testimony, and the possibility of the Lord's call on his life too. The best part was that he was open to hear it! I could remember a time when he didn't want to hear anything about "*God stuff*".

The next day I went to work but spent my lunch hour in my office finding scriptures I wanted him to read. I put together a letter and a list of scriptures he should read. I sent it off that same afternoon on the overnight express. He got my letter just a few days later and began reading. It was funny how law enforcement began to think we were writing in code or something using the Bible. They couldn't believe this could actually mean exactly what it was. I didn't care. For the first time we were in a real honest conversation about religion but law enforcement thought we were using religion to pass messages. It was comical. Not too long after, I received a call from him and he told me he had begun to read what I sent him and he was finding it all amazing. He asked how soon I could go see him because he wanted to ask me questions. For a moment, I questioned his motives and if he was trying to use this to get me to visit more. About three weeks later I made reservations to go see him again. This time while preparing to go, I took two small squares of toilet paper and fed them through the typewriter and typed up some powerful scriptures I wanted to share. After typing it out, I rolled it up tightly in my hand so I could put it in his shirt pocket when we embraced. It worked perfectly. Our visit went well. All we talked about was the Word. He had lots of questions concerning the disciples and their many flaws. It was the weirdest thing. Everything had begun to change in our visits. I was so blessed when he said he felt I had jinxed him on my last visit because when it came to dealing with that difficult inmate, he remembered what I had said about how he would be held accountable to God. He ended up giving this guy a "pass" (*a break*). He had never done that before. A couple of other inmates asked him about it. He told them that he had another plan in mind and they shouldn't worry about it.

Roland was amazed at the lives of the disciples. He talked about Peter and Paul and what crazy characters they were because they also had their faults. He was amazed at how God would forgive their imperfections and still use them. We discussed what the Word said about God using any of us. Suddenly, our visits had taken a different path altogether and we were talking about God. He told me he had heard about some of the "carnales" (*Spanish slang for brothers*) who had turned Christian through The Outreach Ministries. He surprised me when he said he had inquired about my family's prison ministry. He had heard about my stepfather's testimony and the work he was doing in the prisons. He heard how all the inmates spoke highly about the "**Prison Ministry**". It never ceased to amaze me how much information this guy was able to obtain while in penitentiaries all over the United States. By now he had heard about some of the other brothers converting to Christianity. He wanted to know what was going on with these brothers that were changing to religion. He had been following their life changes for quite some time. I reminded him how God was doing new things everywhere and how He had the power to change the hardest, most violent man in the world. I explained how God could get a hold of any gangsters off the streets or in prison to serve Him and shame the Devil. He wasn't sure he could do this because he had a lot riding on his life of business commitments. I told him to talk to God about it in his own words and somehow God would, in fact, work things out for good and show him what to do. He just couldn't see himself as a Christian and was sure it wouldn't fit his lifestyle because of his past life. I reminded him about his brothers and how they changed. I told him God didn't care who he was, where he had been or what he had done. God had the power to move miraculously and make the impossible possible for him if he would just trust God with his life. God would take care of the rest. He couldn't believe it would be that simple. He was now down to just over a year before being released back into the free world. He promised he would think about it as he had a lot to think about before going home. I told him I'd be praying for him and that he should trust God with all the things he didn't understand and wait on Him because He has a way of speaking to all of us. Again, he allowed me to pray for him before I left. We held hands as I prayed and again, he said "*amen*" at the end. He kept saying how different of a woman I was now and couldn't believe religion did this to me; but he liked the new me. I prayed all the way back home on my flight that the Lord would deal with Roland and give him understanding of the spiritual things he was reading and had heard about.

A few more months passed before I visited Roland again. We talked on the phone occasionally and by now I was more grounded in my church and in my walk with the Lord. I was still visiting my son at the Youth Authority. I was so excited because he would be home in few months. I thought just how fast the years had passed. I reflected on how they had been the most trying years of my life. My heart was happy again. It was as though I had survived in a long, evil war for the past fifteen years. I was healing from so much pain and learning to trust again.

My visits to Roland had stopped but I would occasionally write. Our letters were always about what God was doing in my life and all the things going on at my church. He would write and tell me how he found all my activities amazing and realized how much I had changed. He still felt happy for me. By now he was reading the Bible on his own. I bombarded him with printed bible studies to read. He had always enjoyed reading anyway.

In April of 1994, my son was finally released from jail. Roland had one of his attorney's send a limousine to the house so my daughter and I could ride in style to pick him up. There were no words to describe my joy and I thanked the Lord that this day had finally arrived. When we arrived to pick my son up, he didn't even want to wait to dress into his civilian "*dress outs.*" He just jumped into the limousine. He made a quick change of clothes in the limousine as we drove for fear that the authorities would find something wrong and change their minds about releasing him. We went for a long ride along the coast. He loved the beach and it was what he had wanted to do when he got out. We stopped for breakfast at a quaint little place by the ocean where Roland and I used to go. It would be our first family meal together in the free world. We went home later that day where he was reunited with his brother. We took lots of pictures. Our hearts were full of joy as it was just the four of us again. My life was back on track. I had a full time job, a comfortable home and now, all my children! How much better could this get? Their father was still out of the picture. Later, I got word that he was in a local Christian men's rehabilitation program. Ironically it was just up the street from the church I attended. I had forgiven their father, Carlos, and continued praying for his salvation. I eventually told the kids about their dad. Only my daughter was interested in seeing him again. The boys didn't care whether he lived or died.

As the months quickly passed, Roland was transferred locally again. The kids had been aware of him since they were much younger. By now he was only nine months away from freedom. He had to spend a few weeks in segregation before being released out to the normal population and before he could have any calls or visits. One day out of the blue, he called to say hello and tell me that he could now have visits and he wanted to see me. He had lots of questions to ask me about things he had read in the Bible. I thanked him for sending the limousine to pick up my son. He was very happy for me and told me of how he felt when he first came home from the same place years ago. He could hear the excitement in my voice that we were a happy family again. The kids all talked to him. A couple of weeks later, I received flowers from Roland at my job congratulating my son's homecoming.

A few weeks went by before I made arrangements to drive out to visit Roland. It had been many years since our beginnings at a local facility where he was first arrested. I began to hear from the Lord prompting me to ask Roland if he wanted to receive Jesus into his life. I remember thinking he would *NEVER* say yes. I thought he was far from that place in his life. I questioned if it was from the Lord at all. I was so sure Roland would not want to accept "Jesus" in his life.

It was now closer to the weekend that I would be driving out to visit him. The prompting within me grew stronger. I was supposed to pop the question and ask if he wanted to receive Jesus. If he said yes, I would lead him in the sinner's prayer. Just the thought of it gave me butterflies in my stomach. It would be the hardest thing for me to do like when I had flown out to break up with him because I had become a Christian. I couldn't begin to imagine how I was going to ask him. I prayed about it for days. I didn't want to feel stupid later on if and when he reminded me how he felt about "religion" but heck, he was reading the Bible anyways. It was the gamble I had to take to be obedient to God. The day of the visit came. I planned to be gone all day but be home the same afternoon which was really cool compared to the other states I had traveled to in the past to visit him. I asked God to help me through this. I arrived at the facility and he was anxiously waiting for me. I recognized several inmates and their ladies from my previous travels. I had done business with some of these folks and it felt kind of awkward. They gestured a hello as I walked past them. My stomach was so nervous. God has such a sense of humor. Once again, Security had put our visit in the segregated area away from the regular population. It turns out he was still in "*Segregation Housing Unit*" (**SHU**) status. The door finally opened and there he stood. Once again, he had on one of those funny jump suits. He looked ecstatically happy when the door opened. He kept wiggling around as security patted him down before entering the visiting area. He smiled the whole time. The guards seemed to be joking with him. They were much more relaxed and friendly with him and not as rigid as at the other prisons in other states. They escorted him towards my table. Many of the other inmates greeted him out loud. They looked as though they were genuinely happy to see him. He stopped a couple times to greet some of them. Security didn't appear to be worried about him but they told him to keep walking anyway. He finally reached my table, he held me for a long time. We sat and began our visit. Neither one of us knew where to start. He told me how happy he was to be back on home soil. He said it seemed like even the guards were happy to see him back. He laughed and said he already knew these "knuckleheads" (*the guards*) from before and they treated him with respect, so differently than the other prisons. He told me he had a good time chatting with most of the guards and (sadly) they all said they were happy to see him again.

I couldn't wait to tell with him how great it was to have my boy back home with us. He knew my joy and reminisced about how his mother felt to see him finally home. Half a day passed in what felt like only an hour. Our visit was so relaxed and it felt like it had been way back when we first started visiting. We didn't talk about any business and he didn't ask any questions about anybody except his family which I would see when I visited my son. He told me again how he heard good things about his born again "carnales" (*brothers*) and how they were in church and recruiting other local "*knuckleheads*" from the neighborhoods to become Christians. This opened the door for me to ask him about receiving Jesus into his heart. He asked me if I had heard the brothers speak. I told him I hadn't because I didn't attend The Outreach Church. He asked about how I was doing in my church. I gave him a glowing praise report about how great I felt and how I was involved in a live drama we had put on at a local cable television station. I told him what it was about and he thought it was great. Suddenly, as I was finishing my story I felt the Lord speak to me saying, *"NOW is the time."* I began to get anxious and told him there was something I wanted to ask him. He said *"Sure."* I reminded him what I had told him some time ago about the Lord using him and having a real purpose for his life. I asked him, *"**Have you ever, I mean, would you ever consider, I've been thinking that**"* All the while I kept fidgeting and was looking around as I tried to get the right words together. He took my hands in his, looked directly at me and asked me why I was looking everywhere but at him and why was I suddenly not making any sense? He was always very keen on picking up on vibes of all sorts and he was very good at reading body language. He knew me enough to know I was nervous. He asked me whatever it was I was trying to say, *"Just say it!"* I looked at him and told him I wanted to ask him a yes or no question and not to trip out on anything but just answer a simple yes or no. He agreed and asked *"What is it?"* I finally told him I had been praying for him and was wondering if he had ever considered asking the Lord Jesus to come into his life to be his Lord and Savior too. There! I finally got it out and I just looked at him for a response while he remained quiet. I put my head down to wait a few seconds for a response when he quietly said, *"Well, I'm not sure I totally understand everything but Yes Rita, I would."* I slowly looked up and asked *"You would?"* He answered, *"Yes, yes, I would like the Lord to come into my life like yours. I was wondering when you were going to ask me if I wanted to do the same. What do I need to do to change and make it happen to me so I can feel what it is you feel because you glow when you talk about God? You look so excited and happy."* It was like time stood still. I wanted to cry as I sat there for few seconds just staring at him totally not believing what I had heard. Oh, how I wished someone could have heard this moment! I told him I was so happy for him and so was God! This was the best and happiest decision he would ever make in his whole life! I rattled on about what a great day this was. Finally, he asked again what he had to do to have God in him. It dawned on me (*Duh!*) I needed to led him in the sinner's prayer. I told him to close his eyes and repeat after me. He did and I began the sinner's prayer. When he got to the part where he repented for his sins and all the bad things he had done to others, he choked up and sounded like he was about to cry. He stopped and apologized to me. I told him it was all perfectly normal and it was the Spirit of God cleansing his heart. It took a few tries before he could get through the sinner's prayer. When we finished he had tears in his eyes and kept saying he didn't know why he was feeling this way. He asked, *"What next?"* I told him to close his eyes and I was going to pray for him and thank the Lord for his salvation. I put my hand over his forehead and began praying. I got a few seconds into my prayer when Security quickly came over and interrupted us and abruptly asked me to remove my hand from his face. I told Roland it was okay, we could still do this. Although this put a slight damper on the moment, I held his hands and continued to pray and thanked the Lord for his decision to invite Jesus into his life. I prayed for the angels of the Lord to encamp around him when he returned to his cell and that he would increase in hunger for God's Word. I cried with joy as I prayed for him. We cried together. This was so amazing and totally out of character for him. I was so overjoyed that I could barely contain myself. He said, *"You know, Rita, I never cried or felt this sentimental and emotional, even when my parents died at different times. It's different, it's a feeling I've never known before."* I told him it was okay and that the angels in heaven were rejoicing over his decision to serve Jesus from this day forward. I also explained how he would be tested and tried but to stay in the Word and talk to God (*pray*) every day. He admitted he felt nervous and different now that he had said the prayer. I promised him I would have a lot of people praying for him too, including the *"brothers"*. It was so amazing because there was only one other couple visiting in our section and we had the privacy of being able to pray and talk and cry without disruptions. I brought it to his attention how God had made this day possible and special. When we hugged to say good bye, he was tearful again. He kept apologizing and I kept smiling, thanking the Lord and reminding him that nothing would be the same anymore. I told him he was a new man. I knew he didn't quite understand what I meant but again, I told him he would never be the same again. I urged him to remember that when he was getting tempted and tried, it was the enemy trying to discourage him. I encouraged him to get hooked up with some of the Christian brothers there at the prison. He wasn't sure that's what he wanted to do just yet. I promised to come back in a week to see how he was doing.

I was on cloud nine all the way home, crying and praising God for Roland's conversion. I kept thinking about the look on his face as he prayed and how he tried to choke back the tears. It was a monumental moment in my personal and spiritual history. I kept praying for him. I was so, so happy all the way home. I wanted to tell everyone and anyone but I didn't know who to tell because no one in my church knew him and my family wouldn't believe it anyway. I had not been in contact with any of the Christian "*brothers*" because I attended a different church. The only other brothers I was in contact with were not Christians. I had been out of that scene for a while now. I was full of joy all week after Roland's decision to receive Jesus into his life. I wondered who would actually believe he had given his life to the Lord. It was like a big secret. It occurred to me that I was getting bombarded with phenomenal spiritual blessings like never before. My second son had been away in prison for few years and had just come home. Then, a few weeks later, my firstborn son came home to stay after being away from us for several long years. Finally, a month later my daughter gave birth to my first grandson. I was happily walking with the Lord and once again experiencing peace and joy from within. I never, ever thought I'd get to feel this peace in my lifetime again. Without any real effort on my part, I was suddenly walking in the most awesome of God's blessings. The kid's father had quit his crazy lifestyle and was still at a rehabilitation facility getting his life together. Roland had just given his life to Jesus. Man! What more could I ask for? What else could possibly top all these blessings? My heart was full of such gratitude. I had lots to be thankful for and I could see God obviously restoring in my life, my children, their father and now Roland. All week long I prayed hard for Roland's newly found salvation for strength and wisdom as he attempted to walk with the Lord. The weekend came and Saturday morning I was off to follow up on Roland's progress with the Lord. When I arrived, he was no longer in the "*SHU*" and had just been released to regular population the day before. When the door opened, he was bubbly and in happy spirits. He was smiling as they pat him down for his visit. Neither one of us knew what to say first. He had a new look about him and he seemed to glow.

I asked him how he felt and how he was doing after one week with the Lord in his life. He explained it hadn't been easy and spoke about how some of the fellows had noticed a change in him. He said he had begun telling the guys closest to him that he had found the Lord and was going to try Christianity. He said most of them were happy and some just respectfully kept quiet. Maybe they were just blown away by the news or wondered how long it would last. I told him it was okay, this was perfectly normal, especially for a man in his position. He said he had refrained from handling business with things like drugs, money, accounts payable and anyone that needed to be dealt with. He had been laying low for a few days until he could feel what he should do next. He continued to ask God for help. By now he was only six months from release and he told me he had a plan he wanted me to hear. Now it was his turn and he said he didn't want me to interrupt him but that I should just be quiet, listen and speak later. I couldn't imagine what he would say except that maybe this new way of life was going to be just too hard for him. Now it was my turn to brace myself for whatever he had to say.

He had a nervous air about him as he held my hands and began to spill what was on his mind. His plan followed. He reminded me that it would be one week before Christmas when he would walk out the doors to freedom and that we should get married just as soon as he left the doors of the penitentiary to have God's blessing. We could honeymoon for a few days and then go home in time for the holidays and begin bonding as a new family with the kids. We would all go to church as a family and I could help him with his walk and show him how to serve the Lord. He went on and on with his plan. He said he had sent word to some people and that I should contact his carnal (brother) to perform the ceremony. It sounded like he had thought out all the details of his plan and he was ready to implement it as soon as I said "*Yes.*" By the time he was done, I was breathless. As I said before, he seemed to have planned every little detail. I was still thinking it was going to be about something else. He continued talking about money he had coming to him and we could buy our own place, etc. I wasn't ready for this at all. He was full of joy and wanted to share his new life and joy with me in marriage.

When he finally finished, he asked me what I thought, I quietly told him I wasn't sure about all this. I had to think and pray about it. He didn't understand what I meant by *"praying about things."* He quickly corrected himself and said he needed to formally ask me to be his wife. He took my hand and quietly asked me if I would marry him and apologized that it was at a penitentiary but he was sure God had sent me into his life to be his soul mate a long time ago. He promised to never bring up old *"business"* especially about Richard. I knew this meant a lot to him but it took me by surprise and I told him I didn't have an answer and I needed some time to think it over. Again, I told him I wanted to pray about it. He didn't understand what I meant. He believed in his heart that it was the right thing to do but he agreed to wait until our next visit for my answer. He was disappointed that I wouldn't give him an immediate answer but he agreed to wait.

All the way home from our visit I thought about the question he had hit me with. In the joy of his salvation I hadn't foreseen or planned on this turn of events. Marriage! What should have been a happy spiritual moment suddenly turned tragic and sad for me. I thought about the whole idea of marriage with him and what kind of a life I would have. I wasn't sure why I was crying. When I got to the coast, I pulled off the highway and parked. I got off the car and went for a walk along the beach. My plan was to get him right before God and slowly and gently cut him loose, maybe go into a men's Christian rehabilitation program. At least now I had the assurance that he had the Lord. I finally made it home. What I find so amazing is how well our children know us and how much they can sense things going on in our lives. When I got home and settled in, they noticed a change in my demeanor and asked me if everything was okay? They were so right. I was feeling overwhelmed. I was honest and told them how Roland had asked me to marry him.

I didn't go back to visit Roland for quite a while. I realized I was still grieving over Richard and in pain over his death. I had not thought about him and the whole ordeal for such a long time until Roland asked if I would marry him. I thought that my life would just get better since I had recommitted my life to God. A couple of times I had the kids lie over the phone and tell Roland I wasn't home when he called because I wasn't ready to talk to him. He kept calling and writing until he was finally able to connect with me. He was wondering what had happened and asked me if something was wrong? He wanted to know if I had an answer for him yet. I told him I was still praying about it. I gave him every excuse I could to stall for more time before I returned for another visit. I needed time and I still needed to hear from God. I prayed and fasted about the whole thing. I asked the Lord to heal my broken heart. If it was meant for Roland and me to stay together even though he was a baby Christian, He needed to show me and give me peace over marrying him. First the Lord would have to heal my pain and give me romantic feelings for him again, I was happy about his conversion, but marriage? That was a whole different story!

Meanwhile, Roland was growing in the Word and kept giving me his little (*but big*) praise reports. I wanted to stay excited for him but I was struggling with the idea of committing to marriage. I continued going to church and staying involved with the outreaches. One day the pastor began a three day series entitled (Wouldn't you know it?), "*Letting Our Past Go & Moving On.*" The timing of this message just blew me away! He encouraged everyone not to miss it because God had given him a special message and he wanted to impart it to us all so we would all grow spiritually. The message was dynamic to say the least. It hit home with me because I hadn't realized I was carrying so much of my past with me. I felt that marrying Roland would somehow keep me connected to my past and I needed to cut it all loose so I could be free from all of it. I didn't know how to walk with God and be connected to Roland.

By the end of the series, I received the answers I needed about my past, present and future. I spent a lot of time at the altar praying and the pastor prayed over me. I left my past at the foot of the cross and asked GOD to carry it for me because I couldn't do it anymore. I cried every day for God to speak to me. At night before going to bed

I would go over my notes and continue to give it all to God. I learned I needed to forgive myself which was something that honestly had not occurred to me. I was amazed at how much I had suppressed and still silently carried inside. It had been a long while since I had visited Roland. I didn't want anything to interfere with the decision God had for me, even if it meant I had to decline his marriage proposal. I finally went to see him when he was approximately ninety days shy of freedom. I sat and waited in the visiting room. This time, when he finally came out, he didn't look as happy as he had before. He had a superficial smile on. He finally made his way over to our visiting table. He was happy that I had come to see him but confessed he had his concerns about me staying away for such a long time. He said he didn't understand that I had to "pray about it". He figured that since he had given his life to Jesus, things would only get better because we could serve the Lord together and suddenly, everything had come crashing down on him. He said he had been in a depressed state of mind such as he had never experienced before but he had continued reading the Word and talking to God about everything. He continued to ask God to make things right for us so we could serve Him together. He said that without a shadow of a doubt, he just knew God has sent me to him. It made me sad to hear him talking this way but I just let him talk until he was done.

Finally, it was my turn and I told him I wasn't going to sugar coat anything. I confessed what I had been going through since our last visit and the changes I had gone through as a result of Richard's death. From time to time he would interrupt me to apologize. The hours passed by as we talked it all out. He asked if God had given me an answer about marrying him. I told him he did and my answer was *"Yes!"* With God's help, I would be walking in faith the best way I could to give it my best shot. He sat quiet for a few seconds then it hit him and he said out loud, *"Yes! Yes!"* It was loud enough that people looked over our table and the visiting room got quiet. Security saw that he was happy and not angry and didn't budge to come over to our table. He looked so relieved and happy. He told me to get a hold of his carnal that went to The Outreach and could perform our marriage. He wanted me to have them set something up for the day he would be getting out and that we would all meet at the City Hall. He said out loud *"Thank you God! I knew He would hear my prayer."* Everyone just looked over at our table. The rest of our visit went well and before you know it, time had passed and it was time for me to leave. We held hands and prayed before I left. I asked the Lord to be in all we did from this day forth and that He would be glorified in our commitment. We also made a pact with each other from that day on that we would bury our past (*good and bad*) and never bring things up about other relationships. He promised everything would be buried and forgotten from this day on and that he would give it to God. I was truly looking at a new man.

Free and Married At Last

December 20th, 1995, five days before Christmas: One of Roland's attorneys sent me in a black, stretch limousine to pick him up. I arrived at the gate on time. They announced his transportation had arrived. I sat anxiously waiting to see him walk out. I was sure something, anything would suddenly come up on their computers and they wouldn't let him out after all. The driver had the door already open so we could quickly leave. He finally walked out in his civilian *"dress outs"* just as my son had when I picked him up seven months earlier. It was Deja vu all over again accept this time it was Roland. He was smiling and very happy. The driver stood by waiting for him to approach the car. He got in and greeted me. The driver closed the door, put Roland's property box in the trunk and started walking around to get back into the driver's seat which seemed like a long time. We began to hear the inmates yelling something out of several levels from the windows. The driver was getting in and situated. He began to maneuver the limo slowly around to leave but was having problems making a U-turn. Roland opened the sunroof of the limousine and stood up to wave goodbye. I remained sitting down. He started laughing. I asked what the inmates were yelling. He asked me to stand up with him and listen for myself. They were yelling, *"Its Rita's time, its Rita's time."* In a matter of seconds, the sounds seemed to double because now it was even louder with inmates chanting and whistling out of every window. Everyone was happy for Roland. The driver was still slowly trying to turn the limo around. Then they began yelling *"Beso, beso!"* (*Spanish for kiss*.) Roland reached over and we kissed. At this the fellows went ballistic! They all started whistling and yelling at the top of their lungs. It was as loud as a football game. It was such an amazing moment. I wondered how security was taking this. The driver was finally able to turn the limo around enough to start driving off the premises. He purposely drove slowly. We continued waving, hugging and occasionally kissing. As we slowly drove off, we could still hear them. We stood there waving until we left the grounds. It felt like we had been in a parade. It was kind of funny. As we sat back down, Roland got very quiet and I noticed he was teary-eyed and somewhat emotional. I had never seen this side of him. I just hugged him and reminded him that the inmates were happy for him. He said he knew it, but a part of him was going to miss all his camaradas (*Spanish for comrades*}. He said *"Rita, I know I'm never coming back behind these walls again and my life with you will be good."* By this time I was in tears too and I thanked him. He later asked the driver to stop by the beach side before we went into the City to get married.

We arrive at the beach and walked towards the water. He was still a bit emotional and quiet. I asked him if he didn't mind if we prayed that from this day forth our steps would be blessed. He agreed. We held hands while I prayed. He told me about how many years he had looked forward to this day when he would be out in the free world again with me. Now, all these years later, we were standing together in the free world.

He reminisced how he had lost me forever but he had never stopped hoping and talking to his *"higher power"* to bring me back to him even after all the ugliness. I told him he must never forget it was only because of God that all this had been possible.

About 45 minutes later, we got back into the limousine and headed for City Hall to meet the minister who would be marrying us.

Roland kept saying how getting out this time was completely different from all the many other times he had been released from other prisons in his 40+ years of incarceration. I told him it was because we were doing things differently and in God's order. We arrived at City Hall, parked and walked around until we met up with the rest of our party. It was Pastor Dell Castro and his wife who pastor a church not far away. With him was one of Roland's "*brothers*," and his wife, who stood in as our best man and matron of honor. We found a beautiful secluded spot on the grounds of City Hall and Pastor Dell began the ceremony.

Roland was so nervous he kept wiggling and moving around. We both fought back happy tears of joy as we began this new journey and declared our vows to each other. We could feel the presence of the Holy Spirit during the ceremony. All the negative thoughts and memories from our past which I had been sure would interfere never crossed my mind and the Lord allowed our day and emotions to be at rest and at peace. God is so good!

We got through it all, took photos and later, the six of us went into town and had a nice luncheon reception at a local favorite place. It was a beautiful day with old friends celebrating a moment in time and making history for our new life together in Jesus. We all spent the day together talking, laughing and sharing. The brothers committed themselves to help Roland in his walk with the Lord ahead as soon as we got back home. Later that afternoon, before they all headed for home they joined together for a time of prayer. They all left, we changed into comfortable clothes and walked to the pier to sit, talk and watch the sunset as we had planned to do on our first afternoon out. We walked to the end of the pier and sat with others who were there with their cameras to catch the sunset. We were both in awe that this day had arrived. He was finally out and we were together in the free world as we had been before except under completely different circumstances. Now we were legally married and we were both committed to the Lord together for the first time. We talked for what felt like hours about so many things that we had never been able to comfortably talk about before without the eyes and ears of the world upon our every move. This time, there was no pressure of who was listening or watching. We hashed out personal things we had needed to settle for years. We also vowed that day (*again*) to leave everything behind us there at that pier. We were on a natural high. It was quiet and tranquil on the pier with a sense of reverence as the sun slowly began to set. The only sound you could hear was the sound of the waves and people taking pictures. Everyone seemed to be whispering quietly as the sun set. It seemed only right and fitting to acknowledge the Lord at this time. We held hands and prayed, giving thanks to the Lord. This day would be forever etched in our memories. It was picture perfect and couldn't have been any better. The peace of God was with us the whole time. There was nothing missing. It was complete, whole and accomplished in a way neither one of us could have imagined with so much history between us. All the bad would be completely behind us now. What a glorious way to declare a fresh start!

The next day, we were out having breakfast and as observant and perceptive as Roland was about his surroundings, he noticed two undercover agents in the same restaurant that we were in that he'd seen at the pier the day before. He made me aware of where they were sitting. He cautioned me and said that we would probably have surveillance for a few days or perhaps longer and that I shouldn't be alarmed. We weren't doing anything wrong anyway so we had nothing to worry about. He told me to just be myself and not look around. All day long, we were checking in at the Western Union office to pick up money being sent to us as wedding gifts from friends and associates from everywhere. A lot of people knew his release date and that we were officially getting married. For me it was the strangest thing to receive gifts and well wishes this way. Each time we went in, we were picking up lots of money from inmates in different states sending wedding wishes. We had more than enough money for our honeymoon for that weekend and by the time we got home a few days later, we still had just over $2,500 left over.

We returned home to greet the kids. They were so excited and happy to have us home. That same night, Roland called a limousine to pick us up at the house and we all drove out to Santa Monica pier for dinner. Later, Roland met his first grandchild, Joseph who was three months old at the time. We all had a wonderful time talking, laughing and bonding as a family. I couldn't have planned a more perfect homecoming. It felt awkward to be in a limousine again; this time under different circumstance. God is faithful.

Our New Life Begins

It Is Christmas Eve 1995. My family on my mother's side still wasn't talking to me. No one knew Roland was out. Now it was time to begin our married life together. Christmas Eve was the perfect time to begin meeting with some of my family as a newly married woman. I figured I would start at my dad's house where everyone was getting together. I was nervous, Roland wasn't. We went to my dad's house for our traditional Christmas Eve celebration. We both felt a sense of joy and happiness. I wasn't worried about what my dad and his wife would say. I felt things would be okay. My dad had no idea about Roland, who he was or what role he played in my past. I had brought different male friends to dad's house before so he must have thought he was my guest for the evening. I wasn't sure how he would react. But I wasn't going to worry about that and figured I'd cross that bridge when I got there. That night we all arrived at dad's place. The kids went in first and as I walked in and hugged my dad and his wife, Roland came right along side of me and greeted them too. The kids did their usual greeting of kisses and went their way. Thank God, we were the first to arrive because I needed to explain to my dad who was. I went over to the couch and sat with Roland. I asked my dad and his wife to come over for a minute. I told them I had something to share with them. They both sat with wonder and

I'm sure they had no idea nor were they ready for what I was about to say. I said, "Dad, I want you to meet," (*my dad was already getting ready to shake Roland's hand*) I continued quickly and said, "...meet my husband, Roland." My dad paused, taken aback and asked, "What?" I quickly told him that we had been married a few days ago. My dad smiled and shook Roland's hand and congratulated us. Dad said he was pleasantly surprised. I told my dad I was very, very happy. He stated he could see that I was. They congratulated us and welcomed to the family. The night went on as other family members began to arrive. No one could believe we had just gotten married. My brother and his wife were blown away as were some cousins that arrived. The whole night was fabulous. We took lots of pictures. It was "Christmas 1995," our very first Christmas together out in the free world and the beginning of many more happy years to come. It was a great time for us both. Traditionally, we don't open gifts until midnight so it was in the early hours of the morning when we finally left for home.

The next day, Christmas Day, we all slept in and got up late. I was in the kitchen making some breakfast when the door bell rang. As I was going to go open it, the door swung open and it was my sister, Klu, who came over to say "*Merry Christmas.*" Just as she swung the door open, Roland was coming out of the room at the same time and we all sort of met up in the living room. She had no idea he was out let alone that we had married. She paused as she recognized him. I attempted to introduce her to Roland but she commented she already knew who he was. I told her we had gotten married last week. She turned around and walked back out the door and left. Roland chuckled and asked "*What happened*?" I told him I didn't think she was very happy about him being out much less that we were married. I knew it wouldn't take her long before she told the rest of the family. Oh well! They weren't speaking to me anyway so it wasn't going to make much of a difference. We went on to visit his brother's family. There it was quite the opposite. It was a very warm and happy reception. They were used to seeing my son at the

Youth Authority where we used to picnic together when they visited their son. Now both our sons and Roland were out and it was one big, happy family reunion!

It was still the holidays. We had been in contact with our dear brother, Dell Castro, who checked in on us to ask how we were doing. He wanted to invite us to the next Sunday night service. We told him we would be going to my church and then meet up with them at the evening service. He said some of the *"brothers"* were waiting to say hello, too. The Sunday came when I would be returning to my church after my so-called two week vacation. No one knew about Roland or any other man for that matter because I'd never talked about my past with anyone. We went to church a bit early so I could introduce Roland to my pastor before anyone else arrived. I pulled them aside and introduced Roland to them as my husband. He and his wife were floored and commented, *"Husband?"* We told them we had been married two weeks ago. We all laughed as they congratulated us. When the service began, I went to the piano and did my usual worship. It was the first time Roland heard me play piano and sing. He stood there stunned and staring at me the whole time. He sat in the front where I always sat. Right after the offering was picked up and before the preaching begun; the pastor announced to the congregation that he had a very special announcement to make. I had butterflies in my stomach as he made the announcement that Sis Rita returned from her vacation as a married woman. They called us up to the front, prayed for us and later everyone came up and congratulated us. It was a very warm gesture on the part of our pastors. That evening we went to The Outreach and met up with Brother Dell, his wife and some of his *"brothers"*; now serving Jesus. It was good to be there with people we knew. The service was dynamic and the music was great. Roland kept telling me throughout the service how he recognized so many homies (*acquaintances*) that he had thought were dead and now he knew that they were very much alive but Christians and serving the Lord. He was in awe the whole time as he looked around. He had never been to a Christian service like this before. Throughout the service he kept poking me to let me know of another and another homie he recognized. I had to keep telling him to be still. Pastor Sonny preached a very powerful message. I could tell Roland was touched and a bit emotional. He held my hand the whole time squeezing it very hard at times. I remember when they made the altar call, many people went up and after a while I asked Roland if he wanted to go up for prayer. He asked if I would go up with him because he didn't know what to do. I walked up with him. A couple of the brothers followed. They began praying for him. He had his hands lifted up and was crying. The whole time he kept apologizing to me for crying. I told him it was okay and that it was the presence of the Lord that he was feeling. He apologized again and after a while, he just broke. The power of God was upon him that night in a powerful way. I cried tears of joy with him. After the service that night, we all went to have fellowship. It was the beginning of our new fellowship with new Christian friends.

After service he was very sensitive and emotional. He told me how he'd never felt this way in his life. I explained to him how he was being cleansed from within. It was as though both of us never had a dark past because everything within *"us"* felt new. We continued going to our little church on Sunday morning then Sunday nights we would go to The Outreach. This went on for months. One day I was amazed how Roland commented he had this idea to bring a couple of his Christian brothers, to our church so they could testify of what God had done in their lives. He wanted to share how the three of them once terrorized their neighborhoods but now through the power of Almighty God, they were winning souls for the Kingdom of God. I could see Roland was growing in faith. Meanwhile, my sister, Klu, had started to come around when she learned how much we were involved in our church. I told her about the special date that had been set where Roland and a couple of his brother's (*Kilroy and Art*) were going to be sharing their testimonies. Unbeknownst to us, she had invited my mom, stepdad Pete, and the men's home to attend. I told her not to worry, there would be other times and eventually God would do all the healing within the family. Weeks went by and the day came for this special service. It was a packed house. My sister came. The time came for the brothers to walk up and begin sharing. As they were walking up to the altar I happened to look back and to my amazement, my family and the Men's Home were all in the audience. I was blown away! I thanked the Lord and began to pray that they would discern Roland's heart. The three of them began to share about their past and how their lives changed when the power of God got a hold of them. Roland was last and he gave a moving testimony how he had put me through a lot through the years but kept praying in his own way for God to keep me in his life, etc. I was praying the whole time. He thanked the Lord at the end for God sending him the soul mate that he had asked for years ago and how now I was helping him with his walk with the Lord. He explained how he used to talk to God about sending him a woman to help him change his life and how God had heard him. I was in tears remembering all the havoc we had gone through together in our past. I was so grateful and humbled by what the Lord had done. After church, everyone came up to shake hands and greet the fellows. My sister came over and began talking to me. She shared how much she had enjoyed hearing Roland's testimony. She could see that he was a changed person. I didn't know whether to go say hello to my mother as she had not been speaking to me but I went up to her anyway and gave her a hug. She didn't say much. Later my stepdad went up and began talking to the fellows and even took some photos with them. He invited everyone for a little fellowship at a nearby coffee shop. The healing began to take its beautiful course within my family from that night on. The most awesome thing was that God did it in His timing when neither one of us had tried to make it happen. Again, God came through.

One night after church, Roland asked Pastor Sonny if he could come preach at our little church because we had decided to leave this little church and join The Outreach church rather than attend two churches. Pastor Sonny said he would check with his secretary.

Rita Rangel

I remember feeling embarrassed that Roland would impose on him because Pastor Sonny was a very busy man. A few weeks later, Roland got word that Sonny would in fact be coming to our church to preach and bless us out from our church as we transitioned. Our Pastor Danny was in awe that Pastor Sonny would be coming to preach at his church. He had everyone passing out flyers that Pastor Sonny was coming to speak at his church on a Friday night. The Friday finally came when Pastor Sonny preached at our church and later pastors Danny and Sonny together prayed over us and blessed our move to the Outreach. It was a uniquely beautiful service that night. Our Pastors were so honored to have had Pastor Sonny come preach at their church. The following week, we began attending our new Outreach church. We had a lot of fellowship with some of his brothers. We plugged into our church and got involved in many activities. It was such an awesome feeling hanging out with like-minded folks who understood our past and the struggles that lay ahead of us. The Outreach staff was very helpful and supportive of our new walk. We were always so busy doing things for God. Roland, Ernie and Art were going around sharing their testimonies and also testifying at many events like handball tournaments at various neighborhoods, park rallies, rehabilitation conferences and churches. They were also helping Art promote his new book. We had a whole new set of friends. I stuck close to a God-sent sister that became a very good friend by the name of Cathy Clark who was an Outreach staff member and remains a close friend to this day. She helped us both with solid direction when faced with obstacles and decisions to make. It was only through the power of God and in His timing that everything fell into place the way it did. God's plan in and through us was a divine and perfect one. We both plugged in to many activities and spiritual support that helped us get through by understanding God's promises through His word, prayer and faithfulness of good people around us. At that time Cathy was a big part of that support by giving us Godly guidance to help us make the right choices we constantly faced. She loved us through the challenge of Roland's parole conditions and constant surveillance. God uses circumstances, places and people to speak into our lives. Trust was a real issue with both of us because of our past. It was still difficult to get close to people. I especially didn't trust women. Cathy was someone I learned to trust whole-heartedly with our personal life and the challenges Roland and I faced. There was a time when we were waiting on the home we were trying to get into and she housed us in her home for several months. She gave us her personal suite upstairs. She slept on a couch downstairs. It was truly a sacrificial act of love and humility on her part. It broke my stinking thinking and I learned to trust again because of her. We stood for six years with this Outreach church when we decided to attend a smaller church where no one knew us. We began attending a local small church where we both continued to grow in our Christian walk.

My Life Shattered

We had now been married five years. We bought our three bedrooms, three bath townhouse and we were both working at good jobs. Roland was working as a paralegal for a couple of attorneys. I had my good paying job with the county. My daughter and 2 grandbabies came to live with us.

One afternoon, I got a call that my son had been arrested and was in custody. He was sent to a program for a thirty day evaluation in another county. He didn't want to go but he was court ordered. A few weeks later, he was transferred and when he arrived, he called home and spoke to both my daughter and I. He sounded in upbeat spirits. I promised him I would go see him each week and would be praying for him. My daughter and I took turns talking to him on the phone. I told him he was on the speaker phone in the kitchen. He stated he liked the grounds because it looked nice and so far the staff was nice enough to even let him make a phone call. He gave us the telephone number to the unit where he would be in so we could call to speak to him in the future. They were allowed to receive phone calls from family. This made him happy. We wrote down the number and continued with our telephone visit. I felt so much better after hearing from him. We agreed that we would call during the week to get the schedule for visits and be there each week. We said our usual "*I love you's*" and hung up. My middle son was in jail for not reporting to his probation officer. During this time I also had a retail women's business of clothing and accessories. The business was going great. I was even considering leaving my regular job to concentrate on my business and expand. There were a lot of changes going on, some good and some not so good, but it was all manageable.

On this same evening, I was struggling to sleep at night. I was restlessly tossing and turning. I wasn't really sure why but I began to pray to God just in case there was something I needed to pray about. There had to be a reason for my restlessness. I begin to pray for my boys and my daughter. I asked the Lord to show me if there was something specific I should be praying about. By two o'clock in the morning Roland had gone downstairs to sleep because I just couldn't get settled in. I had to be at work each morning by 5:30 am which meant I had to get up at 4:30 am to get there on time. Just after 3:30 am, I went downstairs for a drink of water and Roland was snoring away, sleeping like a baby. I returned to bed, I continued to pray for rest, peace and sleep because I was very restless. I finally dozed off for a few minutes when the phone rang. I couldn't imagine who would be calling me at this early in the morning except my boss to ask me to fill in for someone that wouldn't be making it in. Unfortunately, it wasn't my boss. The lady on the phone asked if I was Rita. I immediately knew it wasn't going to be a good call. I got a knot in my stomach. I didn't want to hear what she had to say next. She identified herself as staff at the program where my son was. She proceeded to say that he had an accident earlier and had "**expired**". It was as though someone had dropped me in a tub of ice cold water, I froze and was speechless. She asked if I was still on the phone. The word she used, "**expired**," threw me off. I asked if she meant *"expired"* as in dead. She proceeded to tell me that their facility could assist me with inexpensive burial plans if I didn't have the means. I asked for the cause of death but she only said that he had just stopped breathing and they couldn't revive him. I told her

I didn't understand what she meant by *"he just stopped breathing"* because he had been breathing all his life. She said that she really couldn't discuss the specifics with me because I would need to speak to someone else at the facility later but her job was only to notify his family *(next of kin)* that he had expired. I asked if his father had been notified. She said no, I was the only name and number he gave on his paperwork. She encouraged me to call the business office during regular hours. I kept trying to get information from her about the facts as this was quickly becoming really weird. I reminded her that he had called earlier that same day. I asked how it could be that he *"expired"* a few hours later. Before I could ask anything else, she nicely gave me her condolences and reminded me of their program and available funding to help with burial arrangements if I needed help. She commented she really had to go and hung up.

I was completely unresponsive and sat on my bed thinking about the conversation I just had. At this moment, everything came to a complete stand still. I just sat frozen as my mind got lost somewhere. It was so quiet and still! I walked towards the window and looked out. It was dark outside with no movement from anywhere. I wondered what I was supposed to do next. She completely took me by surprise and I was still trying to process what had just happened. I walked back to my bed and just sat there with the phone still in my hand replaying that conversation over and over in my head. I was trying to breathe normally and wondered if this was even true and perhaps this might have been the reason I wasn't able to sleep. I thought about how everything from this moment on was going to change if in fact, all this was true. My world was about to flip upside down. I prayed *"Oh God, Oh God, don't let this be true."* I wondered how these people could just pick up the phone in the wee hours of the morning and tell me my son was dead so casually over the phone. I pictured my son scared and wanting to see me at that moment in time. I can't even remember all the hundreds of things I processed in my mind only that I just couldn't get myself to think straight. I was scared out of my mind. A while later; still sitting there numb with the phone in my hand, I called my sister Klu. I knew when she was awakened during the early morning hours she would figure it was definitely not good. I was barely able to speak because I had trouble breathing normal and make sense but I told her about the call. She was in disbelief. She asked if I was okay, I told her I didn't know. She asked me where Roland was. I explained was asleep downstairs because I was having trouble sleeping. I asked if she thought it was true. She advised me to go downstairs; wake Roland up and tell him, then go get my daughter and tell her. Again, I asked her if she thought this was a mistake. She prompted me to focus because I wasn't making much sense and go wake up Roland. I don't know why I didn't think to tell him earlier. Somehow I forgot what to do. She said she'd be on her way and would call the family for me. I asked her to call my job because I didn't know what to say. I walked downstairs and gently sat next to Roland. He was a bit startled and asked what was wrong. I started to explain the phone call I had just received. He sat up and asked me to repeat myself because I wasn't making much sense. He was in total disbelief. He hugged me and said it had to be a mistake because we had just spoken to him a few hours ago. He walked me upstairs to wake our daughter. I opened her door and whispered (*so as not to wake up the kids*) for her to come into our room. She came into our room, sat next to me and quickly asked me what was wrong. I told her I had some disturbing news. I slowly began to explain to her about my phone call. She immediately felt it just had to be a mistake or a prank call because we had just talked to him a few hours ago. That made perfect sense and I wanted to believe he was okay and perhaps this was all just a mistake. We all sat there talking. She began crying as did I. We held each other and could hardly wait until we could call and talk to someone. It was still early morning and we would have to wait a while. My heart was struck with such grief at the thought that this could possibly be true. Roland made coffee and by now we were sitting at the kitchen table. He suggested we all stop and pray that God would help and give us all peace as well as direction in what we should do and how we would handle this nightmare if it was in fact, true. My sisters began arriving with my mother shortly after. We were getting ready for our phone call. I had an intercom speaker box in the kitchen. It would be a while until we could call. I was still in shock mode, nauseated and numb not knowing what to feel or say the whole time. I sat quietly waiting for regular business hours to call the office. I thought about how I would never see my son again nor did I have a chance to say goodbye, however our last words had been, "I love you." So many things went through my mind. I thought of the day I brought him home from the hospital as my firstborn baby boy and remembered breast feeding him for the first time, the time he fell and cut himself learning to ride a tricycle and the day I dedicated him in church. So many memories flooded my mind. I was emotionally caving in and at times found it hard to catch my breath. Nothing made sense as though this really wasn't happening. Nothing could ease my pain and I was desperate to see him once more. It was inconceivable, overwhelming and mind-boggling how this could happen to my son within a few hours of our last conversation. I was thinking about what the staff had said, how *"he had an accident and just stopped breathing."* We spoke to him in the afternoon and he died four hours later.

I sat and wept for my son. I was completely heartbroken that he had died alone, scared and surrounded by complete strangers. *"I should have been there with him"* were my thoughts. How I regretted sending him with his dad. If only I had maybe done this or that differently, etc. I went from shock, numbness, and disbelief to deep sorrow, pain and anger. I began to question God *"Why? Why God? Where were you when my son needed your protection?"* I know we aren't supposed to question God but at the moment I couldn't understand how my God who had always been by my side and there for me, could allow this to happen. I remember saying to God, *"Why didn't you just kill him at birth instead of giving me twenty nine years with him and he had to die like this?"* I was filled with anger at God. I couldn't believe He could allow something this horrible to happen to us. I had no answers or words of comfort for my children. We were all in so much pain. I went to the living room and sobbed as I went through family photo albums. I couldn't imagine what to do next. The thought of making funeral arrangements sickened me. There seemed to be something so unnatural about my child going first instead of me in my older age. It wasn't anything we wanted to do or were financially prepared for. As the hours passed, more of my immediate family began to arrive and to offer support in any way they could do. My mother began to cook. Everyone was doing something or helping with other things like taking care of the kids. As I looked around, it all seemed like a nightmare in slow motion. Unfortunately, it wasn't a bad dream; it was in fact, very real. I had experienced grief and sorrow before but NEVER anything of this magnitude.

My son was in jail and I thought about how he was going to take this. I wondered what to tell him so he wouldn't blow it and get in trouble. I had spent many years in prison/jail ministry; we knew what to do in times of a death in an inmate's family. Suddenly, the reality hit me that it was now my turn. We pulled our resources together to get word to my son. My family called around to facilitate telling my son. I hurt for him and how he was going to feel not to be here with his family during his time of need too..

A couple of weeks later early in the morning, Roland was just lying there and asked why we as Christians, weren't able to retaliate? Why we were expected to take the back seat? He had this idea of revenge staff and it involved explosives as he had done in the past to send a message to put these people on notice. He explained how we wouldn't have to be personally involved but through his contacts, it could easily be done. This would send a clear message to this facility that they messed with the wrong family. He had a plan devised that no one would ever be able to connect this to us. I told him we couldn't and that the Lord wouldn't honor our case if we used violence for violence. This ticked him off and he said he just didn't understand how an establishment could not be held accountable to anyone because had it been him, he would have been in prison for murder. Our faith was being tested. As I listened to him, my old nature actually liked the idea about explosives but another part of me knew if I wanted to keep it real in my walk with the Lord, I had to do this right. He couldn't see the difference in street criminal activity and legal murder or legal cover up tactics. He felt helpless, disrespected and angry. We decided to wait (*out of respect for my son*) until the funeral and burial process was over before we decided what we were going to do if anything at all. Meanwhile, my family and friends got together and held a big car wash locally to raise funds for funeral expenses. I had attended many car washes and fundraisers in the past for other people but now it was my turn for my son. Everyone worked so hard nonstop to raise money. Some were on the streets holding picture posters and bringing in more cars to wash. Others just pulled over to ask what it was for and just donated money. My daughter was out there holding a poster too with her brother's picture on it. I held back my emotions as I watched everyone working hard and at the same time I was comforted by all the love everyone was demonstrating to make this happen. There was even a niece that was breast feeding at the time and her shirt was moist with milk as she washed cars waiting to go breast feed her baby. It was so moving to me. After the car wash, we all got together at the house. Mom had cooked something to eat. A few went into the kitchen to count the money, others went to rest in the living room and others told their stories about their experiences of what people were saying and how many just donated cash. After they counted the money, we all went into the living room to announce how much had been collected. There were quite a few at the house. The living room was packed. It was an emotional time and I thanked everyone for their love and support for my son. My daughter sang a song she wrote. It was here that I announced to everyone that I was going to pay for a private autopsy and with God's help, we were probably going to take legal action. We ended our meeting in prayer.

We got a date at a local mortuary and planned the service. We pulled out resources together in making the programs, putting the music together and getting for the funeral services. We eventually made it through the evening service. There were so many people there and I was blessed with the love and support of many of the brethren. A letter from my son in jail was read at the evening service and my daughter also sang her song. It was all so touching yet sad. His father was there with his close friend, Pastor Gilbert. Truthfully, I had so much I wanted to tell him because I had been quiet for years with him but God told me not to say anything and just leave it alone. As the evening services proceeded, I sat and reflected on so many memories of my son's entire life. his pre-school & kindergarten days and how he cried and begged me not to leave him at school; what a little helper he was growing up; his little friends he made at school; his years of training in Karate; his activities as a Royal Ranger in church; his first girlfriend on and on. I couldn't help but look over to his father and remember the fifteen years of misery he gave us. He had not been a good husband or father to these beautiful children either. Most of all, he was never there in their time of need at home, school, or just growing up, period! The service was a fog as I sat and looked at his coffin asking myself, "*What's wrong with this picture? He's twenty nine years old.*" He had his entire life ahead of him like completing college, getting a steady job, buying the car he wanted, eventually getting married and starting a family of his own. Our kids are supposed to bury their aged parents, not the other way around. It was heart-wrenching and excruciating for me to remain graceful and civil at the same time. It didn't feel real at all except I looked around and saw my family and so many people there. Everything that night seemed to be happening in slow motion. I looked over to my daughter and felt her pain for her brother.

Mothers go through so much with our babies because many of us are single moms and constantly struggling to keep balance at home, work, try to stretch out our time for our kids and fill in for the absentee parent out selfishly doing their own thing. I didn't want to dwell on the negative and was continuously asking God for His comfort and strength to get me through this night as gracefully as possible. I remember asking God to allow me to be a better woman after all this was over and not a bitter one. I struggled with this throughout the entire ordeal of my son's death and burial services.

There was a truly ironic moment that occurred at the evening service that I wished I could have caught on video for other dads to see and hear but it was one of those quick, spur of the moment revelations. I had several displays of my son's photos in the lobby. At one point after services, I was standing there with my daughter just looking at our photos. Her father walked up to us and stood there looking at all the photos with us. The room was full of people talking and it was very noisy. It was a moment in time that could not have been pre-planned and nothing would have prepared me for what took place next. He looked at me and sarcastically yet jokingly commented how there were so many photos of us all on display and why I didn't bother to put any of him in our photos? I didn't say a word and kept looking straight. Our daughter innocently turned to her dad and said, *"Daddy, you were never around to take pictures with us, you were always gone."* I was dumbfounded and speechless. He too, was taken by surprise with this reality check from his own daughter. He laughed it off, hugged her and said *"I know, mija (Spanish for daughter), I know."* He turned and looked at me too. She didn't think anything of it either. You could see she spoke from the heart. Funny, but just for that moment, I actually felt bad for him. What a powerful moment **"out of the mouths of babes"** I thought. So many men not involved in their children's lives wonder why their children are all messed up. Our son had been so emotionally wounded by his dad. Sadly, his last days were an argument between them about how Carlos had never been around for them. It just breaks my heart that there are so many dead-beat dads out there with no clue that their selfish behavior has long term, catastrophic effect on their children. Children carry deep-seated wounds that take years to repair and for the most part, never do.

Somehow, by the grace of God, we were able to get through the evening services. I had a lot of thinking to do as to what I wanted to do about my son's death. I didn't know what I should do to go about seeking justice but I just knew I had to do something! I also knew that if I wanted to grow in my walk with the Lord and keep it real, I had to also walk in forgiveness to Carlos for his years of neglect. I needed healing too. We had suffered for so many years without his help or input with the kids. It wasn't easy to deny the flesh and walk in forgiveness and mercy just as God had done with me. I needed to get out of God's way and allow Him to work things out on my behalf because I felt so much anger and hurt towards him. He was singing his Christian oldies and everyone liked them but no one had any idea of the wreckage he had caused with his family. He had never asked his children for forgiveness either. I had to do the possible on my part and let God work out the impossible.

The funeral service the next morning was even harder to get through because it was time to let him go and it would be the end. I didn't know how to say goodbye. How does a mother say good bye forever? I chose not to go up and see him in an open coffin. It just wasn't a memory I wanted to stay with. I had instructed the funeral director that after everyone was finished going up and it was my turn, they were to close his casket. That's exactly what they did and I began to make my way up to say my goodbyes. It was the longest walk I ever had to take in my life. I didn't want it to end. My final moments passed too quickly and I wanted to hang on to him, his coffin, his flowers, his hand, something, anything! But all I had was our memories. I couldn't breathe right. I wanted to scream as loud as I could and say *"I love you, mijo"* (*son*), but I could hardly speak. Funny, because I had rehearsed in my mind how I would calmly walk up say goodbye and stay strong for my daughter but once I got there, I fell apart and caved in. I stood quietly sobbing. I knew everyone was waiting. The reality hit me that there was nothing more I could or would ever do for him anymore. What was done was done and final. I felt my legs buckling and I didn't want to make a scene so I hurried to get in the car and get through it all. It always brings tears to my eyes to remember this farewell moment. Unfortunately, all I had to hang on to were these two days of memories from the family, things said from his friends and a song that was sung by my daughter.

We made it to the burial site. It was a beautiful sunny day with a breeze. I stayed for most of the services and stoically sat there going through the motions but I felt deeply melancholy. This was heartbreaking for me because it was truly the final of all finals. This was the final chapter of my son's life on earth. Unfortunately, it was also the beginning of our life without him. I would never wish this experience on another mother. What an unbearable pain. This isn't the way we are supposed to part with our babies. After all the people left, the real challenger of living our life without him was just beginning. It didn't seem so bad before because I was preoccupied with the funeral arrangements and surrounded by all the people at the house. But now it was terribly difficult to live as though my son was never with us. I went through many times in my head how I wished I had done things differently. I was angry with myself for sending him to his dads, yet it had become unbearable at the house with him. I wondered what his last thoughts were. I tried not to think about the way he took his last breath because it tore me up inside. At times I thought I'd go nuts. By the time all the services were over, Roland had calmed down and decided to try and get justice the honorable way and was willing to pool whatever resources he could to help win this case.

I took a thirty-day leave of absence from my job. After deep thought and thinking, I decided I would in fact file a wrongful death suit against this facility. I began to interview several attorneys to take on this case. I prayed for God to direct me to the right attorney. After several weeks, I was able to retain a law firm that agreed to take my case pro-bono.

The day finally came when we officially filed our lawsuit in Court. On this day, we staged our first big demonstration at the front steps of the courthouse. We were graced with quite a bit of protestors in attendance as well as substantial media coverage. My attorneys were actually surprised at the amount of people who showed up to demonstrate with me. We started our demonstration with prayer. We all stood in a circle and held hands praying for the favor of God to be with us as we filed our case. We prayed that the message would go out and impact the public in our favor.

My story was seen and heard by thousands of people and organizations throughout the five years of my struggle for justice. I was continuously asked to go speak about my case at numerous places.

The Fight Is Over
Or Is It?

After this long five-year uphill battle for justice, thousands of hours in rallies, demonstrations, press conferences, television station interviews, thousands of dollars (*out of pocket*) expense for this struggle, we reached a settlement and it was finally all going to end. My eyes filled with tears that "***the struggle was over***". We received our copy, got our things and left. I cried all the way home. It was the strangest feeling knowing it was all over. I don't know what I expected but this was it! I came home so mentally exhausted yet knowing it was time for closure and soon all this was going to be completely over and behind us. All these years came to an end that day.

A few months later, I held a celebratory victory luncheon at sea. I had rented a big yacht who had prepared lunch for all my family, staff, and supporters who had worked so hard to help this cause for justice on behalf of my son. It was a bittersweet moment. Our victory celebration was a mixture of emotions. We were all happy and yet sad with the grief that my son was permanently gone. My daughter was very emotional and tearful that day. My other son was still being detained. Several people got to speak and share what was on their mind. We ended it with a prayer of thanks for our five year victorious battle! We were just a few people compared to the upward strenuous battle against all these political giants. I thanked everyone in an emotional speech for their support and sacrifice. It felt like I was a Moses leading all these people in the direction of victory not knowing how to get there but trusting God to part the waters for us all. Thank God for a great understanding husband and a big family that started and finished with me. We lost a few along the way but others filled in. This experience wasn't anything any mother would want to experience in a lifetime to bury your child. I am grateful to the Lord for gracing me with His supernatural strength these past long difficult years. He was and continues to be my daily strength in time of trouble or need. My heart's desire is that I would encourage someone who has or will go through a similar injustice in their lives, to be confident that through the almighty power of God, He can make a way out of no way, part the waters in their time of need and finally; make the impossible possible!

28

Oh No, Not Again

It is the year 2004; my business is going strong and has been able to survive all the strenuous times. I was slowly packing all the work stations away. It was all over now and it was time to move on. I even printed my story behind my business flyers that sat on the counter of my business as people checked out to pay for their merchandise. I met a lot of remarkable people with interesting similar stories of their own. I met many who had read about my son's story. Many customers continued to come back to the business which was nice. They would tell their friends about my unique shop and the story behind it. My store manager, Anna, was a delight to our many visitors. She too, would answer questions for those who came in that had heard of my story. Eventually, the economy began to take a turn for the worst. In the months that followed, I had to make a decision on whether to renew my business lease another five years.

My husband, Roland, began to have stomach pains. He went to see doctors and they told him it was nothing to worry about but he continued to feel sick for months. One evening, I closed the store but worked in the back till late. When I got home, I was upstairs putting away some laundry. I got a phone call from someone asking for me by name. Oh, how well I knew those night phone calls and that tone of voice when they asked *"is this Rita?"* It could only mean bad news.

For a minute, I thought it was about my son. I paused for a minute; the lady asked if I was still there. She identified herself and the hospital she was calling from. Almost exactly the same call I received about my son. She was calling to inform me that my husband had driven himself to the hospital earlier that day because he wasn't feeling well. He filled out paperwork and was waiting when his health took a turn for the worst. He was now in ICU, intensive care. She said his condition was very serious and I should try and get to the hospital as quickly as possible. My heart sank to my feet. My daughter was home. I gave her the news and left driving as fast as I could to the hospital. When I got there Roland was semi-conscious and couldn't talk. I did most of the talking. He would squeeze my hand to say "yes" or "no." It was difficult and frustrating to say the least. The reality of his condition began to sink in. I felt alone and scared. I knew this was very serious and began praying. I called pastors that I knew, family and his brother, to come right away.

By the next day, they had put a tube down his throat to help him breathe and he was now on a life support system. It really didn't look good. He wasn't squeezing my hand anymore but he could still hear. My heart gripped me with fear at the thought of losing him. We kept praying for a miracle. We prayed with Roland and shared the word with him. He could still hear because there were times he would respond with tears. When we were alone, I would quietly whisper personal things in his ear and he would have tears streaming down his face. I knew he could still hear me. He stayed in ICU for two and a half weeks. It was the end of November going into Christmas; his favorite time of the year. Several of his Christian "*brothers*" had heard about his hospitalization and began to arrive and pray with him. It was exhausting and draining not knowing how he was and waiting on his condition to get better every day. Sometimes I would go out to the visiting room with the others and just try talking to people to get my mind off of his deteriorating condition. I silently felt somewhat scared and tried not to think of the worse but it was all the doctors kept telling me. They only gave me bad news after more bad news because he was going from bad to worse. Funny thing is he was health conscientious, ran every day, exercised, was a vegetarian and took healthy vitamins and shakes. I wondered how this could be happening to a healthy person.

At the end of the third week, the doctor took me aside and said that I needed to consider pulling the plug as Roland was pretty much gone. I thought what a horrible thing to say! I called his brother who met with me and the doctor the next day. I wanted to discuss any possible alternatives. Unfortunately, there were none. The doctor stated it was a decision I had to make and I needed to give him my decision in the next seventy two hours. As another day passed, I sat by his bedside and replayed what the doctor's had told me and how difficult this decision would be. Honestly? I was still hopeful that he would get better and go home in a few days. I prayed whatever God's will was, that I would have peace and strength within me.

On December 1st, 2004, in the early hours of the morning, just after 3:30 am, Roland took a turn for the worse. They called a *"code blue"* and he had to be revived. I stood there watching his lifeless body and reminiscing about all our years together good and bad, our wedding day and how he wiggled with nervousness as we repeated our vows. It was sad that our life altogether came to this moment. I thought *"How could this be happening?"* Few hours later I began to call his brother and my family to come quickly. The family arrived right away and by now it was about 8 o'clock in the morning. Several were there with me in the room when the nurse walked in to tell me that **"he is going"**. She explained the numbers on the machine. She said once it hit zero, he would be gone. He was in the high 80's and was slowly coming down. I had a feeling of anxiousness to somehow stop the machine. There was still so much more I wanted to say and didn't know how to react to this. I kept praying. I kept touching him and speaking into his ear of how much I loved him. I wasn't even sure he could hear me anymore but I spoke to him anyway. Again, I sat and reflected on all our memories. It's the only thing I could do as I watched him leaving me right before my eyes. Oh how he just loved

Christmas time. Ironically, he walked out of Prison at Christmas time and now he was going to leave at Christmas time. I never would have imagined he would leave so soon and not like this. Time seem to be slipping away fast as his lifeless body lay there. Everyone began to softly sing some hymns. As the singing continued, there was a moment when suddenly the machine began to make a funny sound. The numbers were in the 30's. I buzzed the nurse quickly. She came in, went to the machine, turned to me and said *"I'm very sorry but he has expired."* Oh How I hated the word, *"expired".* It was the same words they gave me when they told me my son had "*expired*". I asked how that could be possible because the numbers were still in the 30's and hadn't hit zero yet. She explained that sometimes this will happen and patients didn't always make it to zero. She apologized and confirmed once again, that he was definitely gone. I was startled and thought *"Oh no, not again."* I couldn't think of what to do or say next. I simply stood there looking at him. I couldn't cry and had no emotions. I think I was in disbelief. The hospital gave me some private time with the family. They allowed me to stay as long as I needed. More family and friends also arrived; said their goodbyes and expressed condolences. Although I knew that he was in a better place and went to be with Jesus, it still pierced my heart. Someone suggested we all join hands for a word of prayer.

I thought about how I didn't have to make that dreadful decision to disconnect Roland after all. For that, I was grateful. It was one of the hardest things (*as with my deceased son*) that I had to do again. Everyone slowly exited and it was going to be my turn to say goodbye alone. I remember thinking, *"Not again",* it was a difficult thing to do then come home without him permanently. It was all so very familiar and so final again but I got through it. Family came to the house to stay with me and hang out which helped. Once again, I had this feeling like this was all just a bad dream I had gone through before. I felt numb and empty inside. Thank the Lord for family and fellowship that came together to spiritually and emotionally support me by simply hanging out when they did and allowing me to cry when

I felt the need or just comfort me. Through the years my family (*and I*) had ministered at so many funerals and now here I was (*once again*) planning yet another funeral for the second time in my life. One of my closest girlfriends, Julie came to help me put a video presentation together accompanied by music. I looked through many pictures and memories. We finally were able to complete the video. God Bless a local pastor who offered his church to host Roland's memorial service. Everything else fell into place and so many people offered to help that night. It was a gloomy, cold and rainy. Oh, how I dreaded this night to come and when it did, I wanted it to be over with quickly. The service turned out great. Many of his friends and acquaintances spoke. The family sang two of Roland's favorite oldie songs from our ministry CD. There was fellowship afterwards due to many people that had come from everywhere near and far. We only had the evening memorial service as Roland was cremated.

After the services was over and company was gone, the most intimate part of Roland's departure was about to unfold because I had to continue my life without him. The nights and mornings were the hardest to get through because he just wasn't there when I awoke to have my coffee or went to sleep. In the months that followed, I began to gather his clothes, shoes and things in boxes and in time, donated his things to a local men's rehabilitation home for other men to be blessed. Just as I done with my son, it was yet another difficult task. With God's help, I got through it all.

As the months slowly passed, it got just a little easier to get used to. My Christmas three weeks later was the worst! As hard as I tried to be strong, it was sad and empty. It was during this time we were celebrating our wedding anniversary and now I was left with the memory of his death instead. I felt like I wore an inner silent cloak of loneliness that I did not share with my children or anyone. I smiled and interacted with people, friends and family superficially but as soon as they left, this inner loneliness would take over. I felt somewhat ashamed for feeling this way and putting on a facade that I was alright. I didn't think anyone could really understand the sorrow

I carried. It was literally one day at a time. Seeing his family was like being with him again. We all talked about him and our times together.

A few months went by and I planned a burial at sea for him. Ironically, it was what Roland and I had discussed and agreed upon when he began getting sick. He told me he knew he was going to die. I remember telling him *"you're not going to die silly, quit being a baby"*. Now, I was glad for those talks we had because I knew exactly what it was he wanted. He expressed how he wanted to be buried at sea where we were married and later, wanted me to take everyone to lunch at the same restaurant in Santa Barbara where we had gone after we were married. I made all the reservations and everything was set in motion. It was time to put this chapter behind me as well.

The day and time came and everyone reported to the dock in Santa Barbara. We all boarded the big yacht. Pastor Dell Castro who had married us was now about to bury us. He conducted Roland's burial at sea which was going to be his first time conducting a service of this type. I had butterflies in my stomach just being in Santa Barbara without my soul mate. What a magnificent, beautiful day at sea too and the scenery was breathtaking. It was a quiet 30 minute drive into the ocean. Everyone had their own thoughts; quiet conversations and enjoying the ride. We rode out to sea for thirty minutes when the skipper turned the engines off. He gave Pastor Dell the signal to begin our service. Pastor Dell began with prayer and reminisced a bit on Roland's life. Some of his friends spoke as well. I also had several picture posters there with our memories. Later, the time came when I was to let Roland go into the water. I was handed his ashes and the hard part came. I began to slowly let his ashes go. Being as I'd never done this before, I wasn't sure what to expect or what I'd feel. Many thoughts crossed my mind as I slowly let him go and said my goodbyes. Everything was quiet except for the sound of the wind, the water hitting the boat and my racing thoughts. I began to feel myself caving in and broke down sobbing as I released the last of his ashes. I had sort of prepared myself to be strong not break down and do this with dignity but at the end, it went quite the opposite. Everyone stood quietly and simply allowed me my time to get through this. It was one of the most difficult yet familiar experiences I ever had to do. As I sat there after letting the ashes go into the ocean, everyone began to quietly sing hymns which soothed my pain and began to toss their fresh flowers into the sea where I had let Roland's ashes go. It looked beautiful as the colorful flowers floated on the water. It was a feeling of disbelief that I was doing this. Everyone continued to sing as my brother in law also let Roland's sister's ashes go with Roland. Our service lasted an hour. I heard the engines start up and we slowly started heading back. My mother embraced me as I wept. That was comforting.

Everyone was given their directions to the restaurant where we had reservations and would meet later. It was such a tranquil, sunny, breezy day. We sat out on the outside patio next to a big pond with running water where Roland and our guests sat after we were married. It was so serene and soothing. We broke bread together and had a beautiful time of fellowship just as Roland had requested. Our married life had begun at this little restaurant and now it had ended here. Afterwards, we all walked around town stopping at various shops. There was a big city celebration of some sort going on so there were a lot of people everywhere. It turned out to be a perfectly peaceful day such as I had never experienced for a time like this. I didn't feel sad anymore and I embraced the love of my family, friends and Roland's memory. It was how I got through it. Everyone commented how perfect the day was. I thanked the Lord for this picture perfect day and now it would be time to move forward.

I still had the business and I threw myself into work which helped. I had lost two very important men in my life. I had my good days and hard days but I learned to take them one day at a time and live my life as positive and productive as I could. I still had my son and my daughter to live for and I needed to be there for them.

Months later, the economy continued to take a turn for the worst and my lease was up at the shop. I decided I would not renew my lease and close the business. By this time, money was tight and times were getting much harder. Leaving the business when I did turned out to be a good business decision because shortly after, the economy took a hard nose dive. By this time foreclosures were at an all time high, banks were crashing and people began to lose their jobs as well. My business would not have survived another five years. Finally, the stress of all the responsibilities of running a business was gone and I didn't have to worry over it anymore. I returned to a regular eight to five job. It was a job I was only too familiar with and it was working with parolees. Funny how, ready or not, life goes on and time waits for no one.

Six months after Roland's death, I got a phone call from a close friend that advised my children's father Carlos "Jr" had been admitted to a local hospital with diabetic complications. I took my daughter to see him. We walked in and he was conscious and his typical silly self. He expressed how glad he was to see his mija (*daughter*) and me. I took a seat to let her visit with him. He was joking around and talking about how he would probably be going home in a couple of days. I went to speak to the nurses and they told me how very ill he really was. Shortly after, I called our son to tell him about his father. He hadn't spoken to him for years and was still very angry at him for his abandonment and lack of interest in their lives. He said he didn't care and wasn't interested in visiting him either. I prompted him to make the effort to visit his dad and make amends as it would be good for his soul and it would help him to be a better father, son and person in general. He said he still didn't care. I told him his father was actually very critical and urged him to come anyway in case he didn't make it. I went back to the room. They were talking and having a good time. He asked for his son and I told him that he was going to get a ride soon. I wasn't even sure if he would come or not but I didn't have the heart to tell him what his son had actually said. I just prayed that our son would reconsider and come see his dad. After a few hours there with him, we headed home. Later I received a call from my son who said he had in fact, changed his mind and would go visit his father to tell him how he felt about what a rotten father he had been and say what he felt to his face. I told him that was fine and that we would all meet there the next day.

The next morning came and we all walked in together. As soon as he saw his dad who had become critical by now, he walked up, kissed and hugged him and began to sob. He told him he forgave him and how he really loved him. They both cried as they made their amends. I was blessed to see all this atonement unfolding before me as they made their peace. Both my children stood by crying. Little by little, his condition worsened and the doctors advised us that he was only going to get worse. As I sat there observing all this, I thought about the year 1968 when we married, our innocence, our marriage and the start of our little family. He never did come to realize the catastrophic damage his bad choices had on his children and how hurt they were with him all these years. Now here they were at the last minute trying to catch up and deal with all those suppressed feelings. I was thankful that my son had a change of heart. I knew it would be better for him to say what was on his mind once and for all. Just as I had suspected, my son really didn't hate his dad but was only very hurt and wounded by him for so many years. As I watched on, I thought *"wow, what a waste of many precious years"*. The kids waited on their dad hand and foot, helping to feed him and make him feel as comfortable as possible. It was awkward and heartbreaking at the same time to watch. These kids loved their dad more than he ever knew. Although they didn't have many memories with him as children and the ones they did have, were not good. His singing partner in the ministry, Pastor Gilbert and another Pastor Mickey, also arrived and prayed for him. Later we all sat and talked in the visiting room. The next day, his condition became graver and he was no longer able to speak. He communicated with the kids by writing notes. My son stood with him all day and night on his last day.

In November 2005, as the family and kids were saying their goodbyes he went to be with the Lord. I reflected once again as I sat in the distance looking on and reminiscing on my life with him too, how we had met in church through our pastor parents and how our marriage was supposed to be a marriage made in heaven because we were both brought up in ministry. Unfortunately, it turned out quite the opposite because it was a fifteen year long marriage of misery and anguish. I thought of how I lost my innocence with him and the three beautiful children we had together. It was a bittersweet moment. I wondered where all the years had gone and sad that it had all come to this. Being in this room with him dying, the kids and us all saying our goodbyes brought back memories of Roland and saying our good bye to him six months ago. It would be time to plan yet another funeral for our little family. I thought to myself, *"not again."* It had indeed been another painful reality I would have to walk through together with my children. Ironically, I had lost my first and last love six months apart. Wow! What were the chances of this happening? But it did!

I started to make arrangements for the funeral service including the songs to be sung with my family, photos to put out and a program. It was a morbidly gloomy experience. Carlos' memorial service was held at a local church. Lots of people came together to make his memorial service a nice one. God Bless our brother Willie G. whom Jr. had sung with in concerts for many years in other states performing *"Oldie"* concerts back in the day with other well known artists. Willie shared and sang at the service as did my family. Several people spoke as did our son. I was so proud of him for making the good decision to make amends with his father before his death. We had a very nice time of fellowship after the service. It helped the kids too. It was the weirdest experience because many of the same people expressing condolences at Roland's memorial service also attended Carlos' *(Jr.)* service and expressed condolences to me again. Both had been cremated. It was time to put yet another personal chapter behind me and move forward. I was tired of gathering personal things. The kids had cleaned out their father's apartment and put things in storage. It seemed like the last few years we had been packing things away; first for my son, then for Roland, my business and now the children's father. It would be a test of time and spiritual strength to continue going forward to see what God had for me now. I have heard it said that our lives play out in chapters. We close one and start another. This was one of those times I closed another chapter and opened a new one.

My Journey Now

I have changed and grown so much since my conversion in 1994. It is why today I try to be more understanding of those who struggle with their walk to stop smoking, drinking, doing drugs and personal demons they struggle with. I feel that as long as someone keeps trying and go to church (*although struggling*), seeking God and hearing the His word, eventually in God's perfect timing, they will be totally delivered as I was. When the awesome transforming power of the Holy Spirit begins to work, nothing or no one can stop it. I kept praying, pushing and coming to church seeking Him. My heart was sincere. I began to put my hands to the plow once again and prayed each day that He would keep me. I know now that all my self-condemnation came from my old school upbringing. I had to have my own breakthrough and deliverance from my personal demons trying to knock me down every day. I now know that I serve such a mighty sovereign God who loves me just the way I am as I continue to walk with Him one day at a time. I no longer live in condemnation of my past. I don't forget it but I have learned to practice an attitude of gratitude on a daily basis thanking God everyday and finding the good in all the negative the world throws at me. It wasn't easy but I had my own personal spiritual experience which was so real and powerful to me. I will *NEVER* take my walk with the Lord lightly. He's healed and shown me total forgiveness of my past wreckage as a PK and I am honored to have lived as the daughter of a pastor and survived. I have a much deeper understanding of it all now and all I want to do is enlighten someone else that may have shared the some of my experiences.

In his own time, my father returned to God and forgiveness in his life again. Dad has continued to attend a small Spanish church where he and his wife serve the Lord together. He too, is a different person today including his thinking. For that, I am grateful to God for his restoration. It was a humbling experience for him too. You see, Jesus forgives and forgets unfortunately, people don't! He has chosen to go forward. I have had discussions with him about my life as a pastor's daughter and it's clear today that he no longer practices legalistic thinking and has a better and open understanding of a balanced life. I have moved ahead and not looked back anymore. I walk in forgiveness and live my life better and not bitter. I've learned so much through my journey. The Lord has restored everything I had lost in the past and made everything new in my life again. God is ever faithful to His Word. In His mercy He has fully restored my relationship with my family and my children. I can love and respect myself today.

I continue to play the piano, sing and go out to encourage others via speaking engagements anywhere the Lord opens a door. He has renewed my tired and distorted mind that when I began singing again some years ago, it just flowed out like second nature. I remembered all the music and the words. It has a completely different meaning today. I value and respect my walk with the Lord. I never take my restoration for granted and I am completely humbled and grateful when invited to speak or sing. I appreciate every opportunity I am given to encourage someone about the goodness of God in my life. Had it not been for the awesome keeping power of God in my life, I would not have survived the death of my little brother Jonathon, my other brother Isaac, my son, the unexpected death of my husband Roland, the death of my first love and father of my children, Carlos

"Jr", and finally, the latest death of my beautiful pastor mother who went to be with the Lord on May 17, 2012. Ironically, she passed on my father's birthday. It seemed to be loss after loss after more loss for several years. I never could have survived all this pain had it not been for the saving, keeping power of God in my life.

Since my husband's death in 2004, financially it got harder to keep my head above water and slowly watched as things slipped out of my hands when I was so used to living comfortably and being well taken care off. I went to live with my sister, Klu who ironically was a big support system when I was lost in my wilderness and today continues to be that support. We have shared so many experiences together. Ironically, she too recently lost her soul mate as I did. We still continue our sister talks, trips, dinners and adventures together. She opened her doors for me to come live with her as all her babies were grown and gone. She continues to be a blessing and support system in every imaginable way. How time flies and changes our lives. It is in this room and in my van that I was prompted to pursue finishing this book. I didn't know it but the Lord had it all under control even when I didn't understand what was going on in my life and had more questions than answers. He assured me that He had a purpose and a plan for my life all along. I needed to trust him, serve and thank him for the process. It's funny how God has a way of orchestrating our lives because it was during this window of time He prompted me to finish my book which I had started writing just over twenty five years ago. When I fell (*backslid*), I figured I had forfeited the opportunity to finish it. The Lord should me it was just another chapter and gave me the green light to finish. It has been challenging to say the least, but I was strongly inspired to finish it. Time on my hands turned out to be a blessing for me. I didn't see or understand it all but God had it all under control as part of His unique plan for my life. Often we don't understand things going on in our lives but if we would just be still, wait and trust that He knows what He's doing, we would be spared a lot of hardship later. This time was set aside to be my time alone with the Lord to pray, sing, laugh, cry and go through a cleansing period as I completed this book. It has been a painful journey with the purging of things in my life that I didn't even know were still there. I had shelved away countless memories, good, bad and painful. This journey caused me to take a better look inside myself at how quickly time passed me by. I realize how much I have survived during the most painful and insane years of my life. For that, I am eternally grateful and blessed to have lived through it all. I now have a real sense of accomplishment within me to have finally finished this long overdue book. Unfortunately, my mother went to be with the Lord and was never able to see the book completed. Oh, how I wish she could have been here for this moment. She taught me (by example) to forgive people who have or will hurt me. I still have my dad who is up in years and fragile in health but He encouraged me to finish the book as well.

Eventually, the Lord brought me to join forces with my church family, with Pastors Mario and Arleen. I have known this pastor since his youth when he was in the men's rehabilitation home getting his life together and would sometimes travel with our prison team to give his testimony; never thinking he would become a pastor. This church is where the Lord led me to after my pastor's closed their church a few years ago. The Lord has such a sense of humor because it's also the same church where my daughter received the Lord when I was released from jail on my ordeal. Wow, I would have never thought this is where I would land today. It is an awesome church filled with believers from all walks of life. We are all one big happy family working together for the Kingdom of God. Sometimes I play the piano and sing. From time to time I will share a sermon the Lord places on my heart. I also help out with the Women's Fellowship projects like the Spring & Winter Teas, breakfasts and bi-monthly fellowships, etc. and have also started a "Widow's" support group. I enjoy coming to the house of God. My pastors are supportive of me whenever I am asked to speak at women's conferences, retreats and other special occasions. Today, God has given me a better understanding of balance, boundaries and modesty. I'm actually thankful now, that I was brought up the way I was because it's helped me to walk the straight and narrow path with balance and moderation. Needless to say I go to the movies now without feeling guilty or condemned as I was taught. I wear pants, make up and some jewelry too! All this with a healthy sense of modesty as mom used to say. It's not to say that I don't believe in traditionally taught values, I do but I also have a sense of openness and balance. No more condemnation thinking. I want to always present myself as God's daughter in good taste and allow HIS spirit to flow through me and not work hard to show myself. I believe the greatest testimony is the one people (*unbelievers*) see through us in our daily walk because I strongly believe our personal testimony speaks volumes. I can forgive more easily and I have His peace, love and discernment to walk in Him and just keep it real! Things are not as bad as they used to be. I see and understand things differently today. Thank you Jesus for clarity and breakthrough!

I pray that we would all take thoughtful inventory of where we are in our lives and check our attitudes in regards to our pastors and their families. Don't wait for the pastor's children to come and engage in conversation with you. Go out of your way to greet them, make them feel welcomed, needed and loved by you. Be nice, just because! You will never know what lurks in their lives and one quick loving act of kindness goes a long way. Let us not place higher expectations on PK's or pastors. They are only human the same as you. Should we see something in them we don't' like, pray for them but don't bring it to someone else's attention because then it becomes gossip. Prayer moves the hand of God! We are all only human.

To conclude, I want to give my God all the glory for my journey from childhood to now. If someone would have told me years ago about my journey, I never would have believed I could go through the many things I did in my life and survived all the crazy madness. I felt compelled to share my story as a pastor's daughter (P.K.) because often people are not really aware of what a pastor's kid goes through in a pastor's home life and the challenges we go through with the call of our parents to ministry. After all, we have no choice in the matter because we are automatically part of the package. I want to emphasize the fact that the devil is out to discourage and eventually take us out away from what God has planned for our lives. He's no respecter of a person's life nor does he have a limit to what he will do to knock us out of line of God's divine plan for our lives. He used discouragement on me until I totally let *HIS* hand go. It was a matter of time that I was out doing unimaginable things that I never knew about or was exposed to because I was a good girl at one time and I had learned so many things in the world that were foreign to me. At first, it seemed perfectly harmless and quite frankly, it was fun and satisfying (*so I thought*). The enemy started off slow and easy making things look like fun. Before I knew it, I was totally consumed by this lifestyle that had me bound and I was too deep to turn back. Oh how I missed my once simple innocent life that I thought was boring and dull. By this time I clothed myself daily with guilt and condemnation. Just when I thought it couldn't get any worse, it was all just the beginning until I learned what real low was and again, he reminded me how I was too messed up to turn back to the God whom I once served. I was sure there was no forgiveness for the things I had done or had been involved with.

No one but no one would have guessed my parents were pastors and that I came from a good Christian home. My self-worth was chattered and something of the past because I didn't know what that was anymore. It's like I went to hell and survived. I saw, hung out and partied with so many other P.K.s, not to mention all the spiritually wounded back sliders and fallen ministers I rubbed elbows with in my endeavors. It was like witnessing a spiritual war with so many casualties in spiritual body bags. Alive but dead! I realized later, how close I had come to ending up in one of them bags myself.

It is my desire to simply bring awareness and sensitivity to congregations that maybe just have no clue (*or don't care for that matter*) what it is to be a pastor or a pastor's kid. To all backsliders and fallen ministers, there is in fact forgiveness. Unfortunately, God forgives and forgets but people don't. You must get to the point where it is just you and Jesus and get it right because he is waiting there where you last left him and wants more than anything, to bring you home again. He will work out all the details later, just come home. If he was able to forgive me; dear God, he will forgive you. He's a forgiving, merciful, on time God and I pray my book encourages you.

I can see how He had his hand upon my life all along. I don't know why certain things turned out the way they did or why life took the course it did. I know that other things occurred because of my own bad choices. I reaped the consequences of running from God and my calling. It cost me and it cost me good but it's just like the enemy to completely destroy and take us out (*if he can*). Thank God for the prayers of so many people in my life. The bottom line is that upon making a complete circle in life, He was able to welcome me back with open, forgiving arms and set my feet on solid ground as He restored me back to the woman I am today. Although it wasn't and hasn't been easy, I now know that He had a plan for my life all along. I came very close to throwing it all away.

Today, I am dedicated to the reaching of other PK s, pastors and ministers who are lost and finding it hard to find their way back like me. Finding my way back home was one of the hardest challenges for me. ***The higher the call, the harder the fall*** is what I always heard growing up. The call to ministry is no picnic. I believe that's why God calls on whom he calls because ministry is not for anyone. Today, I walk in forgiveness from all those who violated, hurt and damaged me. I'm free now and I want to speak freely about my experiences to bring light to other PK'.s that are lost and wounded by none other than the church itself. I desire that there be openness with ministry; especially our traditional Spanish churches that teach holiness based on legalistic practices such as the way we dress, the color of our hair or cosmetic makeup issues. There are many who know all the holiness rules and regulations but disgracefully gossip about other sisters in the church, criticize the pastor's or their children. At least that has been my observation. They live one life at home and another at church. This is such a turn off to their children and others in our communities watching how we live our lives. We wonder why we have so many lost PK's gone wild out in our world just like I was. No one, but no one would have ever believed I was the daughter of a pastor. To be perfectly honest, I didn't care whether they did or not. I always blamed church people and allowed all the anger to consume me inside. I developed hatred towards all so-called-Christians. I was wrong. My walk should have been my own personal walk. I should have never worried or cared about those kinds of people. No one ever gave me a chance while growing up in church because I was rebellious. Being a PK shouldn't be a declaration of a hopeless dead life. Sadly, I learned that often, God's people behave in ignorance of His word. We didn't have a choice in having pastors for parents. I believe the Lord would have us live in love and modesty. We don't need to look; talk or act like the world but keeping our testimony pure and humble preaches a much louder message. All of our walks in Christ are different and unique. My salvation and walk isn't and won't be like yours because I'm working out my own stuff as you need to do yours. I thank God Almighty for delivering me from destructive, legalistic thinking and practices. I have a true and genuine relationship with my Lord. It's what we do in secret that pleases or displeases God anyway.

If you are a preacher's kid or a backslider who was once in ministry, I beseech you from the bottom of my heart to invite God back into your heart. We make awesome ministry vessels, even through our failures. Why? Because we survived the traps, tricks and lies of the enemy and we lived to tell. We already know the ins and outs of ministry. Been there, done that. If you can just get to that place of not caring about what "*people*" think or what they did or did not do for us and our family, we would be a lot better off and much happier than walking around wounded by it all. I learned that every time I remembered a bad and hurtful experience as a PK and backslider, I relived it all over again and again. It made me even madder and bitter inside. I no longer choose to empower others to have that kind of effect on my life anymore and be short-changed. It's exactly how the devil wants us and unfortunately, we go for it. Yeah, he wants us wounded so we live our lives angry, away from God and bad mouthing the things of God when all along its ignorant people that don't have the love of God in them and neither will we. Unfortunately, we become like them. Remember, the devil's complete plan is to steal, kill and destroy our lives and at the end, he wins yet another soul. He knows his time is short and we PK's carry a special anointing upon our lives. He's threatened with that. He's a liar, deceiver and counterfeiter of anything God has for us. I think he's lied to you long enough!

I challenge you to consider forgiving yourself and others, who may have hurt you, even if it's your parents as in my case or other people who made your life miserable like mine. Not forgiving them puts a stronghold on our own lives. We get stuck there and never quite grow! We need to rise above the madness and press forward to whatever unique plan God has for our lives. Nothing's changed my friend. Where do you think you can go where can you hide? How can you continue without God in your life and expect to be genuinely happy? We ourselves walked away and left Him! He's still there by your side and isn't going to force your heart. Our Heavenly Father longs for us to come willfully to him. Once we commit, *IT'S ON!* We can't care what people say. Our time is limited and the enemy's objective is to take us out. Satan's playground is in fact, our minds. He would love nothing more than to cripple and distort our minds and thoughts. It's where he dwells! Shame the devil and do what is right. Whatever happened to you as a PK or in ministry is the past and can't be changed but your future CAN! It is what it is. It may not be fair either but I believe God has a purpose and a plan for our lives as PK's or restored ministers; otherwise, the battle for your soul wouldn't be this hard. We are not alone, it just feels that way. Your feelings will lie to you. Let God use you to be different and radical. *WE CAN COME BACK STRONG MY FRIEND!* I promise you, He will put a new song in your heart and give you fresh ideas in serving Him. Give your life to God. If He could restore me, he can restore you. I was all messed up mentally, emotionally and spiritually. I was so broken that I honestly believed there was no hope for my miserable life. I believed He couldn't repair me anymore. Not so!!! Here I am today, blessed and delivered from my own defeated stinking thinking. My talk is my walk, no one else's. Someone needs your help too. I pray the Holy Spirit will touch your life as you read my story and be encouraged in a sweet but powerful way that would ignite and challenge your heart to come back home with a new heart and new desire.